# Crazy Makers of the Sm

*Do any of these sound ~~familiar to you?~~*
*(Hope you don't check them all!)*

- ❑ **Overworked**—Working too many hours. Can't take a vacation. Don't feel comfortable getting away. Things always come up to keep you in the office.
- ❑ **Strapped**—Cash crunch, now or chronic. Sudden downturns. Can't get needed capital. Not paying yourself enough.
- ❑ **Blahs**—Not doing what you love. Mired in minutiae. Having to manage/administrate all the time.
- ❑ **Help wanted**—Can't get quality help. High turnover. Dead wood. Stuck with people who aren't doing the job.
- ❑ **Dysfunctional family**—Employees squabble, shirk, run the show. There's one bad apple.
  Your hardest-to-replace employee drags the organization down.
- ❑ **Empty pipeline**—Lost one big customer. Don't know how to market or reach new people. Business used to just come in, now it doesn't, and you hate selling.
- ❑ **Roller-coaster**—Boom and bust cycle. Goes way up: overwhelmed. Goes way down: over-anxious.
- ❑ **Handcuffed**—Only you can run the business, so you're chained to it. Never without your cell phone or pager.
- ❑ **Juggler**—Balancing two endeavors: your old cash cow and your emerging business. Both demand your time and energy.
- ❑ **Fading**—Want to pull back and focus on something else. Can't because managers aren't good enough to take over.
- ❑ **Henpecked**—Problems with partner or key person.
- ❑ **Near-sighted**—Lack of vision. Lost sight of where you are going. Caught in the trees (or swamp); can't see the forest.
- ❑ **Trapped**—Caught in a dilemma, no alternative is attractive, can't see a way out.
- ❑ **Your unique crazy-maker**

|  |
|--|
|  |

*If you are nodding your head and saying, "Yes, that's me!"*
*then this book is for you.*

# How To
# Grow Your Business
## Without Driving Yourself Crazy

### Tools to tackle barriers to
### growth, profitability, and ease

by
Mike Van Horn, MBA

© 2002

the business group

PUBLISHED BY
**The Business Group**
135 Paul Drive, Suite 300, San Rafael, CA 94903
www.businessgroup.biz
800 367-9848

# How to Grow Your Business Without Driving Yourself Crazy

by Mike Van Horn

Published by The Business Group
135 Paul Drive, Suite 300, San Rafael, CA 94903
Tel: 1-415-491-1896, 1-800-367-9848. Fax: 1-415-491-1855
books@ businessgroup.biz

Printed and Bound by Media Litho, City of Commerce, CA
Cover Design by Pete Masterson
Illustrations by Brian Narelle and Ruth Marcus
Book Design by Ruth Marcus, Sequim, WA

Library of Congress cataloging-in-publication data
Van Horn, Mike, 1942-
    How to Grow Your Business Without Driving Yourself Crazy / Mike Van Horn. —
first edition
            p.          cm.
    Includes index and book and resource list
    ISBN  0-9714114-2-5
First Printing, 2002

1. Small business 2. Entrepreneurship 3. Management 4. Organizational Change
I. Title

                            CIP
Printing number

10 9 8 7 6 5 4 3 2 1

# CONTENTS

## PART IV: MAKING IT HAPPEN

## APPENDICES

*To three generations of Van Horn women*

*Daughter Rebecca*

*Wife B.J.*

*and Mom*

# Acknowledgments

Thanks to all the Business Group Members and other business owners I have worked with. You have taught me at least as much as you've learned from me. Remember all those problem-solving notes I scribbled on the flipcharts? They're all in here. I've disguised your names, but you'll find yourselves if you look.

Thanks to my wife B.J., who listened patiently as I tried to make sense of these ideas, then offered suggestions that helped me pull it together; to daughter Rebecca, who transcribed it all and ran the office while I was out playing author; to my mother Becky whose belief and support has got me where I am; and to my in-laws, Andy and Betty McCabe.

Thanks to my illustrator Brian Narelle, who did *not* model my Mr. Crazy logo on himself; to book designer Ruth Marcus, the fastest graphic designer in the west; to cover designer Pete Masterson, who in his role with Bay Area Independent Publishers Association has connected me to many essential resources; and to my copy editor Carolyn Holden.

Thanks to my Business Group leaders, and especially to Eva Shoshany, on whom I rely for design feedback, and about whom I most often say, "Wow, I wish I'd said that!" Well, Eva, I did; it's all in here. Thanks to Linda Anderson, Paul Butler, Jim McCraigh, and Janet Thompson for your support and encouragement; and to Dave Levinson, CPA, aka "Dr. Cash Flow."

Thanks to mentor and inspiration Jim Horan, who gives me $10,000 ideas every time we brainstorm; to Janet Tokerud for getting me back on track every time I bust another schedule; to Robyn Levin, a fountain of creative ideas for marketing and promotion, who exhorts me to think big; to Sylvia Todor, who speaks marketing prose; and to Linda Whitney and Laura Pederson-Schulz for transcribing my mumbling dictation.

It takes a community to raise a book, and I am surrounded by the best and most supportive.

# WHO SHOULD READ THIS BOOK

I wrote this book for owners of businesses like these. Maybe you will recognize them:

- A mom and pop retail store. Mom and Pop are always there. Only *they* know how to do certain key things, and they can't trust anyone else to make the deposits. They can never take a day off together.
- A design company with the owner and six other designers. Every job is a struggle with deadline and budget. He longs for the time when it was just him.
- A rapidly-growing, wildly successful restaurant. It has doubled in size and gone from twenty to fifty employees. "I feel like I need to wear a nametag so my kids will recognize me," sighs the owner.
- A home-based graphic designer. She has to juggle it all—doing the work, generating more business, getting the invoices out.
- A personal care salon. The employees never seem to have enough clients or make enough money to be happy. The owner feels like she works for her employees.
- A bakery with thirty employees. The owners by far work the longest hours. They have hired managers to reduce their load, but the employees go around the managers and come to the owners.
- A non-profit organization. "My board members just don't think like business people. Yet they expect me to produce results and stay within budget. I have nobody to talk with!" complains the Executive Director.

These are not high-tech, venture capital-funded endeavors. These are Main Street companies run by people dedicated to doing the best job they can. They are successful, but they work way too hard. They are profitable, but they don't take home as much as they want or need. They have grown, but they would like to be larger.

Many started their businesses from nothing, out of a garage or back bedroom. Some bought out former employers; others took over a family business. Some have been in business for decades; others are brand new.

Very few of them set out to be business managers. "My husband and I have art backgrounds. We never had formal training on how to run a business. Now we have six employees," says the co-owner of a print shop.

Many came from the corporate world. "When I was with the bank, I routinely put together deals of two hundred million dollars. That was nothing compared to the stress of meeting my ten-person payroll," says a former investment banker who took his "golden parachute" and started the studio he had dreamed of for years.

If this sounds like you* then read on.

I have worked with well over a thousand companies like these. Every one of them thinks his or her business is unique, but when it comes to the barriers to growth, profitability, and ease of operation, all businesses are pretty much the same. I hear the same laments over and over again, and the advice I give has been boiled down to a handful of ideas. I turned these ideas into a workshop that we have given since 1994. That workshop is the core of this book.

My philosophy is that business owners already know most of what they need. A few basic ideas applied judiciously can go a long way for you. This book is full of questions, to help you apply these ideas to your own situation. It is also full of examples, since I know that business owners learn a lot more from each other's examples than from some outside expert.

Every piece of information in this book has been tested against the toughest of audiences–small business owners. I avoid unnecessary jargon and jazzy concepts because I focus on helping you implement simple ideas that can have real results in your business. You can rest assured that it is practical and in plain language, so that you can go back to work and apply it next Monday.

P.S. My company, The Business Group, leads ongoing problem-solving groups for business owners. The changes we talk about in this book are easier to make when you have the support of your peers. If making some of these changes seems daunting for you to tackle on your own, take a look at Chapter 18, which tells you how to put together a business owners group for problem solving and accountability.

## FOR THOSE WHO WORK WITH SMALL BUSINESSES

This book is also useful to professional advisors of small business owners: consultants, coaches, accountants, business school instructors, business incubators, small business development centers, and franchise organizations.

## FOR FLEDGLING BUSINESSES ALSO

People just getting started in their own businesses can get a lot from this book. There are many books that tell you how to launch a business, but very few that address the question, "Okay, I'm up and going. Now what?"

This should also be useful to students in business schools, especially those in entrepreneurship programs. Not everybody in an MBA program intends to work for a large corporation.

# MY PHILOSOPHY OF BUSINESS

- **Growth**. Business growth is not an end in itself, but a way to achieve other important personal values: stability, wealth build-up, making a desired contribution to the community.
- **Profitability**. Profitability is the signal that you are doing a good job, and it is the engine of growth and creativity.
- **Ease**. Business needn't be a constant struggle. Your business works best when you work smoothly and without undue stress.
- **Balance**. Set your business up so that you have the desired balance between business and the rest of your life, and between the various things you do in your business.
- **Satisfaction**. You are in business to do what you love and what you do best. If you're not doing this, why put up with the hassle?
- **Integrity**. Your business is a reflection of your core values. There is no reason at all why your business can't combine high personal integrity, satisfaction, contribution to your customers, and great prosperity.
- **Community**. In today's world, business—and especially small business—is central to our sense of community: the relationship of businesses to each other, businesses to customers, employers to employees, and businesses to the surrounding community.
- **Humor**. Let's not take all this too seriously. We're here to laugh and have fun and enjoy ourselves. I try to convey this in my book, starting with the illustrations.
- **Sharing and learning**. I believe in the Power of the Group. I don't know all the answers. I would love to hear from you.

## WHO I AM

I like working with small business owners. After I got my MBA from UCLA, it took me a very short time to discover that the corporate world isn't for me.

I like problem-solving with people who have a direct stake in the outcome; who will say, "Yes!" or "No!" and not "Well, we'll bring it up at the next committee meeting."

Over the years, I have started and run a handful of small businesses, some quite successful and others not. A restaurant. A motel. An export management firm. Several real estate partnerships. A company that produced technical conferences. And my current company, The Business Group, which started in 1984. I'm sure I've made every mistake in the book.

Small business is one of the most dynamic sectors of our society. Small companies generate a tremendous amount of creativity, vitality, wealth, and new jobs. It is exciting to work with people who pour heart and soul into their endeavors, and to help them reap the rewards. I enjoy my work!

But I don't work all the time. My wife (of a quarter century) and I love to hike and sail and ski, and we live in a great place to enjoy it all. My family contributes to my business. Wife B.J. is the resident Human Resources Genius and daughter Rebecca is Office Manager. Life is good–and not all work!

Mike Van Horn, San Rafael, California, 2002

## Chapter 1

# What Drives You Crazy about Growing Your Business?

*I decided to start my own business so I wouldn't have to work so hard. Sure enough, I only have to work half time. And it doesn't matter which twelve hours a day I work.*

Lament of the overworked business owner

Does the following scenario sound familiar to you? You run your own business and it's going well. You've had a lot of success. But as you grow, a funny thing happens on the way to the bank—or to the beach. You hear yourself saying things like this:

*"Double the size of my business? I would have to work twice as many hours."*

or

*"As my business grows, I become more of an administrator and manager. I no longer get to do the work I love."*

or

*"It's so hard to find the good employees I need in order to grow. I hire these people and I end up doing their jobs as well as mine."*

Do you find yourself nodding your head? Then keep reading.


## THE PARADOX OF GROWTH

The bigger you get, the harder it *can* be to grow yet further. This is the "paradox of growth" for small businesses. It hits every kind of business: consultants and personal practitioners, professional service firms, retail stores, general contractors, small manufacturers. It hits fledgling businesses and long-established businesses, and businesses ranging in size from one person up to a hundred or more employees.

I hear their complaints: too often, growing their business collides with the desire for profitability and ease of operation. The growing business dominates their lives. They work longer hours, and have less time for family and personal interests. Their revenue grows, but their profit does not. They have to work harder and harder without earning any more money. Their headaches increase but their paycheck doesn't. No wonder growth loses its allure.

Yet growth is important for the continued viability of their businesses. Staying the same has its costs as well.

As I have worked with these owner-run companies (well over a thousand by now), I have noticed that the situations they encounter, and their reactions, sound very similar. The challenges to their continued growth fall into a handful of areas. I have found myself giving the same advice time and time again.

From this, I have developed a simple formula to crack the barriers to growing your business. That is what this book is about. It lays out an approach to tackle *any* barrier to growing your business and shows you how to apply it to numerous common situations.

## MUST YOU CHOOSE BETWEEN GROWTH, EASE AND PROFITABILITY?

Business owners often tell me, "I am not much interested in growing my business, it's as big as it needs to be. I don't want to be like one of these rapidly growing dot-com companies." If I ask them what they *are* interested in, they respond, "I wish I didn't have to work so many hours." or "Without growing larger, I'd like to become more profitable." They are more interested in improving the *ease* of operation and the *profitability* from operation. If they are working 80 hours a week, maybe they want to cut it down to 55—while keeping their company profitable and successful.

In truth, the same things needed to grow your company are also needed to operate with greater ease and profitability. You can apply the tools in this book to operating with greater ease, increasing your profitability, or growing faster. Or you can have all three.

## HAVE ALL THREE: GROWTH, EASE, *AND* PROFITABILITY!

Come on, say them all in one sentence: "Growth, ease, profitability." You can have all three if you want. They can all fit together. When we say we want to grow our business without driving ourselves crazy, we are really saying that we want to grow with ease and profitability. This book is a road map to growth, ease, and profitability.

First let's take a closer look at the barriers to growth.

## WHAT DRIVES YOU CRAZY?

What is the difference between a company that seems to grow with ease and one that has a lot of problems growing? In the latter case, very often it is the owner's unstated attitudes and management style that get in the way.

You may respond, "Well, in my case, it's the problems we encounter selling in such a competitive market." However, if I explore this with you, we may discover that your real difficulty in selling is related to the need for better tracking systems, or for more consistent effort, or for better training of your sales people. Or it may be related to your own attitude toward marketing and selling.

Tough competition, unresponsive customers, tight labor market—these things are true for everybody. Look instead at the things that are special to your situation. Start with your own (often-unstated) beliefs, attitudes, and work habits.

Below are examples my leaders and I hear all the time in our workshops. Which of these resonate with you? Use these examples to help you see the barriers that are limiting your own growth or ease or profitability. I recommend that as you read, have a pad or notebook handy, and write down the ones that pertain to you.

### You can't find and keep good people

"I can't find good people to hire."

"I'll train a good person; then they quit and become my competitor."

### You don't know how to get there

You would like to grow, but it gets fuzzy and murky when you figure out what that actually means for you, or how to go about it.

"I get so tangled up in day-to-day operations, I lose sight of my vision."

"I look at people who have grown larger businesses, and wonder, 'How did they do it?' It seems beyond me."

"I can see where I am, and I can see where I want to get to, but I sure don't see how to get there."

"Sure I have a business plan, but things change so fast I get knocked off course before the ink is dry."

### Only you can do the job

"No-one can do this job but me. I can do it so much faster and better than anyone else can. It takes more effort to manage my employees than to do the job myself."

"It's hard to let go and turn things over to my employees."

### Growth is dangerous, painful, unpleasant

"As we grow, I find I've become a manager and administrator. I don't enjoy managing and I have less time to do the work I love."

"Growing exposes me to more hazards, more stress."

"I feel overwhelmed by things I know would be useful tools." E.g., the computer, the Internet, your website, interpreting financial statements, doing employee performance reviews.

### Growth comes at the expense of having a life

"Double the size of my business? I would have to work twice as many hours!"

"How can I do all my work, yet set aside time to do all the things I must do to grow the business?"

"I will have even less time for family, recreation, other things in life."

### Growth is costly

"Sure, our revenue has gone up, but the amount I take home has stayed the same, even shrunk."

"There's not a big enough market to justify me bringing in other people."

"To expand, I would have to rent more space, buy more equipment, hire more people, and pay for all these things before I have enough work to afford them."

Other growth barriers fall into familiar categories.

### You have reached a plateau

You grew rapidly up to a certain level, then growth tailed off. No matter how hard you try, you just can't break through.

Your business market is mature; you see little room for profitable growth.

You don't know how to do the marketing needed to reach the next level.

Your product lines or services, your packaging or your way of doing business may not carry you to the next level.

Your vision is murky or limited; or you have lost track of the stepping-stones.

You have reached the end of your comfort zone. The desirability of further growth is a push/pull for you. You are attracted to it; yet you are afraid of it.

You have outgrown your systems—the ways you manage your business.

Some key ingredient is missing: capital, know-how; a critical skill, type of support or professional input.

### You have a hidden fear of success

You can't envision yourself running a company as large as you say you want.

Been there, tried that, got hurt, backed off. The nail that sticks up gets pounded down.

You believe you must take care of other responsibilities first.

You must be prudent, conservative, not take big chances.

### You have a "culture of smallness"

Business culture is usually thought of in relation to a large company, but your small company has a business culture as well. When you start out, you do everything in ways that seem natural to you, and it works. As your company grows, if you do not change, these outmoded ways of doing business become a part of the molasses that keeps you from growing further. Here are some common ways that business owners and employees continue to "think small":

Lack of controls, systems, routines, or written policy. Little or no documentation on how things are done. "We make it up as we go along." "We all know our jobs; we don't need to write it down." "If I put it into policy, then I'm stuck with it."

"We are all one big family." "We all do many jobs." Dislike of hierarchical structure. No boundaries. "If I write job descriptions, then people won't want to do all the little tasks outside their designated job."

"My door is always open." (I.e., you may interrupt me at any time.)

"We started out as hippie entrepreneurs, and profit was suspect."

"I promised I would never become the boss I hated at the corporation. But now my employees run all over me."

All profit is shielded, hidden: "Life is a write-off." When you earn extra money, you spend it. "As year end nears, we calculate our expected profit, then go on a spending spree, to buy all the things we need for next year. Otherwise it all goes to taxes."

### Your revenue grows but your profit does not

"We went from a half million in sales to a million, but am I taking any more home? Not a penny. In fact, I'm not always taking a regular pay-check." This is a key crazy-maker. It is discouraging; it saps your energy; you feel burned out; you question where you're going.

What are other drags on your profitability?

You focus on break-even instead of break-out. (If break-even is the level of revenue you need to just cover costs and survive, then in contrast, break-out is the level that allows your operation to thrive.)

Your overhead is too high. You haven't adopted the maxim, "Spend no overhead before its time."

Spending runs away from you. When money comes in, you spend it. You lack a budget or budget discipline.

Your work is too time-intensive. You are not leveraging your time and effort.

You under-price. "I provide more but I charge less, because I'm small." This is a formula for staying small—or bankruptcy.

You sell to the wrong customers. You are distracted from serving your good customers by the time and effort you spend on unprofitable or prob-lematic ones.

If you are under-performing financially, add to this list.

## GROWTH BOOSTERS—THE OPPOSITE OF GROWTH BARRIERS

For any of the statements below that are sore points for you, go to the chapter shown in parentheses.

- Get clear on your vision, your goals. Get help on clarifying these and figuring out how to get there. (Chapter 3)
- Create systems and procedures that replace things that only you (or a key person) can do. (Chapter 7)
- Find advisors who have been where you are going. (Chapter 6)

## TABLE 1-1. LIFE STAGES OF AN ENTREPRENEURIAL COMPANY

| Life Stages | Biggest Challenges | Typical Leadership Style | Attitudes Toward Profits & Finances | Choice Points or Turn Backs | Leadership Traps, Dead ends, Mistakes |
|---|---|---|---|---|---|
| 1. Start-up. Fledgling | Selling. Closing deals. Swing between marketing and doing the work | Wear all hats | Will do any job. Under-priced. Fail to charge for all work. | Am I cut out for this? Or should I get a real job? | Can't do it all, but can't afford the needed help. |
| 2. Up and running. Entrepreneurial | Making payroll. Finding and keeping good people. Keeping the business flowing | Oversee everything | Need to get paid for the work you do. | Should I grow and manage others or stay a one-person business? | Fills in for everyone to the point of burnout. Not getting paid enough. |
| 3. Established. Profitable | Run day-to-day operation while keeping an eye on the big picture. Finding time to develop new products and services. | Manage the supervisors | Each job must be profitable. Dump unprofitable business. | Should we remain a mom and pop shop? | Hard to give up control and let others do their jobs. Poor managerial and administrative skills. |
| 4. Adding organization and structure | Turning what key people know into procedures and systems | Manage the managers | The entire business must be profitable. | Should we sell out to a larger company – or grow by buying smaller ones? | Difficult to overcome "culture of smallness." Swing between laissez faire and micro-management. |
| 5. Growing sophistication | Establishing multiple locations or ventures; making remote operations work. | Build a team of top-quality execs and technicians | Assured of cash flow. Need to be paid very well. | Should we go public? | Not thinking big enough about the strategic mission. |
| 6. Cruising along | Keeping interested | Allow GM to handle day-to-day operations | Maximize value of company | Should we renew our vitality by buying small hotshot companies? | Complacency. Get overtaken by hotshot competitors. |
| 7. Ready for an exit strategy | Looking for new challenges (or retirement) | Find people good enough to run the company. "I'm half-way out of the door." | Make the balance look great. | Should I pull the equity out to bankroll my new venture? | Lose interest and squander assets. Or stay in too long because others are not trusted. |
| 8. Getting out | Letting go | Finding the next challenge. | Send my checks to Maui. | Should I keep my hand in as a consultant to the company? | Get sucked back in because successors were not prepared properly. |

- Find out how you work best, and set it up so you do more of that. (Chapter 3)
- Guard your time jealously. Not just the time you spend doing your work, and focusing on strategic concerns, but also the time you set aside for yourself and your family, for renewal and recreation. (Chapter 11)
- Promote yourself to CEO of your company. To do so, you must also hire or promote someone to fill the role you are vacating. (Chapter 8)
- Be a master team builder. Bring in top quality people. Hire people who are better than you. Set the parameters, then trust them to do their job, and hold them accountable. (Chapter 6, 8)
- Fake it till you make it. Look and behave as large as you want to become. Create your image and identity to reflect where you are going, not just where you are—or where you have been. (Chapter 3)
- Learn to sell value, not just time. Always focus on the benefit and value you bring to your customers, not just on what you do. (Chapter 11)
- Set up an accountability system for yourself (as well as for your key people). Have peers or mentors who can help you set goals and commitments and stay on them and problem-solve when you slip. (Chapter 17)
- Keep your antennas out for both opportunities and challenges. Build a network of reliable sources of forward information. (Chapter 3, 6)

## THE LIFE CYCLE OF A BUSINESS

The crazy makers on the preceding pages can pertain to any size or type of small business, and especially one that is run by the owner. In addition, some things are more likely to pertain to a particular stage of growth.

Table 1-1 on the preceding page shows the life cycle of an entrepreneurial business, including for each level the biggest challenges, typical leadership styles, attitudes toward profits and finances, choice points or turn backs; plus leadership traps, dead ends, and mistakes. See where you fit on this table.

***...Or just drive yourself crazy.*** Sometimes when I tell people that our theme is "grow your business without driving yourself crazy," they retort, "Too late, I'm already crazy!" So as a spoof, I created a flyer for the contrasting version: "How to Drive Yourself Crazy without Growing Your Business" (See next page).

# How to **Drive Yourself Crazy** Without Growing Your Business

The workshop every Business Owner is afraid they are already taking!

Tools to tackle the problems of having too much money and time on your hands

## What You're Afraid You Will Learn

### What others are saying

*"Oy, oy, oy!"*

*"I have to wear a nametag so my kids will recognize me"*

*"No time for a comment, I've got to keep working."*

*"I went into business so I would only have to work half time. And it doesn't matter which 12 hours a day I work!"*

➤ How to break the limiting mindset that you can run a business and have a life at the same time

➤ 99 important additional tasks you can do on evenings and weekends

➤ Five ways to do your employees' jobs on top of your own

➤ How to wear 8, or 9, or even 10 hats at the same time

➤ Time-tested ways to juggle many things, dropping only a few

➤ The four almost magic ways to avoid taking a vacation

**When:** Workshops begin every night, and last forever
**Cost: $1 million** (More if you're smiling)
**Call today:  1-800-BURNOUT** to reserve space.

**The Crazy Biz** is always lurking around nearby, waiting to overtake those who lose site of who they are, what is important, and where they want to go with their business. There are no groups, you are on your own.

**www.crazybiz.com**

This is a spoof. But if it seems all too real to you, sign up for our real workshop, How to Grow Your Business Without Driving Yourself Crazy.

## ROAD MAP TO GROWTH, EASE, AND PROFITABILITY

This book provides the tools to tackle all these crazy-makers and get on the path to growth, ease, and profitability. Many companies grow like gang-busters and do not seem to run into the same kinds of barriers. Why not? Those people are no smarter than you are. The difference is, they apply the kinds of things described in this book. This stuff ain't rocket science. It's about applying a set of simple ideas whenever you encounter a business problem. It would be presumptuous to call these tools the "secrets of business growth"—they are there in plain sight.

## ASK YOURSELF . . .

At the end of each chapter are questions you can use to apply the topics discussed to your business. I recommend that you use a notebook to answer the questions for yourself. The greatest value you can get from this book is not from the ideas it contains, but from reflecting these ideas off your experience and business situation.

You will get the most from this if you write out the answers. You don't need to answer all the questions. Focus on the ones that have the most meaning for you – your "hot-button" issues.

Think about the way your business operates, and the way you run it.

1. What stops you from achieving your objectives and realizing your vision?
2. What barriers have you run into?
3. What challenges have been the hardest for you to overcome?
4. In what ways do you have a culture of smallness?
5. How do you resist going for as much as you can?
6. Is there a way in which you fear success or fear failure?

## TABLE 1-2

### Business owner's agreement to make specific improvements

When a business owner joins one of our Business Groups, the group leader has them identify the barriers and challenges they face, and make an agreement to make specific improvements. Here is the questionnaire we use. Some of the questions will be easier to answer after you have read later chapters.

_____          _____

Your name                                                                          Date

1.  What is your biggest barrier, your key challenge, your toughest business problem?

2. What is your desired outcome? How would you like it to be? By when?

3. What has kept you from achieving this outcome up till now?

4. What have you tried?

5. What have you avoided doing?

6. What is the value of this outcome to you? Be as specific as possible.
    - Monetary value, wealth
    - Ease, reduced stress, well-being
    - Satisfaction, sense of accomplishment
    - Other values

7. What is the cost to you of not attaining this outcome, of staying as you are?

8. What *specific improvement* do you want to make first?

9. To achieve this desired outcome, what support do you need? What support could The Business Group and your leader provide you?
    - Problem solving. Where will the ideas and feedback of the group be most needed?
    - Accountability. Where do you most need the group to help you stay on track with this?

10. What course of action must you commit to in order to bring about the desired outcome?

11. What might hinder you from completing this course of action? What misgivings or reservations do you have?

12. Are you willing to make this commitment? Yes or No?

## Chapter 2

# Growth, Ease and Profitability

### Questionnaires and checklists to assess your business

The crazy-makers in Chapter 1 are heartfelt sentiments of business owners, as well as symptoms of needed underlying change. In this chapter
you will find questionnaires and checklists to help you identify "hot-button issues" that are impediments to the three themes of this book: Growth,
Ease, and Profitability. Use them to clarify the desires and the barriers you
face in each area and identify your strengths and weaknesses.

### THE BUSINESS VIABILITY TEST

When can companies operate with greater ease and profitability, and grow
without driving themselves crazy? Let's start with a look at how your
small business appears when it is operating smoothly. Table 2-1, our
"Business Viability Test," has two contrasting profiles. Column 1 is "The
Route to Growth, Ease, and Profitability." These are the operational building blocks of growth, ease, and profitability. Column 2, in contrast, is headed "It is Hard to Get Over the Hump: Business Drives You Crazy."

It's not necessary or even feasible that your business operates entirely
in Column 1. However, the more often your business tends toward Column
2, the less likely it is operating with growth, ease, and profitability.

Conversely, you can increase your growth, ease, and profitability by tackling Column 2 items individually.

Of course, there is a range of options for each row. In Item 7, for example, between "Your customers pay as they go" and "You pay costs up front yet have a long receivables cycle" would lie "We invoice right away, and customers pay within 30 to 35 days."

One strong Column 1 entry can outweigh a Column 2. The real problems arise when Column 2 items come in combination. For example, if you are in a low-margin business—groceries, bookstore—you can counterbalance low margins with strong cost control and rapid inventory turnover. However, if you find labor costs creeping up and stale inventory building up, growth, ease, and profitability evaporate.

This list was inspired by a jewelry-maker. He had to buy his gold and gems up front, paying cash. He had a big inventory and had to pay his goldsmiths as they produced his pieces. The pieces didn't sell instantly, and after shipping, it took months to get paid by the jewelry stores. He increased both his ease and profitability not by growing, but by shrinking. He slashed overhead and focused on high-margin pieces where the high price compensated for the long cash cycle, and by doing personal commissions where customers paid a big up-front deposit.

For almost every business I have worked with, there is some way to attack the Column 2 cluster. On rare occasions, however, the best solution may be to close up shop, as in the case of an independent bookstore trapped in a small location with declining foot traffic and then hit by chains and online booksellers. We came to the conclusion that it was no longer a viable business.

## GROWTH, EASE AND PROFITABILITY ASSESSMENTS FOR YOUR BUSINESS

This next section discusses the three themes of growth, ease, and profitability individually and presents questionnaires to help you assess where your business is now. The Questionnaires are designed to identify your "hot button issues" and areas of strength. They can be used to establish targets for improvement in weak areas.

To use the questionnaires:
1. Answer these questions for yourself. (Remember, you can download them from our website if you wish.)
2. Rate yourself on each question.
3. Look for the questions that you ranked 2 or 1. Prioritize those. Those are you "hot button" issues. You should not select too many. Choose one, or at most two, from each questionnaire.

4. Total each questionnaire, add up the 4s, 3s, 2s, and 1s for each. High scores are better.
5. Compare the three. The questionnaire where you have the lowest score is probably where you feel the greatest stress. Surprise, surprise! You already knew this!

## THEME 1: GROWTH

### *What is growth?*

Some people have told me that the phrase "grow your business" is grammatically incorrect. You can grow vegetables or flowers; but you cannot grow a business. Such people have clearly never owned a business. Whether you have potted plants in your apartment or run an agri-business giant, you know that growing plants is tricky. It takes the right combination of resources: soil, water, sunlight, fertilizer. You must be eternally vigilant for weeds and pests. You must trim and prune. A good dose of caring is essential.

The same is true for a business. Small business owners experience the process of growing—or trying to grow—their businesses in very personal terms. Big corporations can talk about increased market presence in abstract terms, but small business owners experience the gain or loss of each customer; the success or failure of each marketing effort; the effectiveness of each salesperson. Growing a business is clearly the key to one's livelihood, security, and retirement. But for many small business owners, it's even more—their business is an expression of who they are, of what they most enjoy doing, and their passion. GROWING a business brings financial rewards, but also allows for making a greater contribution by providing products and services to more people.

For many of the people I work with, their business is just a tool. They start up, buy and operate, and sell or dissolve businesses as a matter of course. They use their business as an instrument to attain other ends—and this is fine. Even so, they are very clear that the "grow" in "grow your business" is an active, transitive verb.

For other business owners, lack of business growth—when growth is desired—is seen as a personal reflection of who they are. This may or may not be a healthy attitude, but it's undeniably true. So, when I discuss growing your business, I mean more than increasing revenues and marketing share and customer base. I also mean expanding your ability to express yourself in the world through your chosen vehicle, i.e., your business.

### *Why grow?*

What are your reasons for wanting to grow your business? They might include:

## TABLE 2-1. THE BUSINESS VIABILITY TEST

| Column 1<br>The Route to Growth, Ease, and Profitability | Column 2<br>It Is Hard to Get Over the Hump:<br>Business Drives You Crazy |
|---|---|
| 1. Your markets are steady, foreseeable. You have regular, reliable customers. | 1. Your markets are uncertain. You face rapid and unpredictable change in your markets. You face huge swings in business—feast or famine. |
| 2. You have a unique, protectible niche; you can set yourself apart from competitors. | 2. You face highly competitive markets and strong competition. Customers can easily switch. |
| 3. You can set prices to operate at "breakout" level, factoring in a reserve for hazards, maintenance, and financing growth. | 3. You under-price and feel you cannot raise prices to give an adequate margin for fear of losing customers. |
| 4. High margin on sales gives you flexibility in pricing. | 4. Since prices are squeezed, you face chronic low-profit margin. |
| 5. Your overhead is low compared to your revenue swings and gross profit margin. | 5. Your overhead and fixed costs are too high for your level of sales and profits. |
| 6. You have low or no inventory, or else rapid turnover. | 6. You have high inventory costs and slow turnover. |
| 7. Your customers pay as they go. You have good trade terms with vendors. | 7. You pay direct costs up-front (inventory, materials, labor), yet have a long receivables cycle. |
| 8. Your profit from operations is sufficient to pay yourself well, to reward your people, to build up a cushion, and to contribute to financial incentives and retirement plans | 8. Low profitability means you don't pay yourself—or your people—enough. You suffer from burnout; and your best people go elsewhere. |
| 9. You find a way to free yourself up to focus on business development, to look at the big picture, and to relax. Your revenue allows you to hire the help you need. | 9. There is a constant time crunch for you and key people; it is hard to carve out time for strategic activities. You are always handling details, putting out fires. |
| 10. You leverage your effort by selling value, not hours; by turning your personal service into a product; by building a top-quality team to do what you do. | 10. It is hard to leverage your efforts. It seems you have to do it all, and that revenue is tied to your personal efforts. |
| 11. You have stability in your labor force, or else, it is easy for you to get new people trained and up to speed. | 11. You face high turnover of people, thus high training costs or inconsistent and mediocre performance. |
| 12. You have top-quality employees, allowing you to focus on key tasks and do what you are best at. Operations run smoothly even when you are away. | 12. You burn yourself out. It all falls on your shoulders. |
| 13. You have cost-effective marketing. Marketing and selling costs per customer are much less than profit per customer. | 13. Your marketing is expensive and time-consuming. It is hard to tie marketing effort to sales results. |
| 14. Your workflow is smooth; there are no bottlenecks. Your production control systems monitor quality, scheduling, ordering, and costs. | 14. Your production isn't efficient, due to old, slow equipment or a poorly designed workspace. You are operating near capacity with little slack, leading to overtime costs, waste, and returns. |
| 15. You can spend a small amount to test the market and see if further investment is justified. | 15. A high initial investment is required for you to grow, and there is a long lag time until the investment is repaid. Your investment is vulnerable in the face of market uncertainty. |
| 16. You know what the keys are and you have good systems. "Cookie cutter" formula can be duplicated and taught to your team. | 16. You lack a proven growth formula. You make it up by the seat of your pants as you go along. |
| 17. Banks call offering to lend you money. | 17. Your lack of consistent profitability, plus credit problems, makes it hard to borrow money. |
| 18. Outside financiers (bankers, investors) see the potential and offer you money. | 18. It is hard for you to demonstrate good business prospects; thus it's hard to raise capital. |

- **To make more money,** not just more revenue, but also more profit
- **To increase the stability** of your business, broadening your base so that you are not tossed about in the storms
- **To use your overhead more efficiently**, more cost-effectively
- **To make a greater contribution,** by making your valuable product or service available to more people
- **To operate with greater ease and profitability**; that is, with less effort and more reward.

## When not to grow

You may *not* want to grow your business when:
- You have gone through a large growth spurt and you need to digest the growth you have made.
- You are as large as you need to be, and growing larger would require a huge investment for an uncertain return.

## What if you stay the same?

Is it worthwhile for you to take the steps needed to expand your business? If you are not sure, then ask yourself, what is the downside to operating at your current level? For example, at your current size, are you:
- Whipsawed by the slightest market shift?
- Vulnerable to the incursions of larger competitors?
- Unable to take an extended vacation because you cannot afford good backup?
- Unable to earn quite enough to justify essential overhead costs?
- Unable to find enough challenge?

If these are all too real for you, then growing your business is probably worth the effort.

## What is your desired growth track?

In the following profiles, there is no right or wrong answer. The purpose is to identify where you are. Which fits best for you? Or perhaps there is another description that better describes your situation.

| | |
|---|---|
| **Fast track growth**<br>(50% or more per year) | Likely requires substantial financing from outside—either equity or debt. Influx of new expertise—especially related to how to grow. Requires a high-leverage business plan, changes in the mode of operation, and new key players. |
| **Organic growth**<br>(20% to 50% increase in revenue per year) | Growth is a strong objective, but it relies on increasing current markets. Uses existing business model or an evolution. Uses bank financing and line of credit, or internal financing. Does not radically change the current operation. |

**Incidental growth**
(0% to 20% per year)

Growth is not the aim; ease and profitability are.

**Small business spurt**   A very small business—since it starts from a low base—can have a huge percentage increase in sales merely by applying business discipline, such as bringing in good help, adding systems, improving marketing and strategic time use.

From these profiles, you can describe your own desired growth track.

## Questionnaire #1: Growth

**How does your company rate
on these keys determinants of growth?**

| | **4** Yes almost always | **3** Pretty good | **2** So-so | **1** Rarely or never |
|---|---|---|---|---|
| 1. Do you have a solid vision for the growth of your business? | | | | |
| 2. Do you have a strategic growth plan based on your proven strategies? | | | | |
| 3. Do you regularly review progress toward your goals and stay accountable to your commitments? | | | | |
| 4. Do you set your priorities according to what's most important to move you toward your goals? | | | | |
| 5. Do you have the team needed to power your desired growth? | | | | |
| 6. Does your management style allow you to keep focused on your strategic aims? | | | | |
| 7. Do you have strong role models, advisors, and strategic alliances? | | | | |
| 8. Do you have a firm grasp of why your customers do business with you instead of someone else? | | | | |
| 9. Do you keep attuned to the opportunities and challenges in your marketplace? | | | | |
| 10. Is your marketing capable of producing the growth in sales you need to achieve your goals? | | | | |
| Total | | | | |

### Where do you have the most problems with growth?

If you answered with 1 or 2 to any of the above questions, refer to the following chapters or references to help you clarify the challenges you face.

| | |
|---|---|
| 1 or 2. Developing solid vision and a strategic growth plan | Chapter 3. "Your Vision of Business Success" |
| 3. What approach to setting goals and being held accountable would work for you? What goals or targets should you be held accountable to? How could you be held accountable? | Chapter 16 & 17 |
| 4. For which of your goals would it be particularly important to have a prioritized project plan? | Chapters 14 & 17 |
| 5 Where are the biggest holes on your team? What one position could you fill, or what personnel shifts could you make, that would make the greatest impact? | Chapter 6 |
| 6. How could you change the way you run day-to-day operations to help keep your focus on strategic aims? | Chapter 5 |
| 7. What role model, experienced advisor, or strategic ally would be of greatest benefit to you? | Chapter 6 |
| 8. Would you be willing to call your best customers— the kind you would like more of—and ask them why they do business with you instead of someone else? | Our book, *The Magic Chain of Marketing* |
| 9. Where are you most likely to get surprised by outside events or trends? What could you do to stay on top of things proactively? | Our book, *The Magic Chain of Marketing* |
| 10. What parts of your marketing are working and where does it need to be upgraded to achieve your goals? | Our book, *The Magic Chain of Marketing* |

## THEME 2: EASE

### What does it mean to operate your business with ease?

What is ease? People told me I shouldn't focus on "ease" in this book. They told me that business owners understand growth and profitability, but that ease is a fuzzy notion. I disagree. People who *lack* ease of operation sure know what it's about! And they want it. For many business owners, ease of operation is a more important goal than growth and more profit. But if you don't understand ease, here's an analogy:

Imagine an engine that is well-tuned and just hums along, even when pulling huge loads. Now imagine another engine that's knocking and sputtering. It's hard to start, hard to keep going and uses way too much energy. It can't haul the load it should—and throws off dark fumes. The former is operating with ease, the latter is certainly not.

This analogy applies well to the way you work in your company. Ease does not mean kicking back, loafing, or coasting along. Rather, the work flows. You and your people work hard and produce results. And you can see the results of your efforts. You enjoy what you are doing. Your time is used well. You have the desired balance between different work activities and between work and the rest of your life. When you can work hard and still feel energized the next day, you are operating with ease.

Nor does ease mean "stress-free." But the stress of your job comes from tackling tough—yet solvable—problems, making tight—yet doable—deadlines. It is not the stress of going up against impossible situations, intractable conflicts, or problems that never seem to get solved.

We are very familiar with the opposite of ease: Working too hard; feeling tired, discouraged, or burned out, or working much harder than needed. Business owners tell me when they lack ease:

"I wake up stewing at 3:00 AM."

"I break commitments to myself and my family so I can work more."

"It's Friday, and I'm thinking, only two more work days until Monday."

"It's affecting my health."

"It's never-ending: no matter how much I get done, there's always more."

"Even when I'm on vacation, my pager and cell phone interrupt the tranquillity."

When you operate with ease, you put in the effort and get a satisfying result. You have good people who help produce the result, so you can focus on the big issues. When you leave at the end of the day, you can put it out of your mind until tomorrow. You go on vacation (*without* your cell phone or pager) and you are confident things will run smoothly.

When I ask business owners what they would include as part of ease of operation, their answers fall into these categories:

*In the dictionary, ease is defined as freedom from labor, pain, annoyance, concern, anxiety, difficulty, great effort, financial need. Ease is a quiet state of mind, financial plenty, comfort, well being, happiness, contentment, and calmness.*

• Getting to do what you most enjoy in your business

• Having a work style that fits you and draws on your strengths

• Satisfaction with the work you do and the results you produce

• Getting desired financial reward from your effort

• Having the desired balance between business and the rest of life

- Creating the opportunity, time and resources for activities outside of work
- Getting to make the contribution to your community that you want to

Ease is both an attitude and a result. As an attitude, ease—or inner peace—can help you get through the toughest situation. It is more a function of who you are at the core, which is beyond the scope of this book. But ease as a skill is what this book is about. When you tackle the barriers to ease, your feeling of ease increases. If you then learn to pay attention, upticks in your feelings of unease become a sensitive indicator of things that remain to be dealt with in the way you do business.

## What is your desired ease profile?

| **Hard charger** | I love my work. Long hours don't bother me. I want to improve my effectiveness and productivity and my executive touch, so that I can take on more. |
| **Work smarter, not harder** | I've put in the long hours and achieved great results. Now, I want to maintain—or even improve—the results yet cut back the hours. To do this, I need to run a great management team. |
| **Absentee owner** | I want the business to run well without me. I'll be there part of the time and maintain oversight, but I want others to make it go. I'm going on to something else. |
| **Looking for an exit strategy** | I already have one foot out the door. I want to assure continuity and maximize the value of my asset so I can sell at the best price. |

## The unease profile

What is the contrasting nightmare of slogging that limits your ease of operation? When people aspire to one of the levels in the Ease Profile, but do not accomplish it, they might describe a corresponding negative profile:

- I am burnt out, discouraged. I am working far too many hours with too little effect. I feel like I am banging my head against the wall. I am not producing the results I want. It seems I can never get the job done. There is always more to do.
- We just do not work smart. We make mistakes, and have to do things over. We are always over budget and behind schedule. The burden always falls on me. I am stressed; I can never relax; I stew about it all night; I never get any time off.
- If I am not there, things fall apart. I cannot rely on the people who work with me to do it right. Customers and others make demands that only I can fulfill.

- If I am not working, the whole thing stops. If I am not billing, my income stops. The company has no value except for the hours I put in.

## Questionnaire #2: Ease

**How can you increase the ease with which you run your company?**

| | 4 Yes almost always | 3 Pretty good | 2 So-so | 1 Rarely or never |
|---|---|---|---|---|
| 1. Are you satisfied with the balance between your work and the rest of your life? | | | | |
| 2. Does your role in your business build on your strengths and what you most like to do? | | | | |
| 3. Are you good at leveraging your effort (producing greater results and returns for each hour you work)? | | | | |
| 4. Do you use your own time well; i.e., are you able to set priorities, set a schedule, and stay on it? | | | | |
| 5. Does your company culture support you in working the way you want, and getting done what you set out to do? | | | | |
| 6. Do you make it a habit to reduce routine activities to systems, procedures, and policies that others can handle instead of you? | | | | |
| 7. Do you pay yourself what you are worth? | | | | |
| 8. Do you have the right people working for you, who free you up to focus on what you need to do? | | | | |
| 9. Are you good at building and guiding a team, and fostering teamwork? | | | | |
| 10. Do you have the outside professional advice and support you need? | | | | |
| Total | | | | |

## Where do you have the most problems with ease of operation?

If you answered with 1 or 2 to any of the above questions, here are questions and suggestions to help you clarify the challenges you face, plus references to chapters where you can further pursue the issue.

1. Describe the balance you would like between work and the rest of your life. What gets in the way of having that? What is the effect of having poor balance? What do you wish you could do even though it seems unrealistic? — Chapter 3. "Your Vision of Business Success"

2. What personal strengths should your business be built upon? What do you most like to do that you are not doing in your business? In what ways does your business, as it is currently structured, operate from your weaknesses? What is the impact of this? How could things be restructured? — Chapter 3

3. Do you find it difficult to leverage your efforts? Why? What have other people in your situation done to leverage their efforts? What is a conceivable way to leverage your efforts? — Chapter 11, "Recapture Your Time"

4. What pulls you off your own effective time use, priorities, and schedule? — Chapter 11

5. How does you company culture hinder you working the way you want and getting done what you want to? How should it be? — Chapter 12, "Build a Culture of Growth"

6. What activities would you like to reduce to systems, procedures, and policies? What do you do that you wish others could handle? — Chapter 7, "Get the Secret Knowledge out of Your Head"

7. How much are you worth? How much should you be paid? How much would you have to pay someone to perform the roles you currently handle in your business? How much could you make working for another company? — Chapter 3

8. Who should you bring in to free you up? — Chapter 6, "Hire Wonder Woman or Superman"

9. How should your team operate? What could you do to foster better team work? What people would be better team members? — Chapter 8, "Promote Yourself to CEO"

10. What outside professional advice or support would be the most liberating for you? Would help you ease your job the most? — Chapter 6

## THEME 3: PROFITABILITY

### What is profitability?

We all know what *profit* is: the surplus left over from revenue after covering expenses. *Profitability* is the measure of profit generated on an ongoing basis. Profit is generally measured in dollar terms; profitability is measured as a percentage of sales. You need to focus on both.

For many small businesses, profit equals the owner's paycheck. If your profitability from operations doesn't generate enough cash flow, you don't get paid. The first step is to figure out how much you need to pay yourself—to cover your basic needs and desired lifestyle, savings and retirement, and to pay your taxes. Then, figure out how much money your business needs to bring in to cover its expenses and pay you this amount.

This is an eye-opening experience for business owners. Your initial reaction may be dismay: "How can I ever bring in that much revenue? Am I doomed to just scrape by?" But, given your financial goals, you can begin looking seriously at how to restructure your business to give you what you need financially—or else get out of it and go on to something else.

## The uses of profit

As your attitude toward profit shifts from (a) what's left over that you use to pay yourself to (b) a resource you use for critical business needs, you can plan your operations so that they generate profit from ongoing operations to cover such items as:

- Fund for expansion or upgrades
- Cushion to cover downturns
- Fund for bonuses and financial incentives and profit-sharing
- Retirement programs for you and employees
- Debt repayment
- Return on your initial investment
- Last but not least, paying taxes

Using the above items, you can create a profit budget for the coming year. Your accountant may gnash his or her teeth over the above paragraph, correctly pointing out that many of these items are business expenses, not profit. I agree. However, for small business owners who are trying to make a transition from a cover-the-costs mentality to a generate-a-surplus mentality, developing this profit budget is invaluable. These are the very items that they otherwise fail to account for in their planning, their projections, and their pricing decisions. The format for a profit budget is found in chapter 13.

Here are several ways that small businesses should look at profitability:

- **Profit is ROI—return on investment.** You (and perhaps others) put capital into your business and you expect to get it back someday with a suitable rate of return. For an established yet vulnerable small business, a suitable ROI can be from 20% to 30% per annum.
- **Profit is ROE—return on effort**. Many people start their businesses

largely with sweat equity, putting in thousands of hours of their own time—unpaid—to get the business up and running. Can you ever recoup the value of your time?

A business run by the owner should look at profit as the financial return per unit of your effort. For example, suppose you work 2,000 hours in a year, and your company's profit is $250,000. For that year, you could say that you had a return of $125 for each hour you put in. If you want to operate with greater ease, make sure you don't increase profit by dint of harder work and longer hours. More on this in chapter 11 in the section on "Leverage Your Effort."

• **Profit is a tuning fork**. It tells you how well tuned your business instrument is. When you are doing things right—working productively and cost-effectively, selling the right things to the right people, serving your customers well, treating your own people well—profit is the measure that amply demonstrates that.

The opposite is also true. When your business is not tuned properly, it sounds the discordant notes of low productivity, unhappy employees, dwindling customer base, and mounting losses. Profit is acknowledgement that the business is tuned properly.

• **Profit is flow**. Profit provides the surplus that helps you weather the lean times. Profit allows you to be generous.

• **Profit is energy**. Many small business owners say they are more interested in achieving their vision than in making a big profit. But without adequate profitability, you get worn down, burnt-out and discouraged. An unprofitable business fails unless outside money is continually pumped in. You cannot make the contribution you want without bringing in a good profit.

## What is your desired profitability profile?

| | |
|---|---|
| **Torrents of cash** | I have a high-margin, low-overhead business. It should throw off a lot of cash flow for myself and others, e.g., investors. |
| **Profit is our energy** | Besides paying ourselves well, profit is our company's engine of growth—especially since bankers and venture capitalists aren't flocking to our door. |
| **Enough to live well** | I'm in business to do what I love. Business must meet my financial needs both now and later. |
| **Profit is secondary** | I don't need to take a lot of money out of the business. I'd rather plow it back in, pay people better, give bonuses, and build up value. Profit just goes to taxes anyway. |

**Go-go start up**          Rapid expansion and market penetration are much more important in the short run than showing a profit.

## *The unprofitability profile*

Here is a contrasting nightmare of slim pickings:

- I have a high-overhead, low-margin business. I can never get ahead. It is a struggle just to cover my monthly requirements. I am always putting more of my own money into the business.

- The company operates hand-to-mouth, break even. There is rarely enough to pay for needed improvements, upgrades, or growth.

- I will never be able to retire. If I stop working, that's it. I have never put any money away.

- I have always run my business to minimize profits. Life is a write off. I spend money rather than pay myself. But I cannot get a bank loan, and I have a poverty mentality.

- I have no reality on actually earning a profit, or even enough revenue to have a going business. I am always in start-up phase. This business seems more like a hobby than a going concern.

## Questionnaire #3: Profitability
**How can you increase the
profitability of your company?**

| | 4 | 3 | 2 | 1 |
|---|---|---|---|---|
| | Yes almost always | Pretty good | So-so | Rarely or never |
| 1. Do you insist that each activity and product line is profitable? | | | | |
| 2. Do you have clear financial objectives and targets for each time period, and regularly compare them with actual figures? | | | | |
| 3. Do your financial systems and controls give you the timely feedback you need to make good management decisions? | | | | |
| 4. Do you know how profitable your next sale will be? | | | | |
| 5. Do you know the profitability of each part of your business? | | | | |
| 6. Does your pricing give you adequate margins on sales? | | | | |
| 7. Do you analyze the rate of return and payback period of major expenditures before you make them? | | | | |
| 8. Is your cash flow adequate to maintain healthy operations? | | | | |
| 9. Do you have the outside advice you need, including a forward-looking financial advisor (CFO)? | | | | |
| 10. Do you watch expenditures like a hawk, even when times are good and cash is rolling in? | | | | |
| Total | | | | |

## *Where do you have the most problems with profitability?*

If you answered with 1 or 2 to any of these, here are follow up questions and suggestions to help you clarify the challenges you face. The numbers below are keyed to the questionnaire above. (This topic is covered in greater depth in chapter 13 , "Build a Culture of Profitability."

1. Which of your activities or product lines are not profitable? If you do not know, what would it take for you to find out? What could you do about the unprofitable parts of your business? What would it take to make them profitable? How can you justify continuing with unprofitable segments?

2. What would it take for you to have clear financial objectives? What help would you need? What information? Can you set targets for each time period? What systems and what help would you need to compare your performance with your projections?

3. What should you know about your business performance to make good management decisions? What figures would give you that? What system would help you develop those figures? What information would you have to track?

4. To know this you must know your gross margin.

5. To know this you must separate revenues and costs for each part of your business and know the growth margins. What additional information would you need to know the profitability of each part of your business? What systems must you add or refine to track it? What help do you need?

6. Why are your prices too low? Where should you increase prices, increase volume, decrease costs, or decrease overhead? What are your assumptions about pricing that keep your prices too low?

7. What are the big expenditures that you have made, or need to make? How can you recoup these costs? How would you allocate these costs to your sales? How would this effect your prices? What is the payback period? Are there big costs which you may not be able to recoup (such as equipment) that cannot be paid for before it is obsolete? Or employees who cannot earn enough to cover their own salary?

8. How much cash flow do you need? If you do not know, how can you find out? How much financial cushion should you have to cover the variability of your business, the unexpected ups and downs? How much do you need to pay yourself, to cover unexpected things, to lay the groundwork for growth, pay your people better, pay taxes, or repay debt?

9. What outside advice do you most need that you are not getting? How could you get it? How could it pay for itself?
10. Where do you know that you are spending more money than you should? What would it take to keep tighter reigns on your expenditures?

## ASK YOURSELF . . .

1. What is your Number 1 hot button issue regarding Growth?
2. What is your Number 1 hot button issue regarding operating with greater ease?
3. What is your Number 1 hot button issue regarding desired profitability?
4. How has poor financial performance limited your growth and ease of operation?
5. Have you or your company reached a plateau? What has slowed your desired further growth?

**Extra credit**

6. Which of your barriers lies at the root of the others?
7. How much would it be worth for you to overcome the barriers described above?

## GROWTH, EASE, AND PROFITABILITY ASSESSMENT

For help with a growth, ease, and profitability assessment, or for personalized assistance, see the Book and Resource List (page 277).

## Chapter 3

# Your Vision of Business Success

### *Where you want to go. How to get there.*

*Keeping your business vision in sight energizes you to
crack through the barriers to growth.*

Now that we've completed our focus on the barriers to growth, ease,
and profitability, let's next turn 180° and look at your vision of
growth, ease, and profitability.

What do I mean by a vision of business success? It is a positive, concrete,
and energizing declaration of satisfying achievement in your profitable
enterprise. This is built from the dictionary definitions of vision, business,
and success. Think about each key word in this statement:

*Positive. Concrete. Energizing. Satisfying. Profitable.*

These are the foundation stones of a compelling vision of business success.
The question I want you to be able to answer is this one:

*How can you structure your business so you can get exactly what you want?*

If you don't have a business vision, this chapter will help you develop one. If you already have one, it can help you refine it so it provides an even stronger motivation to guide your actions.

## A COMPELLING VISION OF BUSINESS SUCCESS

The best vision statement for a small business is concise and concrete. There's no need to be elaborate. Your vision statement is basically the completion of this sentence: "I/we will have the business we want when..." We ask business owners to paint a brief picture of their business vision. Here are some examples:

"We want to have five or six stores in the three-county area."

"We want to be recognized as the leader in our marketplace in this metropolitan area."

"I want to grow the business to a size so that it can be sold for $10 million within ten years."

"We want to have a national reach, with enough representatives so that people in any major market can find out about us and do business with us."

"I want to expand from being a small service provider in one market to selling our packages nationally. "

"I want our business to provide for our financial needs, to run well in my absence, and be large and profitable enough to weather financial storms and downturns."

"I want my business to grow enough so that I once again get to focus on the design work I love, rather than being stuck in day-to-day management as I am now."

"Once I sell the three stores that don't fit our theme, I'm turning day-to-day operations over to the General Manager and returning to college to get my degree."

Once you have your vision statement, you need to flesh it out with dollars, numbers, and dates—but a brief, inspiring statement remains the heart of it. The questions in this chapter will take the mystery and grandiosity out of the process.

## BENEFITS OF A VISION; THE COST OF NO VISION

The two statements below were made by the same person; the second one after she answered the questions in this chapter.

### Statement #1. Lost sight of her vision

"My employees are so aggravating. I have to do their jobs as well as my own. I'm always so busy I never have time to do what I need or want to do. My daughter said the other day, 'Mom, you are always so busy.' Sometimes I think I'd just like to sell the business."

### Statement #2. Reconnected with her vision

"I got into this business because I like to design the products and oversee their production. My design eye has brought us our success. To tap into my creativity I must keep up my energy. I can't work so many hours. I must free myself up to be the designer, and not be the manager of employees and details."

Once she reconnected with what she loved about her business, she gained better perspective on how to deal with the difficulties. It became clear that she needed to hire a general manager to handle day-to-day operations. Her question shifted from, "Can I afford to hire a GM?" to "How can I afford *not* to hire a GM?"

Lack of clarity on your vision of success is one of the greatest causes of unsatisfying business performance. A vision statement has several benefits:

It keeps you focused on where you want to go.

It helps you get back on track when you are pulled off.

It helps bring into focus the barriers to achieving your goals.

It provides a touchstone to decide whether proposed activities or strategies are on target.

It inspires and energizes those who work with you. Your goal thus becomes a shared goal.

But you need a *written* vision statement—not just a good idea in your mind. Formulating a vision statement benefits you and your business because it brings clarity to what you want, what you value, what you're good at, and what you love. When you lose sight of these things, you feel confused, dissatisfied, frustrated, and stuck.

### Why business people don't have a vision statement

Despite its importance, many business owners do not have a business vision statement. Here are some of the reasons why:

"I am just struggling to get by day-to-day, to keep the doors open, and provide myself and my family with a living. Why do I need to worry about some grandiose vision?"

"I am swept along on the tides of business fate. The gods laugh at those who dare make a plan. Who am I to create a vision?"

"I've had several business visions but I've made little progress toward them. I know how I'd like it to be, but day-to-day demands keep me from focusing on that."

If you feel this way, look again at the vision statements at the beginning of the chapter. Do these statements seem grandiose or unattainable? Your vision needs to be challenging and inspiring, yet reachable and practical.

---

### TABLE 3-1

### *A Vision of Business Success is Compelling When ...*

your business helps you get what you want in life

you get to do the work you love

your business is built on your personal strengths

your business is built on your personal values and ethics

your business supports the rest of your life

you offer something people want and you sell it to them profitably

you move with opportunities and challenges

---

## THE SWEET SPOT OF BUSINESS SUCCESS

SWEET SPOT OF BUSINESS SUCCESS

Your business is most satisfying to you when you are doing things you love and have passion for, when you are doing what you're good at, and when people are willing to pay well for your service. This is illustrated here as three partially overlapping circles. The intersection of these three circles is the *sweet spot of business success and satisfaction*. This is the route to growth, ease, and profitability.

Business owners know this, but sometimes—in the crush of day-to-day operations—forget it. You lose sight of how important it is for your business to grow from your strengths and desires. You may question whether it is even possible. It is important to ask and re-ask these questions from time to time. All the businesses that we work with re-examine these questions at least once a year. This is not a once-in-a-business-lifetime exercise; your answers change over time.

## QUESTIONS TO HELP YOU GENERATE YOUR VISION

For a larger company, a business vision normally starts with strategic questions of products, customers, market share, and return on investment. However, for a small business owner a vision statement encompasses more than the path of your business. It is more personal because your business is so much an expression of you; therefore, the personal elements become the foundation of your vision.

Answering these questions will give you the raw material to fill out your own vision of business success. Your vision statement doesn't have to incorporate all of this information. There are a lot of questions; answer the ones that resonate with you and ignore the others.

Watch especially for those questions that seem important but for which you have no answer.

The questions preceded by "**" will help you identify the barriers to achieving your vision of success; your answers to these will be issues to tackle as you read the rest of this book.

> *There's no reason why your business can't combine high personal integrity, satisfaction, contribution to your customers, and great prosperity.*

This is a great exercise to undertake with someone else: your business advisor, partner, spouse, or top manager. Answer the questions on your own, then discuss your answers. Get feedback. Brainstorm on the fuzzy parts. Far too many business owners neglect these questions. I've seen the look of shock that crosses their faces upon reading the first question, "Why are you in business?" "Well, I never asked myself that question before." We ask our member businesses these questions every year. Your answers change. Your desires and circumstances change.

### Get what you want from your business
Your business should help you get what you want in life.

1. Why are you in business? Where are you going with your business? What is your personal mission or calling or driving force? Where is the excitement for you? What do you personally want to accomplish? For example:
   a good living, security, wealth build-up
   follow your passion, practice your craft, do what you love
   create something valuable
   achieve a worthwhile goal
   leave a legacy for your family
   make a contribution to your customers, to your community

professional acknowledgment, recognition
live a desired lifestyle
the opportunity to pursue another interest
community, connection, belonging

What are your life goals outside your business? How does your business contribute to these? Is there is a larger contribution you want to make through your business?

What is the wildest, far out idea of what you could accomplish with your business? What is a prudent, practical, reasonable idea of what you could accomplish with your business?

   **How are you unclear about what you want from your business or how you will get it?

2.  How much do you want to take out of your business as your paycheck? How much wealth do you personally want to build up? By when?

    How large does your business need to be to provide for your needs and wants?

    ** What gets in the way of achieving your growth and profitability goals?

3.  What business are you in? What do you sell? To whom? How? What benefits do you provide to your customers? For what problem is your business the solution?

    What do you *want* to sell? Who do you want your customers or clients to be? Who do you not want to work with?

    ** Are you unclear about what business you are in? Do you lack a focus and feel pulled in more than one direction?

    ** Where do you have difficulty communicating your benefits and uniqueness, or attracting the customers you need?

### Do the work you love, and build on your strengths

Structure your business so you get to do what you love and what you do best.

4.  What do you most enjoy about your business? Where is the "juice" for you? What is your driving passion?

5.  What are your greatest strengths? What strengths do you bring to the business? How can your strengths be best used in your business? How is the business built around your strengths?

** What do you like the least about your business? How are you a bottleneck to achieving your business objectives?

** How do business circumstances thwart you using your greatest strengths?

** What are your greatest personal weaknesses? In business, what tasks and responsibilities are you not good at? How could your business compensate for them? Could you delegate those parts to someone else, or change the way you do business so that these parts are eliminated?

To catalyze thinking about your strengths, start off being imaginative and wildly impractical. If you could have it *exactly* the way you want it— ignoring the cost—how would your business be organized? Complete this sentence: "What I really wish I could do, that I've never admitted even to myself, is . . ."

Remember: You are in business to do what you want and what you do best. If you don't ask for it, you surely won't get what you want. If you do ask, even if it seems totally impractical, you may be surprised at what turns out to be possible.

Write a job description for yourself, describing your role in the business you envision. How could your business be reshaped to get as close as possible to this ideal role?

## Balance business with the rest of your life

6.  What is your best work style? Doing what? Not doing what? What are your desired workload and work habits. How many hours per day or per week would you work? What would your ideal work-month look like?

    Who should your key team members be and how would you work with them?

    ** What hampers you from working in the way you want, doing what you want, or working your desired hours? How would you like to reduce stress and increase your ease of operation?

7.  What is the desired balance between business and the other parts of your life? How can you achieve your desired balance in these areas?
    time off
    recreation, health, fitness, well-being
    family and friends
    avocation
    community
    spiritual

** Where are things out of balance for you, and how could the balance be redressed?

** How do you need to change your own role to do what you enjoy and what you do best, and to free up time for things outside the business?

## Build on your values and ethics

Your business can be a reflection of your core values. There is no reason at all why your business can't combine high personal integrity, satisfaction, contribution to your customers, and great prosperity.

Some say that the things they value most in their personal relationships seem difficult to include in their business:

"I value openness, honesty, and generosity, yet in my cutthroat industry—with customers and employees always trying to squeeze another nickel out of me—these seem like impractical ideals."

Yet, time after time, business owners tell me that their "Doing what you love" circle *must* include running their business in a way that is in alignment with their personal values and ethics.

You are in business to get what you want. By definition, your values, i.e. what you value, are what you want. When we ask business owners what they value most and what they want from their businesses, here are the things we hear most often:

prosperity, security, wealth, legacy

independence

integrity, ethical behavior, activity aligned with core values

satisfaction, joy of work, labor of love

creation, craftsmanship, artistry, high-quality work

accomplishment, contribution

recognition

communication, connection, community, cooperation

to give back, teach, mentor the next generation, be a good community citizen.

8.   What personal values must be the bedrock of your business? How is your business built around your preferences and personal values?

** Where do you have trouble embodying your values and preferences in your business?

How can your business be a better vehicle for your preferences and values?

## Have a business that works

Make sure you offer something that people want and that you sell it to them profitably.

9.  How large do you want your business to be? What would it look like, and by when? For example:

    Your size, i.e., revenue and profitability, number of employees or locations

    Your reach, i.e., geographical extent and market niches

    Your scope, i.e., the breadth of what you do or sell and what you will no longer do

    Your industry position compared to competitors

    Your workplace and the work environment

10. What sets you apart from your competition? If I ask your preferred customers why they do business with you rather than with someone else, what would they tell me?

Surprisingly, many small business owners have trouble answering this question. Even though you provide excellent service and products and have happy, loyal customers, you aren't sure why. Ask them. Call your best customers—the kind you want more of—and ask:

"Why do you do business with me, rather than with someone else?"

Then, ask a couple of follow-up questions:

"How can we serve you better? How could our service to you be more complete?"

"Where could we make improvements in our service?"

11. How could you take better advantage of your competitive strengths?

    ** In what ways do you feel you have no competitive advantage, that you are selling "just a commodity"?

    ** What are your greatest competitive weaknesses? How could you compensate for them?

12. Do you have a "business endgame" in mind? By when? For example: Sell your business to a) another business owner, b) your employees, or c) a larger company.

Sell the assets, shut the door, and head into the sunset.

Get your desired income or cash flow as long as you want to (or can), then cease operation.

Turn it over to your children (or another family member).

Go public, bring in other investors, or form an ESOP, then replace yourself.

Retain ownership indefinitely, but gradually cut back your involvement, leaving day-to-day operation to others.

** You don't see an endgame; you're just working away.

If you are considering more than one of these, which ones? When will you decide? (By when? or What must happen first?) What will your criteria be?

Are you in agreement on your endgame and time frame with your partner, co-owners, or spouse?

    ** If not, what must you do to come to agreement? What is the cost if you fail to do so?

What should you be doing to prepare for your endgame? (Most likely, there are things you should do now that will help you prepare for *any* of your choices.)

    ** Are you having difficulty progressing toward your long-term goal? What difficulty or dilemma do you see? E.g., *"I don't see how I can come out with enough money for my retirement." "I don't know how I could sell my company."*

## Move with the opportunities and challenges

Keep on top of things and move with the times.

13. Where are the greatest opportunities for you and your business?

    What strategic moves do you need to make to take advantage of any of these?

    To get where you want to go, with whom should you link up? What strategic alliances or linkages should you seek out?

14. What outside challenges can affect your business success, either positively or negatively? For example:
    in your industry, among your competitors and/or vendors
    within your market or customer base
    technology developments
    economic conditions
    changes in laws and regulations
    local business environment, global trends

## *Resolve the dilemmas and uncertainties*

15. What major dilemma must you resolve to achieve your vision of success?
    For Example:
    balancing two lines of business
    doing paid work and developing new work
    sustaining the old while allowing the new to emerge
    retaining your personal touch while improving efficiency and productivity
    being caught between what you love to do and what you feel you have to do
    you knowing where you want to go but not knowing how to get there
    you wanting to grow, but not having the energy, resources, ideas or knowledge needed
    you wanting to grow your business, but fearing the consequences of growth

16. Is a major transition or fork in the road approaching? Is there a tough choice you must make?

   As you envision where your business is going, will you reach choice points or forks in the road? For example, "As our business grows, I may want to establish a regional presence. On the other hand, I may be satisfied being a leading player in our metropolitan area." "I am satisfied with our current number of stores, but we may decide to build a web-based e-business component as well." "I'd like to work another ten years, but I'm not sure my health will let me."

   In such a case, state when and how you would decide which choice to make. What are the signs you look for? What is your window of opportunity? When will it be too late?

## STEPPING-STONES TO YOUR VISION

We can envision the way we want it to be, and we certainly know our current reality. Use this page to describe a series of concrete steps to get there from here. Start at the bottom ("now") and work up to "your vision" at the top.

   To make your vision of success a reality, you must also envision a series of discrete, possible steps. Without these, your success remains unattainable. This is like crossing a swift creek: you see your goal on the opposite bank, but you can't get there without spotting a sequence of stepping-stones that get you all the way across.

   This is the precursor to long-range planning. To complete this, you need no action plan, and only the loosest time frame: "This year I can do this, next year I can do that, and then maybe by the following year I will be ready for the next step." If you slip a year, it is not critical, as long as you stay on the path.

If you can't see all the steps initially, don't despair. Spot as many as you can, take the first steps, and create further ones as you go.

|  | Your Vision of Success (Looking ahead about __ years) |  |
|---|---|---|
| Major business inputs you will need (Capital, expertise, role model, new form of organization.) |  | Personal events that will affect this scenario (Kids, family, parents, your health) |
|  | Stepping Stones or Milestones<br><br>• <br>• <br>• <br>• <br>• <br>•  |  |
|  | Where you are now |  |

## THE THICKET

Sometimes the stepping-stones to our vision are obscured by the thorny barriers we face, seemingly as impenetrable as the thicket faced by Prince Charming as he sought to rescue Sleeping Beauty from the castle. The thicket of barriers you identified in the earlier chapters may seem equally daunting, and may even discourage you from pursuing your vision. The first step in tackling them is to gather them all in one place, as on the illustration below. Then surround your thicket of barriers by the resources you already have (on the left) and the resources you need (on the right).

Your Vision of Success

Resources you already
have that will help you
tackle these barriers

Additional resources
you need to tackle these
barriers

"The Thicket"

The barriers that stand between
you and achieving your vision

Where you are now

See an example of what a composite of the Stepping-stones and Thicket might look like filled out two pages below.

If you fill out these charts for yourself, make sure you state your stepping-stones and barriers as concretely as possible. You want statements that are definite enough for you to take action on. For example:

| "FUZZY" Problem statements | "CONCRETE" Problem Statements |
|---|---|
| We want the business to be big enough to provide us a good living. | To pay ourselves $120,000 per year, the business needs to grow to $1.5 million. |
| All I do is put out fires. | I need to focus 75% of my time on strategic tasks that move us toward our long-term objectives. |
| I don't delegate well. | I hire good people, but I don't give them enough direction, and I'm always correcting them. They stop taking initiative. |

Now that you have identified barriers that hinder your vision, let's turn our attention to how to resolve them. I recommend you keep your Number 1 barrier in mind as you read through the next few chapters on the problem solvent.

## ASK YOURSELF . . .

1. What is your vision of business success? State it in just a couple of sentences.

2. In contrast, where is your business now? Describe it in a couple of sentences.

3. What are the top two barriers to your business growth? State them concretely by completing this sentence: "I have trouble growing my business because…" Refer back to these as you read the upcoming chapters.

4. What parts of your vision will re-energize you when you get stuck in the thicket of your barriers?

**Extra credit**

5. Outline the stepping-stones to achieve your vision, starting from where you are now.

## TO TAKE THIS FURTHER . . .

Our annual planning workbook, *Success in 20_ _,* which we update every year, is full of questionnaires and templates to help you answer for yourself all the questions in this chapter.

# STEPPING STONES AND THICKET—AN EXAMPLE

**Horizon:** 7 years

### Vision of Success
10 retail stores in 5-county area, with web-based customer order system. Sell the chain for $10 million.

### Thicket of barriers.

We have trouble growing because . . .

We find it hard to keep the employees who are good enough to run stores for us.

I'm the bean counter, she's the creative style selector. We sometimes run it like it's two separate businesses.

We are both too hands-on; we make too many tiny decisions, even though we've hired people to handle those functions.

It's hard to convince banks of our growth potential.

We need to devote an unpredictable amount of time caring for our aging parents.

### Now
2 stores, run by my wife and me. We work constantly, and don't make enough money.

### Stepping-stones & Strategies
### (Read from bottom up)

Grow by buying small, floundering stores with good locations in our target communities. Next store: Millwood.

Develop systems and procedures for our two stores, that can be duplicated for the new stores. Upgrade our Point of Sale system

Have the courage to hire experienced managers, give them performance incentives, training, and then let them run a store.

Use Store #2 as training ground for new managers.

Lease a new, centralized warehouse and e-commerce sales center.

# Chapter 4

# The Problem Solvent

## *The five elements needed to overcome any barrier to growth*

For any barrier to growth, ease, or profitability, the solution includes these five elements:

**1. Help & support**
What help and support do you need (whether or not you know where to get it)? Internal staff, outside professionals, or advisors.

**2. Systems & procedures**
How can you ease tasks and increase productivity by systematizing things you do intuitively?

**3. Skills & capabilities**
What management skills should you or your employees gain or upgrade?

**4. Changes in workplace, equipment & materials**
What new materials, fixtures or equipment, or changes in your workplace, will help you tackle these barriers?

**5. Work on yourself**
How do your management practices, work habits, beliefs and attitudes get in the way of achieving your objectives and overcoming your barriers to growth?

These five elements are the heart of our approach to tackling barriers to growth. We call them the "problem solvent." A solvent is something you apply to a blot or stain to dissolve it and wash it away. Apply this solvent liberally to any problem you face in growing your business. Asking these five questions about any barrier helps shrink it down to a more manageable size. For example:

**Your barrier**   "I can't grow my business because I can't find good people, and it's easier doing the job myself rather than managing others."

You may state such a barrier to growth as an immutable fact; however, it could be tackled by applying the "problem solvent," e.g.:

**Help and support**

You could:
– Hire a professional to help you craft the job description, interview and screen candidates.

– Hire outside professionals to handle certain jobs, like bookkeeping.

– Brainstorm with your advisors where to find good employee candidates.

**Systems and procedures**

Perhaps you need to:
– Break your jobs down into pieces appropriate for the people you can hire.

– Develop procedure manuals for your jobs, and make your employees' jobs more straightforward.

– Upgrade your computer systems to ease data entry and record keeping, so that lower-skilled people can perform them.

**Skills needed**

You could improve your ability to:
– Size up good job candidates.

– Write job descriptions.

– Train and manage employees.

**Workplace, equipment & materials**

Change the office layout so that you and your employees can work more productively.

**Management** Question your belief that "It's easier doing the job myself."
**habits,**          Work on your habit of taking back delegated jobs,
**attitudes,**       or hiring people but not giving them enough training
**beliefs**          or oversight.

In this chapter, I will briefly explain the five parts of the problem solvent. Each is then covered more thoroughly in the following five chapters.

## ELEMENT #1. HELP AND SUPPORT

The first element to the problem solvent  is getting the help you need to tackle the barriers to growth.

You can't do it all. And even if you could you shouldn't. As your business grows you need more help both from employees and from outside professionals. The employees can be full-time or part-time, ongoing or just when you need them. They can be hired from outside or promoted from within.

Inadequate help from quality people is one of the leading barriers to growth, ease, and profitability. This is true whether you have a one-person business or dozens of employees.

Many business owners resist hiring people they know they need: "I can't afford to hire", "I can't find good people", "I am the only one who can do this job", "I actually enjoy doing these routine things."

But here is the truth: If your time is worth $100 an hour and you do your own administrative tasks, which someone else could do for $15 an hour, then you are overpaying your administrative assistant by $85 an hour.

Even if you can do the books twice as fast as a competent bookkeeper you are still better off hiring a bookkeeper and focusing on the growth and profitability of your own business.

Time after time I have worked with business owners who initially resisted hiring needed help; but when they finally did so they could not believe they waited for so long. Here are a couple of before and after examples:

• **A one person marketing consultancy:** "I will never have another employee. It takes more time to tell them what to do than to do it myself." Then the crunch came: "I just can't get all this work done. I am burned out!" She gave in and hired a part-time office assistant from the local college. "She is great! I did not realize how much time I spent being the go-fer. My billings have increased 50% since I have more time available."

• **Owner of four stores:** "I can't afford to hire a general manager. I just don't have the sales to justify it." The crunch: "I am so fed up with managing the employees in my stores, I don't have enough time for merchandise selection and displays and promotions." She hired a general manager. "He handles the employees a lot better than I do. I have just finished designing a new line and then I am off on another East Coast buying trip. I am excited!"

You must ask yourself this crucial question: Who is the highest skilled person you could bring in to help you achieve your vision and overcome the barriers to growth? Who could give you the most support and free you up to pursue what you most need to do?

For a one-person company this might be a part-time administrative assistant or bookkeeper. For a company with a handful of people it may be a field rep, foreman, office manager, or technical assistant. For a mid-sized company it may be a chief financial officer, a marketing strategist, a sales manager.

When you ask yourself what help you most need to boost your growth and profitability, don't limit yourself by what you think you can afford. Instead ask yourself what it costs you *not* to have the needed help.

### Getting the outside support you need

As your business grows you need additional types of outside professional support as you outgrow some of your current sources of support. For example:

"Even though we have been with our bank for ten years and had an excellent record they turned us down for needed financing for our expansion." Time to shop for a new bank.

"Our CPA was so focused on tax documentation that he could not really grasp my need for forward looking financial analysis." Time to find someone to act as your chief financial officer (CFO).

"I had been loyal to Joe's advice for years but when we were ready for our regional rollout it became apparent he was out of his league." Time for a consultant experienced with larger, rapidly-growing companies.

## ELEMENT #2. SYSTEMS AND PROCEDURES

When your business is small you do things in unique and idiosyncratic ways. You make things up as you go along. As your business grows you need to get more systematic. You must turn all the idiosyncratic ways you do things—and that your key people do—into systems and procedures that others can follow. When you keep doing things the same old way it slows you down. You risk letting better-organized competitors pull ahead of you.

Developing and improving systems and procedures is essential to overcoming almost every barrier to growth. Your must become a "systems demon": learn to take the things you do intuitively and turn them into a procedures manual, a checklist, a template, a computer program. You and your people then perform regular tasks in a consistent way so that things no longer get dropped out. Each person can understand what the others are doing. You are freed from detail and minutiae.

You must also learn to get the "secret knowledge" out of your head. If there is key knowledge that only you have, then you must be involved in every decision. You become the bottleneck, and are chained to the business. Likewise, if key knowledge is held in the head of an employee—e.g., the delivery terms preferred by Customer A—then he or she must handle every transaction with Customer A or else things go awry.

Here are a few examples of "seat of the pants" management, contrasted with systematic approaches that might replace them. It should be obvious that the approaches in the left column are barriers to growth, profitability and ease of and that resolving these barriers requires moving to approaches in the right column.

| MAKE IT UP AS YOU GO ALONG APPROACH | SYSTEMATIC APPROACH |
|---|---|
| Notes from sales calls are written on slips of paper | Marketing database on the computer contains boxes that must be filled in after each contact. |
| Each counter person takes orders differently. Delivery dates are promised to make the customer happy. | Your written terms and conditions are on each estimate. The computerized order entry system won't allow over-scheduling. |
| Whenever employees ask you for time off you work out something with them. | You refer employees to the employee manual, which spells out policy for sick days, vacation, leaves of absence, etc. |
| You spend a lot of time figuring out when you can afford to pay whom, and when to transfer funds from one account to another. | Your written cash management and accounts payable policies allow the bookkeeper to make all routine decisions, and tells when to bring the decision back to you. |

In your business, where do you have similar "make it up as you go along" policies? How do these limit your growth and profitability and require you and your people to work harder than you should?

In chapter 7, "Get the Secret Knowledge out of Your Head," we will explore how to tackle your barriers by improving your systems and procedures and how you go about improving them.

## ELEMENT #3. SKILLS AND CAPABILITIES

When you start out in business you do whatever needs to be done. You wear many hats. Some fit you well, others don't. You make up in commitment and effort what you lack in skill.

Most people don't go into business because they like managing or are particularly good at it. They want to pursue their profession or craft but then discover that to have a viable endeavor they must master some management skills.

Even people who excel in some aspects of managing are poor in others. You love selling and working with your customers, but financial statements make your eyes glaze over. You love financial analysis but managing people intimidates you. You love doing the work if only you didn't have to sell.

As your business grows, missing skills become a bigger and bigger barrier. Here are the ones I hear about most often:

Bookkeeping, understanding financial statements

Interviewing well so that you hire good people

Estimating and doing proposals so that you get jobs—and they are profitable

Getting the best out of your employees

Planning and setting priorities

Scheduling, staying on top of projects

Setting inventory levels

I am sure you can add to this list.

Different skills come into play at each growth stage of a small business. Take a look at a few examples on the next page which are drawn from the table in chapter 1 "Life Stages of An Entrepreneurial Company."

The skills needed to run a successful business fall into several categories. First are the professional skills needed to do the work. These are specific to each type of business. However, some skills are similar for every business and organization:

* Management skills needed to run the enterprise
* People and communication skills
* Self-awareness and self-management skills

Looking at this list, it is apparent that no one person can master all these skills. You have several options:

* You can improve some skills or learn new ones.

- Your employees can learn or upgrade skills.
- You can hire new people who bring in needed skills.
- You hire outside professionals who provide expertise that you do not need all the time.

This is why I say "skills and capabilities." You can gain the skills or hire the capabilities.

When you lack a needed skill it is costly in both time and money. The missing skill becomes a barrier to growth, to profitability and to your ease of operation.

For any barrier to growth, ease or profitability, improving particular skills is almost always part of overcoming the barrier. Look back at your own barriers to growth from chapter 1. Ask yourself, how could improving any skill help you overcome the barrier.

| Growth Stage & Challenge | Example of Skill Needed to Get to the Next Level | Barrier Caused by Lack of the Skill |
|---|---|---|
| 1. Challenge for start-up: Selling, closing the deal. | Understanding the benefits you provide to your customers | You fail to make sales that you should. |
| 2. Challenge for up and going company: Finding and keeping good people | Interviewing, selecting, training and orientation | You hire the wrong people and they don't do a good job. |
| 3. Challenge for established CEO: Run day-to-day operation while focusing on strategic issues | Managing your own time by priorities | You run yourself ragged, stay stuck in day to day minutiae. |
| 4. Adding structure. Challenge: systematizing | Hiring, training, and overseeing managers | Key knowledge that is stuck in your head slows the operation. |

## ELEMENT #4. CHANGES IN YOUR WORKPLACE, EQUIPMENT, MATERIALS

Just as your kids grow out of their clothes, your business grows out of things that have served you well: your office, your shop, your computer system, your marketing materials. Staying with these after you should replace them is a major barrier to growth. Likewise, for any barrier to growth or profitability you should ask how making changes in your workplace, equipment or materials could help you overcome the barrier.

This question pertains to every level of business. For example:

"Working out of my home was so convenient but it was hard to separate work and non-work. The convenience of having an office at home became the drudgery of sleeping in my office."

"I watched my office people sitting there staring at the computer screen waiting for data to download. The next week I bought them new and faster equipment."

"Our sales growth seems capped by the small number of parking spaces we had."

"We still have 5,000 brochures left. But they look *so* 1990's. One lost sale would cost us more than replacing all those dated brochures."

"My open door policy meant I never got anything done in my office. I was hiding out in the supply room to work on the budgets. I replaced my glass office door with a solid one and told people when they could and could not interrupt me."

"Consolidating production from our three shops into the new larger facility dropped our cost of goods sold by 5% and boosted our on-time delivery rate by 50%."

Many people who run a growing business routinely provide the best office and equipment for their people, but it amazes me how many don't even have their own office. "I had to give up my office to the controller." "I like being on the floor." "I spend all my day going from one store to another." Yet lack of a place your papers can call home is a drain on *your* productivity.

Look at the barriers to your own growth, profitability and ease. How could making changes in your workplace, equipment or materials help you overcome them?

## ELEMENT #5. WORK ON YOURSELF

Last but certainly not least!

As you grow, your management style often becomes the bottleneck to further growth. You become part of the problem. For every barrier to growth, ease and profitability—I mean EVERY barrier—you need to ask:

How do your management practices and habits, your attitudes and beliefs get in the way of achieving your vision and overcoming your barriers to growth?

*Is it possible your management style is part of the problem?*

"Management practices, habits, attitudes and beliefs" is such a mouth full. Let's shorten it to M-PHAB (pronounced "Emfab").

Making shifts in your M-PHAB is both the toughest and easiest of things to do. It is the way you have been doing things for years and these habits never seem to change. Yet when they do change it often happens so easily that you do not even notice until afterwards.

The M-PHAB categories can overlap and are closely related, as illustrated in this example:

- **Practice**. Open door policy. You pride yourself on your accessibility.
- **Habit**. You let yourself be interrupted by everything that comes along rather than staying focused.
- **Belief or attitude.** "I can never get anything done." "There is no point in setting a tight schedule, events always overwhelm it."

You may not consciously believe these things—you may even state the opposite—but you behave as if you believe them.

Every barrier that we mentioned earlier in this chapter grows out of an outdated M-PHAB. For example:

**Systems and Procedures.** A situation that limits growth, ease and profitability: You make special deals for each customer but the lack of consistency hurts your productivity, profit margin and level of customer satisfaction. Why? You believe you must make special deals or your customers will go elsewhere. You like wheeling and dealing. You resist going by the book—that is why you left the big corporation. You have hired others like you and so all make special deals with your customers.

**Help**. You hire good people but you don't trust them to do the job you hired them for. You hold onto routine tasks that should be delegated, then complain you don't have time to focus on the big picture.

**Workplace**. To keep payroll down you do the go-fer tasks—cleaning the cobwebs, delivering supplies to crews in the field. Then you complain you are never able to get your most important work done.

How can you change an M-PHAB? It's as if I am asking you to change human nature. We get into this more in the next chapter, but here is an example:

You get fed up with the way it has been going. You just can't seem to achieve your Cost of Goods Sold target, and it's killing your bottom line. You see that your habit of keeping all these figures to yourself is the major cause, because your forte is selling, not crunching numbers. You finally decide that are willing to change, so you put in a system to ensure consistency in order taking, pricing and scheduling. (You already had most of this system—you were just not using it.)

In meetings with your managers you emphasize the importance of using the new system and you get them on board with you. You put your production manager in charge of this system because she will hold you and your other sales people to it, and won't let you backslide. (She has been itching to do just this!) Over the next few months, you work the kinks out and make changes.

A year later you announce, "Our cost of goods has dropped, on-time delivery is up and customer satisfaction has increased. This has lead to a big boost in profits. Thus I am announcing some healthy year-end bonuses."

All because you were willing to change a management habit you had grown out of.

**Use the entire toolkit.** It is apparent that all the parts of the problem solvent fit together and reinforce one another. It makes no sense to separate them: that would be like trying to repair your car with just one tool. You need the whole tool kit. Over the next five chapters, we will look in more detail at each element of the problem solvent and show how they fit together. After that, chapters will focus on a number of the common barriers to growth, ease, and profitability and apply the problem solvent to them.

## TO TAKE THIS FURTHER . . .

Our companion workbook, *Grow Your Business Without Driving Yourself Crazy,* is full of worksheets to help you apply the ideas in chapters 4 through 9.

## Chapter 5

# The Inner Game of Growth

### Your management style, practices, habits, attitudes, and beliefs

*How is the way you run your business
a barrier to your growth, ease, and profitability?*

Why do some businesses grow rapidly while others struggle for growth and profitability? The difference often lies within the noggin of the owner. You are the biggest asset of your business, and more than likely the biggest bottleneck as well.

Alas, all the clichés are true. The buck stops with you. You have to look in the mirror. To overcome your barriers to growth, ease, and profitability, you must work on your own management practices, habits, attitudes, and beliefs (your "M-PHABs"). You must "work on yourself." As we go through the elements of the problem solvent, I will continually talk about working on yourself. (You'll get sick of me saying it!) But this is part of virtually every barrier, so I have put it first.

## A MINDSET FOR GROWTH, EASE, AND PROFITABILITY

When your business grows profitably, when you operate with ease and satisfaction, what are the characteristics of your management style? I see two columns of matched pairs, which on the surface seem contradictory, yet which must be balanced:

| ON THE ONE HAND ... | ON THE OTHER HAND ... |
|---|---|
| Be the visionary, the inspirational driving force. | Roll up your sleeves and jump into the trenches when the need arises. |
| Keep focused on your objectives. Use your time strategically. | Be ready to shift and go with the flow. |
| Persevere. Stay on course. Push on through. | Be ready to turn on a dime to follow opportunity or avoid threat. |
| Do the things you do best. Exploit your personal strengths. | Be a team builder. Work with people who are as good or better than you are. |
| Do what you love to do. | Do whatever needs to be done. |
| Let people do their job. Trust them. | Keep an eagle eye on operations. Don't hesitate to intervene when necessary. |
| Take care of yourself. Schedule personal and family times *in ink*. | Crunch times happen. (Keep them limited.) |

## What gets in the way of a mindset for growth?

Self-defeating management habits, attitudes and beliefs pervade the "crazy makers" we described in chapter 1. If you look at yourself, you may notice contradictory attitudes like these:

| | |
|---|---|
| I can't get all my work done. | I'm not hiring another employee. |
| I must learn how to manage my time better. | I can't find the time to make the needed changes in how I use my time. |
| We've got to stay on budget. | I can't resist making last minute design changes. |
| We've got to watch costs. | I can't be bothered to review the financials. |
| Low margins are killing us. | I can't bring myself to raise prices. |
| I've got to take more time away from the business. | I can't leave my managers alone. |
| I need more employees. | I'm afraid I'll just train my own competition. I'm afraid I won't have enough work to keep them busy. |
| I need more sales. | Marketing scares me. I wish customers would just come. |
| I get so tangled up in day-to-day operations that I lose sight of my vision. | I doubt the value of having a plan. |
| I want to ease up and work fewer hours. | I can't change my belief that hard work is necessary. |

Even when you acknowledge these contradictory attitudes, you may doubt the possibility of doing anything about them. I hear rationalizations like these: "It's the way I have always done things." "It has gotten us this far." "It's just human nature." "I might not be perfect, but what can I do about it?" "It's difficult working on these ingrained habits." "It's embarrassing and uncomfortable and probably impossible."

It is *not* impossible, and you don't have to change human nature to change your work habits.

## HOW TO CHANGE YOUR M-PHABs

To achieve your vision of success, how do you need to run your company? How does your current management style hold you back? To develop a mindset for growth, what changes must you make in your management style and practices, habits, attitudes, and beliefs?

The first step is to become aware of the things you do that get in your way. Notice your "mindset of smallness." Identify the changes you want to make in the way you do things.

We use the "Work on yourself" exercise in our workshops to help identify M-PHABs that get in the way. Try this on your own growth barriers. The categories overlap, so don't worry about whether something is a habit or an attitude.

| Column 1. "Is Now" <br><br> **M-PHAB that gets in your way.** <br> Management style, practices, habits, attitudes, and beliefs | Column 2. "Should be" <br><br> **What your behavior needs to be** to support your growth goals. Distinguish between realistic and unrealistic "should be's." |
|---|---|
| Management style or practice that slows you down | Management practice for growth |
| Work habit that gets in your way | Desired work habit |
| Current beliefs or attitudes that limit you | Beliefs or attitudes that serve you better |

Here are a few examples:

| M-PHAB THAT GETS IN YOUR WAY | HOW YOU WANT IT TO BE |
| --- | --- |
| I spend all my time in the office/store/factory as an example to my employees. | My employees appreciate my contribution and see that it is not linked directly to the hours I spend on-site. |
| If I take time off, I am afraid my employees will resent me. | When I take regular time off, my solutions are more creative; I create more value for the company, myself, and my employees. |
| If I raise prices, I'm afraid I will lose my customers. | I communicate my value and attract people who want what I offer and are willing to pay the price. |
| I have an open door policy but I'm always getting interrupted, so it's hard for me to stay focused on my key responsibilities. | I tell people when I am accessible and when I need my privacy, and expect their help in maintaining my schedule. |

After you have identified the behaviors you want to change, and know how you want to react in such situations in the future, learn to pay attention to the way these situations unfold. You can use these questions:
- In what situations do you act or think in the old ways; the ways you want to move past; the ways you want to change?
- What exactly did you do? Describe your behavior that's out of synch with what you want to do. (E.g. "I can trust my people and leave them alone to do their job until my sales manager comes in and makes another excuse. I get so angry at him, and then I immediately get sucked into doing his job for him.")
- What impact did your behavior have on the situation?
- What kept you from behaving in the way you wanted to? This is not a time to blame yourself for human failings, but just to notice and acknowledge what happened.
- What do you wish you had done instead?
- If you had done this, how would that have affected the outcome?
- How would you like to handle a similar situation in the future?

Once you identify the problem, attitude or habit and know how you want it to be instead, follow a few guidelines:
- Since these behaviors are often difficult for you to see in yourself, it helps to work with others—a consultant or coach or a group of business owners. Describe to them what happens, and how it gets in your way. Relate the circumstances when it comes up, and what you wish you could do instead. Problem-solve how you are going to change it.

After trying your new approach in your workplace, tell your support team how it went. If there were problems, brainstorm how to handle them next time. Trial and error are part of the process.

Often times these behaviors diminish—or even disappear—just by talking about them. How often has someone said to me, "I can never do such and such. It's hopeless." Then the very next time I talk with them, they exclaim, "I did it! I just did it!"

- Spell out the benefit of making these changes—and the cost of not making them.
- Apply the problem solvent to support your desired behavioral changes: I'll give examples of this in chapter 10 after more is said about the problem solvent in the next few chapters.
- Stay accountable by reporting your progress to others. Make a public commitment with milestones and a timeline. This forces you to stay mindful of your goals and to get help with the difficulties you encounter.
- Be patient; it takes time. Don't get thrown off when you backslide.
- Reward yourself for progress.

When these changes do happen, they often sneak up on you. You don't even notice it till later, when you look back and say, "Wow! I no longer do . . ." "I've gotten much better at. . .!"

Watch for contradictory attitudes that together reinforce your growth barrier.

**Issue**

*"Only I can do it right."*                    *"I hire good people, but end up just training my competitors."*

You hire good people, then continue with the attitude that only you can do certain jobs. The result being that they feel constrained in the job, never fully trusted, or not able to live up to the job they were hired for. Thus, you tend to drive them away. They go to work for a competitor, or set up their own similar business.

**Recommendation:** Shift your management style so that it gives them a challenge and responsibility; they then feel better about staying with you and advancing within your company.

**Issue**

*"My customers—and my employees —always ask to talk to me."*

*"My managers do not handle as much responsibility as they should.*

*"I need to watch the numbers. I just have to shut myself away in my office more."*

*"I need to keep in touch on the floor, both to know what is happening and to motivate my people."*

You are operating at two levels—manager and floor supervisor. While it is important for you to keep in touch with what is happening, the question is, how much? You are clearly invading the turf of your managers who should have the primary responsibility for keeping in touch and motivating the troops. Since you are doing part of their job, your managers feel frustrated and take less initiative.

**Recommendation:** Examine your own motivation. Is it possible you are holding on to the floor work—at which you feel more comfortable—to avoid facing bigger challenges?

Do the work you enjoy, but find a way to do it that doesn't conflict with the responsibilities you have given your managers.

**Issue**

*"I am not getting paid enough."*

*"I pay myself last because I have to pay the landlord and my employees first."*

*"I am discouraged, feeling burned out and low energy."*

*"I am letting opportunity slip. This is hurting our business.*

You are your most important employee and you are treating yourself very poorly. You could not get away doing this with another top employee. You say you cannot pay yourself because you must cover these other obligations first, but perhaps you have that backwards. If you take care of yourself, including paying yourself, then your energy returns. You stop dropping things out, and your clients are happier. Your business improves so that you can afford to pay yourself— and your landlord.

If this is not the case, then perhaps your business model is not viable, and you should re-look at the way you do business.

**Issue**

*"I cannot say no to referred business. I am afraid my referral source will dump me."*

*"My good clients pay the price for my lousy ones."*

I question whether a referral source will dump you if you decline business that will not make any money for either you or them. And if it did, why would you want such a referral source?

**Recommendations:**

1. Write a profile of the types of client you want from your referral sources, and also the types of clients you do not want.

2.  *Extra credit solution:* Think about what it would take to convert an undesirable prospect to a desirable, profitable client. This often includes *raising* the price.

> For example, this brief story: "One of my best referral sources sent me this prospect. When the prospect told me what she wanted, I groaned inwardly. I knew I would be likely to spend way too much time on that job to make it worthwhile for my fixed fee. Rather than say no, I quoted her what I figured was an exorbitant price. I was flabbergasted when she got back to me and accepted my price. So, instead of my normal habit of putting in unpaid hours and grumbling about it, I ended up getting paid my desired hourly rate for this unusual work. I found it quite exciting, and she was very happy with the result."

This is an example of transforming a "bad" customer to a "good" one. Note that the key element was the business owner shifting her attitude about what price she could charge.

### Issue

*"I cannot get everything done. I drop things out, and thus I lose clients."*

*"I cannot afford to hire help— even part time."*

**Recommendations.** Sounds like you cannot afford *not* to hire help. If you bring in needed help it frees you up to do the work that you are in business to do. If you please your clients better, they pay you better. You can then pay yourself well and pay your help.

The transition is the problem. How do you finance that? Bringing in new employees, training them, and getting them up to speed can actually put more pressure on you in the short run. You may need to find outside money just to finance this transition. If you fail to do this, however, you may put yourself out of business.

### Issue

*"I can never really get away. I go on vacation and my managers still call me. Why do they call to ask questions that they know the answer to?"*

*What's not said: "I leave my cell phone on even when I'm at the lake with my family. If my managers don't call me, I get antsy and call them."*

Here are some other parts of this dynamic:
- They call you when you are on vacation because you let them do so.
- You show that you are afraid they will make poor decisions.

- They are afraid that if they mess up, you will yell at them. So it is easier and safer to ask you.

**Recommendations.** Either your managers are competent to do their job or they aren't. If they aren't, replace them: they are holding you back. If they are, then let them do their jobs and don't let them delegate back to you.

How can you change this dynamic between you and your managers?
- First, acknowledge that it is caused by your behavior as much as theirs.
- Tell them how important it is for you, for the health of the company and for their jobs, that you and they change this dynamic. Make a pact to change this.
- Announce in advance when you will be on vacation. Evaluate your people: what preparation do they need so they can handle things in your absence without calling you? Ask them what they think they'll need.
- Train and cross-train them to upgrade their skills. The biggest result of this will be confidence in themselves and in knowing you support their independence.
- Sure, take your cell phone with you if you must! But don't leave it on. Designate particular phone check-in times, maybe once or twice a week, and stick to it.

Here's a story:

My husband and I were planning a three-week vacation—our first in years. Our three managers were sure they could handle things, but I was trembling in my boots. After all, they ask me everything as a matter of course. Upon our return, I was delighted to see that everything had gone smoothly in our absence. They had handled all the little crises without missing a beat.

I thought to myself how great it would be to continue this style, even if I were here. If all decisions were routine, I wouldn't be working these six-day weeks. But within two weeks, we were back to the same old pattern: they were again calling me for every little thing.

But I saw very clearly that I let them do this; even encouraged it. I kept sticking my nose into their projects and second-guessing their decisions.

Should I go on a permanent vacation? Very tempting! But what I did was to move my office out of the shop building, so that I was physically separated from them. This removed the source of temptation: I couldn't easily wander around the shop every half hour, nor could they barge into my office at any time. We set up specific check-in times and set protocols for what crises they could call me for. We now hold weekly project planning and debriefing meetings.

What a change this has made! To change our ingrained ways of interacting—both theirs and mine—required making this physical change.

## THE VICIOUS LADDER AND THE VIRTUOUS LADDER

Sometimes when I advise a business owner, nothing I say seems to help. He has already tried everything to no avail. He cannot do A because of B, nor B because of C, and so on through the alphabet until he comes around to A again. It's a vicious circle and there seems to be no way out.

People are often unaware of this until I start writing it all down on the flip chart. The Vicious Ladder on table 5-1 is a very common example. I feel tired just reading this list! Note that the bottom and top items are linked. (Vicious circles and ladders are the same thing; it's just harder for me to write in a circle.)

Once your vicious ladder or circle is written down like this, your first reaction may be dismay: "See how tough my problems are?" But bringing the whole mess into your awareness is the essential first step in doing something about it.

The next step is to identify a way to break out of your vicious circle. It can be a small thing, but one that has a spreading effect. Your goal is to transform your vicious ladder into a virtuous ladder, as shown in the table 5-2.

In this example, perhaps the place to start is with the top two items: raise prices (especially for new customers) and talk with your best customers about why they work with you. You may resist the idea of calling your customers to talk with them about this. But if you do so, it can be an energizing and inspiring exercise. You find out in concrete terms that you provide real benefit to people and they appreciate you for it. They like doing business with you. You hear their horror stories about how they've been treated by your competitors. You learn ways you could do things even better. Occasionally, you'll hear a complaint, which also helps you improve what you do.

### Watching your attitudes change

Talking with customers this way should provide a real boost to your self confidence. It also gives you the ammunition to present yourself more effectively to other people you want to do business with. You have real stories of the benefits you provide, not just an abstract list of items. Your energy and enthusiasm are apparent. People want to do business with you and price is a secondary issue.

This is an example of how small actions can change your attitude and break you out of your vicious ladder. Once you do this, you have created an opening for the other rungs of the *virtuous* ladder to emerge.

"Yes, but," you object, "I can't raise my prices." (Insert *your* list of reasons here.) Here's one such example.

Kate provides a makeover service that appeals to professional, well-to-do women. She has been doing this for a couple of years and is just barely scraping by. Her prices are about half those of her better-known competitor. "But I cannot raise my prices to her level because she has much more experience than I do!" says Kate.

I asked Kate, "Does she provide greater value for her customers than you do for yours?" I had her ask a few of her clients who had formerly worked with this competitor. She discovered two main differences: her competitor could say she had been in business for twenty years, and she had slicker marketing materials. Not a word about better makeovers.

*When you are stuck in a vicious circle, look for the one small change you can make that will ripple through and transform it to a virtuous circle.*

Kate grudgingly concluded that she could raise her price—for new customers—part way up to her exalted competitor. I had her practice stating her new price in front of the mirror, in front of her husband, in front of me, and in front of her business advisor's group. Then we gave her this homework: Quote this price matter-of-factly to one prospective customer.

A week later, I checked in with her by phone and she forlornly informed me that she had not had the nerve to quote the new price. I asked her if she was willing to do it over the next week. She said, "Okay. I'll try." The following week, she excitedly called me and said she had done it! "I quoted the new price and all she said was, 'Do you take a credit card?' No price resistance at all!"

Now, ironically, Kate didn't accept credit cards. We convinced her to establish a merchant account so she could do so. Making this minor change in the way she did business further helped reduce any resistance to her higher prices.

A few months later, Kate was pricing slicker marketing materials and talking about hiring a part-time office assistant to relieve her of some routine duties.

This is an example of how to change from an attitude that keeps you small and stuck to an attitude that allows growth. The attitude change was reinforced by the other parts of the problem solvent that we will be covering: Getting help for the routines of business, improving marketing materials, and installing a procedure to accept payment by credit card.

## TABLE 5-1
## THE VICIOUS LADDER

Each item is linked to the one following it. The last one is linked to the first, so it is also a vicious circle.

- You cannot afford to hire good help because you are not bringing in enough money.

- You are not bringing in enough money because you are having to do all the little tasks yourself, using valuable time that should be spent on billable work.

- You are overworked because you charge too little, or you are not billing for all your work. You underestimate how long a job will take, but since you do not track your time, you do not know how much time you actually spend on jobs.

- You are reluctant to raise your prices, for fear all your customers will leave.

- You feel like you can't afford to turn away any business; thus you take on marginal jobs and customers who complain and try to nickel-and-dime you. You spend more time trying to please so-so customers than your good ones.

- You are not doing your best work because you are overworked, burned out, and discouraged, and you don't have the best available people working for you.

- You are working so hard that you have little energy to clarify and capitalize on what sets your company apart from your competitors. Customers undervalue your offering, and resist paying the price you need.

- Your nose is to the grindstone; thus you have no time to keep on top of new opportunities, to brainstorm new ways, or to develop new systems and procedures to improve productivity.

- You must keep your nose to the grindstone because you cannot afford to hire good help.

## TABLE 5-2
## THE VIRTUOUS LADDER

- Set prices so that all your work is profitable.

- Talk with your best customers (the kind you want more of). Ask them why they work with you rather than someone else. What can you do to serve them better?

- Focus on attracting the customers who are clear on the value you provide and are thus willing to pay the price you ask; communicate the value and benefit of what you sell so that you attract the customers you most want to work with.

- Use the profitability from this work to hire the best people, pay them well, and give them challenging work. Satisfied employees stay longer and are more productive, thus reducing your labor cost as a percentage of sales, and boosting profitability.

- Pay yourself well. The energy and competence generated will provide even more value for your customers, thus bringing them back time after time.

- Satisfied customers keep returning, and their word of mouth brings in others. This reduces your marketing costs as a percentage of sales.

- Your reduced cost of labor and marketing allows you to maintain your profit margin while keeping prices competitive. This solidifies your market position.

- Your profitable operation allows you to build up a financial cushion to weather tough times better than your competitors.

- Profitable operations and good help frees you up to focus on what you need to do to expand your business: to innovate, to promote yourself even more effectively, to provide even more value to your customers, and to expand into new market niches.

What is the difference between the Vicious and Virtuous Ladders? It's an attitude about your business. Such attitudes are deep-seated. Business owners hang on to old mindsets as if they were the family jewels. But they can and do change. It is a major part of The Business Group's work to help business owners change their mindset and attitudes and their performance.

Table 5-3 shows a way you can analyze parts of this Vicious Ladder facing you. It is useful to work with someone else on this, since we are not always good about seeing these attitudes in ourselves. The M-PHAB is the problem statement made by the business owner; the Likely Cause and Remedy were suggested by the business advisor. The owner then objected to the Remedy and the advisor addressed the objection.

There are several benefits to this approach:
- It brings all the attitudes and assumptions out into the open, where they can be addressed. Practical, do-able changes jump out at you.
- You take one step at a time. Since you can't deal with all things at once, select the top "eye-level" issue, the one that underpins others, and where you can produce some positive results right away.
- This takes some of the energy off the discouragement of the Vicious Ladder. Just finding a way to tackle it generates new energy.
- You can easily generate a "To Do" list, with schedule and milestones, and get help staying accountable to it.

## MAKE THE CHANGES STICK

**Set measures for progress.** How will you know if you are making progress on the desired change?

"In a couple of months from now, if I look back, I'll be happy with the progress I've made on this behavior if I...." You must fill in the blank.

Those are the things to watch for.

**Stay accountable.** Fill out the Problem Solvent worksheet (Table 10-1) with desired measures of progress, milestones, and markers and report this to your group or your coach each month.

**Stay mindful.** The toughest part of changing behavior is staying mindful of the desired change. You forget about it. It leaves your awareness. The purpose of tracking and accountability every day is thus twofold: 1) Staying mindful and 2) making progress. The toughest part is staying mindful when we're *not* making progress. It is easy to report progress; reporting lack of progress or backsliding takes courage and support.

**Work with others.** That's why it's so beneficial to do this in a group. People will remind you, "Last month you said you were going to do such and such. What have you done on that over the last month?" "Well, gang,"

## TABLE 5-3 – LOW PROFITABILITY DIAGNOSIS SHEET

| Owner's Complaint | Likely Cause | Remedy Suggested by Advisor | Owner's Objection to Remedy | Advisor Addresses the Objection |
|---|---|---|---|---|
| "I'm not making any money; I'm unprofitable." | Low margin, not enough profit built into jobs. | Don't take on unprofitable projects. | "I need all the work I can get. I can't afford to turn any away." | The time you spend on unprofitable jobs keeps you from going after profitable ones. |
| | | | "Small jobs lead to big clients later." | Sometimes this is true, but make sure you aren't using this as an excuse to avoid going after bigger, more lucrative challenges. |
| | Some of the jobs are unprofitable. | Charge for all the work you do; don't give it away. Learn how to estimate more realistically. | "People don't recognize the value of the work I do that I'm not charging them for." | Then don't do it for them. Explain the value to them and tell them up front you are charging for it. If they don't want to pay for that, then perhaps they are not a qualified client for you. |
| | | Raise your prices. | "I'm already charging top dollar." | Learn to clarify and communicate your value. Find out who is interested in paying for the value you provide, and focus your efforts on them. |
| I'm spending too much time. I'm overworked." | You are doing it all yourself, including low-level field tasks. | Delegate to a field assistant. Focus on key tasks, and on high-paying tasks. | "I can't afford to hire the field help I need." | You can't afford not to. Either: a) You have a viable business and you should focus on doing what makes it viable, or b) You don't, and you should change what you offer. |
| | You lack strategic focus. | Work with the advisor to clarify where to focus your energy and help keep you focused. | "I still will have to do all the regular stuff." | See the response above. Prioritize. Learn to defer, dump, and delegate. |
| "I am having trouble getting the word out. | Timidity. False modesty. Reluctance to tell people your real message. | Work with your advisor to clarify your vision, your desires, your mission, and how to pursue it. | "I'm fuzzy on how to go after my vision." | Take one step at a time. Find an ally to approach first. |
| | You're unclear about what you offer; or are ambivalent about what you want to offer. | | | |
| | "I can't afford to advertise." | Then get publicity. Tell your story to the media interested in the exciting options you offer. | "I don't have time to write all this up." | What else could be more important than this? Didn't you say that a trade publication had approached you? Enlist their help. |

you confess, "I let it slide." "Okay. You let it slide. Now, what are you going to do this coming month?" The group can help you look at the reasons why this goal slipped and come up with some other ways to tackle it in the coming month.

But look, we are not running a therapy group—and that is an important clarification. We are business people and we tackle these barriers to growth as just another problem to be solved. Are you committed to solving it or not? If not, then abandon it and go on to something else. If you're going to solve it, then do the problem-solving that is needed to bring about the desired behavioral change. If you want to whine and moan about how tough it is, that's okay for a little while. We'll all sympathize with you. We've been there ourselves. But beyond that, either get off it and solve the problem, or go whine to your therapist.

**Set a goal with a measure of completion.** How do you know when you are successful? This is not so easy for a behavioral goal like "I need to manage my time better." It helps to initially answer these two questions:

"I'll know when I'm making progress on using my time better when I see that I am..."

"I will be satisfied with my time management when I..."

## CAN YOU CHANGE THE WORK HABITS AND ATTITUDES OF OTHERS?

"How many psychotherapists does it take to change a light bulb? Only one: but the bulb must want to change." So goes the old saw. Employees have attitudes and habits that also prevent your business success. However, if some of your employees *don't* want to change, it comes back to you. Why would you have people working for you who do not want to perform the way you want them to? You can *demand* that they change. If you are signing their paychecks and their M-PHABs are hurting their performance, then you'd think you would have some leverage over them; but this may not be adequate.

So the first thing is to make sure you have the right people working for you. It's often a lot easier to train someone new in a complex skill than to change another's attitudes and habits. Don't get cast in the role of personality mentor, and don't let yourself be held back by people who just aren't going to change.

If you have people who are willing and able to change habits and attitudes, then answer these two questions:

1. How can you set it up so that people who might be reluctant to change to more effective ways of working are willing or even enthusiastic about making changes?

2. How can you support your people in making the changes they want but find it difficult to do?

Apply the problem solvent. What training in job skills, communication skills, teamwork, supervising, etc. would help? What changes in your systems, procedures, and policies—or in your workplace—would support the desired behaviors?

Use the approaches described in chapter 12, "Build a Culture of Growth," and the section of chapter 14 on gaining acceptance of change.

If they agree with you on the needed changes, ask them what would help the most. Jointly set goals and a process to track progress and problem-solve on backsliding.

Allocate time to make changes, especially if they entail training or getting accustomed to new ways of doing things.

If you want your people to change their work habits, you must also work on your habits. You can count on it—you are part of their problem as well. Watch for co-dependency between you and them. How do you and they keep each other in the old rut? How can you help each other change to a new pattern?

Perhaps use an outsider, such as a coach or consultant, to find a way to change these habits. Since you are part of the situation, it is very difficult for you to simultaneously manage the discussion and examine your own behavior. The outsider can help you work out how to introduce needed changes to your team.

> *To change the behavior of your employees, you must work on your own as well.*

Take advantage of a symbolic marker if you can, such as a strategic change in your business, a threshold that you are reaching, an external threat or opportunity, or some special event.

Create no rule or policy change without enforcement. For example, if you set a firm start time at 8:00 AM, then turn a blind eye when people sneak in at 8:15, it's worse than not setting the rule in the first place.

## A team can work on itself

A team of people in your workplace—e.g., the partners, the executive committee, a project group—that is committed to working together productively, quite often gets pulled from its desired mode of working. The team members can ask a similar set of questions:

- What pulled our team off course? What happens that stunts the team's productivity?
- How does the way our team interacts with outside entities contribute to the problems we encounter?

- What do we need to do to get back on course?
- How could the team perform better next time these circumstances arise?

I recommend bringing in an outside facilitator to work with the team on these questions.

## CONCLUSION

Working on your mindset, attitudes, and habits is not easy. It helps to have the support of others. We often do not see these things in ourselves to start with. It is easy to get bogged down. If you work with others, they can help you to become aware of these things, problem-solve how to deal with them, and come up with a plan of action. Specific goals and a time line can help you stay accountable to this.

If you are not willing to look at this aspect of running your business, then some of your barriers will be very tough to overcome. If you are willing to look at these things and deal with them—either on your own or working with others—then you can make huge strides.

## ASK YOURSELF . . .

1. Complete this sentence: "One thing I act like I have under control but really do not is . . ."
2. Fill in the blanks: "The real reason I don't _____ (make calls, delegate, check financials, review performance) is because I am _____ (shy, intimidated, afraid that _____)."
3. What management practice, attitude, or habit slows you down the most? What should it be to support your growth goals?
4. What keeps you in your old way of doing things when you try to change? What could you do about that?
5. If you made the change you wanted, what would be the benefit to you? What is the cost of staying the same?
6. For you to make desired changes in your M-PHABs, who else must be involved?
7. How will you know when you have successfully made the desired changes in your M-PHABs?

## Chapter 6

# Hire Wonder Woman or Superman

## *The help and support needed for growth*

*Who is the highest-skilled person you can hire or promote to free you to focus on growing your business?*

Navelle

M any business owners are held down by having the wrong people working for them.

When you start out, you often do everything yourself. You wear all the hats. Before long, you find you cannot do this. There is way too much to do and you cannot get it all done. Furthermore, you are not skilled at all of the things that must be done, and many tasks are just not a good use of your time.

This seems obvious, yet many small business owners resist hiring the people that really need. Why? Here are the things I hear from business owners all the time:

"I can't afford the people I need."
"Only I can do this."

"Good people are not available."

"What if I hire them and then business goes down?"

"I end up hiring and training my own competition."

"I am not a good manager of people."

"Our current employees get upset if I hire someone from outside to come in above them as manager."

"I enjoy doing these routine tasks."

"I once had employees, I got rid of them, and I am not getting any more."

"I'm not good at interviewing and hiring."

Do any of these sound like you? What is the result? You struggle. You wear too many hats, and stay mired in minutiae. You don't get to focus on the things you enjoy and that will most benefit the company.

The businesses I work with don't have a lot of employees: from one or two to a few dozen. In a company this size, if even one employee doesn't do the job well it can have a huge impact on the performance of the company.

Further, if the owner is wearing many of the hats, adding just one good person—I mean a *really* good person—can make a huge difference. If you have no employees, it might be a part-time office helper; if you have fifty, it might be a general manager. Here are a couple of stories to illustrate:

**She literally rolled up her sleeves.** A client who owned a flooring company had just lost yet another office manager and dreaded the prospect of hiring someone else who probably wouldn't work out. She said, "I don't want to pay much because I can only get mediocre people."

I asked her, "How much would you be willing to pay to bring in someone who could take a big load off your shoulders?" She thought it was a pipe dream. Where could she find such a person?

We brainstormed all the tasks she wished she could hand off to someone else. We built up a list of personal qualities she wanted in this person. Since she'd had a succession of unsatisfactory employees, she was much more in touch with what she didn't want. So her first list profiled "the employee from hell." We then listed the opposites of those negatives and came up with the qualities of the person she wanted. Since she was not a good interviewer, we helped her evaluate candidates.

She hired Cindy as office manager. When I saw her again, she was beaming. "When Cindy came in, I was afraid to show her the mess in the back office. I explained the things we needed to update—the files that needed to be purged, the systems that needed to be developed—

fearful that she'd turn around and walk out. But, she literally rolled up her sleeves and said, 'This is the kind of challenge I love!' In her first week, she made more progress than anyone else had done in that entire year. She's my wonder woman!"

The owner had asked herself, "Who's the highest-skilled person I can bring in to free me up to focus on the needs of the company?" This was the result.

**Let me handle that.** Beth owns several retail stores. Her business has blossomed because she is very good at selecting merchandise, display, and promotion. As she added stores, she spent more of her time on managing day-to-day operations and on hiring, firing and scheduling employees. The bigger she got, the less time she had to spend on what makes her business special.

People in her Business Group urged her to hire a general manager. She said, "How can I justify $50,000 a year or more to have someone come in and manage my stores, when I can manage them perfectly well myself." But she wasn't managing them all that well, and was feeling discouraged and burned out.

Finally she hired Frank to oversee the stores. Before long, every time she voiced concerns about some aspect of the operation—problem employees, cash flow, stale merchandise—Frank would say, "Leave that to me. Trust me to handle that for you." At first it was hard for her to let go of dealing with all the employee issues, but at his urging, she gradually did it. Now, instead of focusing on people problems, she's able to focus on the hot new trends for next year. Frank was her superman.

*If the owner is wearing many hats, adding just one good person—I mean a really good person—can make a huge difference.*

**Wonder Woman or Superman.** I call these employees wonder woman or superman to remind you that you want someone who can work wonders, not someone who is just adequate. Stop singing the "so-so employee" blues: "Since the people working for me aren't very good, I end up doing their jobs as well as mine." Instead, hire the person who can free you up to focus on growth, ease, and profitability.

Here is the key question:

Who is the highest-skilled person you can bring in to free you up to focus on your growth, profitability, and ease of operation?

Your answer depends on the size of your company, your skills, and your needs. In one of our recent workshops, we asked the participants, who would be (or already is) wonder woman or superman for them. Here are some of their responses:

"A business development person who will bring in projects and free me up to design, since my designs are what make the difference in my business."

"My financial controller. She watches cash flow like a hawk, and keeps me out of trouble."

"Someone who has a similar standing in my profession—more like a partner. Complementary to me. We can give each other support and feedback, and build synergy."

"My assistant comes in a few hours every week to help me work through areas where it's hard for me to get going. She helps me think through my marketing strategies and activities over the next few months."

What kind of person do you need to hire to:
> better exploit your company's competitive advantage
> get to the next stage of growth
> get the most from your unique skills and gifts
> compensate for your management weakness
> be the most productive with your time
> make it smoothly through the upcoming transition?

As your business grows and you are ready to move up and take on greater challenges, whom must you hire to fill in behind you?

| WHEN YOU ARE READY TO MOVE BEYOND... | YOU NEED |
| --- | --- |
| being a one person business | administrative assistant, bookkeeper, and/or go-fer. |
| a small office | an office manager, "vice president of minutiae," or controller. |
| your doing all the sales | a salesperson or sales manager. |
| being a small manufacturer | a production manager or expediter. |
| a single location, to multiple locations | branch managers. |

You may hire someone to fill a position that until now you have handled, or that so far hasn't been handled well by anybody. The person you need may be someone already working for you. It may be someone you hire as a full-time, part-time, or temporary employee. It may be an outside professional or contractor. Here is a checklist, just to get you started.

| ADMINISTRATION/FINANCE | MARKETING/SALES | PRODUCTION/TECHNICAL |
|---|---|---|
| Office phone coverage | Marketing strategist | Operations manager, production manager, floor manager, assistant manager |
| Filing, organizing, updating | Salesperson, sales rep | |
| Errands, cleaning, go-fer tasks | Customer service rep | |
| Materials and info assembly | Sales manager | Associate to handle routine or lower-level parts of your jobs |
| Correspondence, mailings | Mail order or web site sales | |
| Shipping, receiving | Phone contact & follow up | Production help, apprentice, trainee, courier |
| Scheduling | Marketing mailings | |
| Logistics support | Handling of inquiries | Contract or project management |
| Procurement | Prepare materials, packages | Technical specialist |
| AR/AP, invoicing, collections | Public relations, promotion | |
| Bookkeeping, accounting | Arrangement of events, presentations | |
| Cash management | | |
| Inventory control | Support at shows, exhibits | |

## Just too miraculous?

Sometimes our definition of wonder woman or superman is a bit too miraculous. "I want someone who is a combination of professional organizer and bookkeeper who can run the office day-to-day and also help me with marketing." This sounds like more than one person. When you try to find such diverse skills in the same person, you are looking for a rare type indeed. As business owner, you wear many hats. You may do your marketing and your own finances. Why can't you find someone who can do everything that you can do? Even if you could, this requirement makes it a much more difficult search. It is probably more fruitful to divide these tasks between two people.

## Organizer vs. doer

"I want someone to help me organize my office, then run things day-to-day." This may be two different people. Someone who can organize and set up office systems may charge $30 to $50 per hour; the person who thereafter runs your office and uses these systems may be worth $12 to $15 per hour. The first person, the organizer, probably should not be (and probably doesn't want to be) an employee; rather, it is someone that you would contract with to help you on a project basis. You can then turn over the ongoing office operation to an administrative person.

## Hire no more than you need

Your small, growing company cannot afford to hire all the employees you need. These people do not have to be full-time. Nor are they necessarily employees: many will be outside contractors. You pay for only what you need.

### Hire vs. promote

The person you need may already be working for you. Do you have untapped potential among your employees? Who have you been over-looking? If you tell your people what you need right now, who will rise to the challenge?

## CAN YOU AFFORD TO HIRE THE PERSON YOU NEED?

Can you afford not to? What does it cost you to not have this person work-ing for you? What is the cost in lost opportunity? What could you do with your time? How could you perform better? How could your company be more productive? (If you don't have good answers for those questions, then perhaps you should not hire.)

> *How do you justify the cost of hiring? Ask yourself: What is the cost of not getting the help you need?*

Remember that you cannot justify a new hire or a promotion by comparing their salary with extra revenue they bring in. Their pay must be covered, not by added revenue, but by added profit, generated by new business or by saving money. Their activity must lead to an increase in the profit of your company greater than what you pay them.

The new business attributed to them can be business they bring in directly, e.g., as a sales person. But it's just as valuable if they free you up so that you are the one bringing in more profitable business.

Here are several ways to justify the cost of a new person:

1. They make you money.
   "I've been delaying filling this position because it's an expensive per-son to hire; but that's a false economy. I see right away that he or she would bring in enough added business—more than would cover the salary—especially if I pay partly on performance-based commission."

2. They save you money.
   "She plugs the leaks in the organization. She catches all the ways that people waste time and money: unnecessary purchasing, poor schedul-ing, too much overtime. She has put a stop to 80% of that. Just that part of her job is worth more than I'm paying her."

3. They free you up, not just to bring in more business in the short run, but to focus on the strategic direction of your company. They help you

go after opportunities that you might miss otherwise. You can increase the capabilities of your company.

"I was doing things my project managers should be doing. They didn't have time because they were doing things the office staff should do. But the office staff was working flat out. By bringing in two interns to help with routine stuff, it freed people all the way up the line—including me. And the interns didn't need fancy offices."

"I hired a licensed contractor to handle all our construction projects. I used to do all this myself. I could do it just fine, in fact I enjoy doing it. I'm probably better than he is. But it was too consuming; it was driving me nuts. I was losing sleep."

"My office manager is wonder woman. One of the most important things she does is to clean up after me—put away the files that I get out, handle the details of all the little things that I start."

4.  They perform an essential function, perhaps better than you can.

    "He catches the details of all of our jobs that I might overlook. This makes our clients a lot happier. He also bills for things that I used to give away."

    "She's better at negotiating with the renters than I am. She gets a couple more percentage points than I would, because she sticks to her guns in ways the renters will go along with. A few percent per month on each lease builds up."

    "I don't think she makes us any money directly, but she is essential for the smooth operation of the team."

5.  They help you avoid risks, hazards, oversights, and blunders, not to mention lawsuits, that may take years to manifest.

    "I don't know if I can justify his salary in the short run, but he is my insurance policy. He will keep me from making costly mistakes."

## SUPER HERO, WHERE ARE YOU?

How do you find the right employee for you? If you are not careful in your hiring, you have mediocre employees who are a lot tougher to manage.

The most successful executives are the ones who build top-notch teams. Start by getting the best people for the position you need to fill, perhaps people who are even better than you. Don't settle for another Joe Blow. Hire a wonder woman or a super man. Here are the keys:

• **Wish list.** Brainstorm what you want. Who would help you most in achieving your goals? Who would free you up? Your answers to these questions are the foundation to the job description.

Don't just brainstorm skills and experience. Focus on the personal qualities of the person who would free you up.

Don't limit your thinking to the people who are already working for you, the people you've had in the past, who you think is available, or how much you think you can afford. Go first for what you want.

• **Job description.** Write down on paper all the skills, personal qualities, and areas of responsibility you seek in candidates. Rank these by (a) Must Have, (b) Want But Not Crucial, and (c) Would Be Nice.

It often helps to start from a description of what you do *not* want; i.e., your "employee from hell." I ask people to think of the worst qualities of former employees. This generates a list real fast! "Offended when I asked her to be on time." "Argued with the customers." "Was afraid of anything new. Got intimidated by the electric pencil-sharpener." "Got defensive whenever I tried to give her feedback." "Never came in with an ironed shirt." "Since she was an assistant manager, thought tidying up was beneath her."

> *Write a job description for the "employee from hell," then think of the opposites, and you've described the person you want.*

Probably your own list is beginning to pour forth now! Write it down, then beside each item, write its positive opposite. "Punctual. Good with customers. Excited by new things. Presentable appearance. Willing to pitch in and do what is needed."

Personal qualities are as important as specific skills. Table 6-1 shows two lists that I made while listening to business owners tell what they wanted and didn't want in new employees. Whenever they gave me a negative quality, I suggested a positive one.

• **Interview questions.** Devise questions that allow you to evaluate how well candidates satisfy your job description. Not only the skills and capabilities, but the personal qualities as well. In many cases, hiring for personal qualities is more important. You can train for the skills.

• **Recruit.** Cast your net as wide by as possible to bring in qualified candidates.

• **Interview and select.** If you're not a good interviewer, get help with this key function. In our book, *Finding & Keeping Good People*, the theme is, "Hire smart so you do not have to manage tough." Evaluate their qualities and test their expertise.

• **Training & orientation.** Get people started off on the right foot, not in just their job responsibilities, but also in interactions with other employees and in your business culture.

### TABLE 6-1
#### Qualities of a restaurant manager

- Be engaged with customers and with employees. Remembers names, faces and preferences. Schmooze, yet be hard-headed.

- Be a go-getter. Be a creative contributor to the business.

- Look for what needs to be done. Be willing to work enough hours to get the job done.

- Stay aware of inventory levels and item costs when making special offers.

- Be willing to fill in for employees who don't show up for work.

- Stay cool in tough times, especially when traffic doubles.

- Be computer-savvy and be comfortable with our performance reports.

- Be aware of what's going on in all parts of the company, esp. disputes, disgruntled employees or customers and behavior that reflects badly on the company.

- Know what to handle on their own, and what to bring to the owner's attention.

#### Qualities of a seminar leader

- Strong constitution, strong voice

- Establish rapport. Get the audience involved. Be an instant storyteller. Have a sense of humor.

- Maintain eye contact.

- Pacing: be flexible, go with the flow, yet stay on course.

- Self-confidence: feel secure in a room full of high-powered, self-assured, argumentative participants.

- Stay in control; project strength. Take criticism well. Be able to deflect attacks. Use challenges as lessons.

- Be able and willing to work hard and travel.

• **Evaluation, correction.** Give them constructive feedback on how they are doing the above. Develop checklists that allow you to do this in a systematic way.

Many small business owners have trouble with interviewing and selecting. You can get help in these areas.

### "I just can't afford anyone"

Suppose you really need help, but you cannot afford it. It's time to do some creative thinking to figure out how to get the help you need in a way that doesn't break the bank. Remember, you don't have to hire full-time people.

Call this "organizational triage." Whom could you bring in for the maximum benefit in the shortest amount of time with the goal of boosting your earning power and creating more business? This might be done with administrative backup, help in thinking through your marketing outreach, or perhaps by making follow-up calls to prospective clients. Who, as an employee, could get you charged up so that you'll use your time more effectively right now?

Start by writing down five tasks where you most need help. Which would provide the most immediate benefit when done? What should you focus on first? Second? What limited result could you achieve that would have the greatest impact? How could you create a small benefit that reverberates throughout the entire organization?

How can you get more from your current employees? Who can step up to a greater challenge? Alternatively, who cannot? Are you being held back by loyalty to someone who cannot (or will not) give you the help you need?

Ask this even about those who are not your employees, such as a bookkeeper who you send your work out to, or a web designer. You can even apply this line of questioning to your customers or your vendors. And finally, you should apply it to your co-owner or partner or business advisor.

## HOW TO FIND GOOD PEOPLE IN A TIGHT LABOR MARKET

**Do you have trouble finding the employees you need?** "It is hard attracting the kind of people we want."

• Be clear on who you need. Look realistically and define your needs carefully. Perhaps you need to redefine your job opening. The description may be too broad, making it more difficult to find someone who can do everything you want. In this case, divide the job into two pieces.

• Make sure you keep the good people you already have. Train your in-house people. If they are capable, promote them, and bring in entry-level people. But if no one in-house is capable of taking on the responsibility you need filled, then don't hobble yourself by limiting the position to fit their capabilities.

### Sell the desirability of working for your company

A woman who runs an auto body shop and who never has any trouble attracting people, comments: "I work hard to make my shop a place people want to work. People are always coming in and asking if we have work available. I get to choose which ones I want."

Look at the challenge of attracting the kind of employees you want as a marketing job—you have to sell the desirability of your company: "Here's why you should work for our company."

Many highly skilled individuals will choose a small company (and the lesser salary usually offered) because they appreciate the autonomy, neighborliness and personal environment; in short, the culture of your small business.

Make sure you have an attractive place to work. Get people excited about the prospect of working there. Offer attractive benefits or extras. Emphasize:

• The work environment, the quality of the other people who work there, and the pride they have in their workplace. This new employee can be a valued member of your team.

• The equipment they will use.

• Training you offer to upgrade their skills.

• Emphasize such things as flexible hours and/or jobs that are less than full-time.

• Show the future opportunity, the increased challenge and the path to promotion.

These guidelines are not limited to high-tech or professional offices; they are applied equally well by general contractors, restaurants, and retail stores that I work with that rely on lesser-skilled and entry-level people.

• Know the salary range. Pay at market or slightly higher. Perhaps offer performance-based incentives.

### *Cast your recruitment net far and wide*

Here are some of the tactics used by companies I work with:

- Draw good people away from larger companies. Many would prefer working for a smaller company. Advertise, "We're a small, friendly company."

- Look for people who live near you, who currently have a long commute. They may be able to regain three hours per day by working for a company closer to home.

- Keep your eye out for good people. When you find them, no matter what kind of company they are working for, give them your card and say something like, "If you know anyone who would be interested in a job at our place..." They may call you for themselves, but they won't call unless they are already thinking of moving on.

- Network within your industry organizations. Even in the tightest markets, people move on. Companies have to lay off good people, and they would like to help them find a new position.

- Ask your employees. Offer an incentive if they bring in someone you hire. One client offers her employees a $500 bonus to bring in people they know who are potential new employees. It's surprising how many workforces are filled with uncles and cousins and nieces and people from back home.

- Bring in interns from local colleges and universities. Offer permanent jobs to the best ones.

- Contact strong candidates who previously answered an ad but then went elsewhere. Keep in contact with them and they may come to you in the future.

## HOW TO KEEP GOOD PEOPLE ONCE YOU HAVE THEM

The cost of replacing a worker is much greater than the cost of keeping them productive. The Number One reason a person will leave a job is unhappiness with the boss. In a small company, that boss is either you or one of your managers.

Treat them well and fairly. Maintain a workplace that is firm, fair, and consistent. Make sure they see the fairness. Employees sometimes have a distorted view of the profitability of a small business. They somehow assume that all the revenue pouring in—besides their pay—flows directly into your pocket. Don't you wish!

Give them whatever they need to do the job: tools and equipment, training, support from below, guidance from above, teamwork from all sides, validation, and authority.

Make sure you hire the right people in the first place, but if they don't work out, let them go. Be ruthless about this. Not only is the pay of the mediocre employee coming directly out of your pocket, but poor performance brings down the entire team. Your best people will get fed up, and may even leave if they see you coddling someone who isn't doing the job.

Manage them well. Many small business owners are not natural-born managers. Tell them what you want from them. Give them training and retraining. Convey your goals and expectations. Set ground rules and boundaries. Monitor their performance and give them feedback on a regular basis.

Trust them to do their jobs. Delegate, then give them freedom to take initiative, and hold them responsible for results.

Acknowledge their successes, troubleshoot their problems, and involve them in solving the problems.

Share information on the operation of your company. If you offer profit sharing, base it on open books, at least on the part that pertains to their bonus. Show them how they can make more. Show them how much you contribute to profit sharing.

Make sure that your managers do these same things with their subordinates.

## Recognize that your employees are temporary

Very few are likely to stay with you for the rest of their working lives, even assuming that you want them to. Prepare for this: cross train and develop checklists and manuals so that future employees can get up to speed faster by having something to refer to.

Ask people what their plans are. What do they see as their career path? People will tell you such things as: "I expect to go back to college in September." "We want to build a house on our lot in Oregon within five years." "I'd like to stay here till my youngest finishes school." "I want a chance to move up the ladder and earn the money I want."

## Help your people do a better job for you

The Number One way to get more from your employees is to tell them what you want. Your employees may not have a clear idea of what you expect from them. Remember, they can't read your mind. What are their daily sales goals and production quotas? One shop owner got tremendous results from putting a small sign up by the cash register, saying, "$1800."

She told her employees this was the amount the store needed to sell each day to remain healthy. Before that, the employees really had no idea.

Ask your people, "How could I help you do a better job for me?" You can ask your employees, your managers, and your subcontractors. This is a magical question. Everyone has an answer. We may not ask it because we're afraid of what we will hear. We fear that people will ask for impractical things that we can't provide for them.

But if you have people working for you who are qualified and capable and want to do a good job for you, they will give you a good answer to that question. They will say things that are completely obvious once you hear them. You'll think, "Ah! Why didn't I think about that before? Why didn't you tell me that before?" "Well, boss, you never asked."

> *How can you help your people do a better job for you? Ask them.*

One business owner asked his managers what kind of incentive system they thought would be best to introduce for the employees. One manager said, "First, remove the disincentives." It took bravery to ask this question and to give that answer. But it led to very productive changes in the work rules.

Ask yourself (or ask your employees if you have the nerve), what do you do that drives your employees crazy? What do you do that gets in their way? What is it that confuses or distracts them, or pulls them off course? What makes them feel angry or insecure? Are there barriers you could remove that limit their performance?

When people tell you what they need from you to help them do a better job for you, then give it to them. Give them training. Give them concrete goals. Set up simpler procedures. Give them the information and tools they need. Give them an assistant. Redefine their job. Get off their backs. Give them some acknowledgement.

(And while you are at it, give these things to yourself as well.)

## HAVE YOU OUTGROWN A KEY EMPLOYEE?

As your company grows, it may leave some employees behind. They may have done well when the company was smaller, but now that it has grown they are being forced out of their comfort zone and they are not able to step up to the challenge.

This is particularly painful when it involves key people who have been with you from the beginning. You have grown and they have grown right along with you. But when you reach a certain level, you see that they aren't keeping up, and they resist further growth. It becomes apparent in their attitudes about the way the company is going. Their commitment diminishes. They lack the skills or the willingness to gain skills. They lack the energy or the ability to take a risk and to take charge.

It is easy to allow yourself and your company to be limited by their limitations. You are loyal to them even though they're not able to perform at the needed level.

To continue on the desired track you must make sure such people do not hold you back. You can reassign their role(s), bring somebody in above them, or you may have to ease them out. Let's face it, they are not happy with the role you want them to assume. They might prefer you stay the way you used to be but that doesn't work for you. You don't want your employees setting your growth strategy.

---

## TABLE 6-2

### *Find good people and keep them productive*

How can you improve the way you do these things?

Design jobs, divide up responsibilities, and write job descriptions.

Recruit; attract qualified candidates.

Interview and select the best candidates.

Assure a good fit, including skills and experience, attitudes, and personal qualities.

Give training. Get new hires started off on the right foot.

Set goals and give guidance and direction; involve people in planning and goal setting.

Monitor efforts and hold people accountable for their actions.

Build teamwork, cooperation, and communication among employees.

Motivate desired performance such as by offering incentives.

Redefine lines of authority.

Manage your managers and train them to be better managers.

Upgrade or install systems, policies, work practices and procedures.

Provide needed support and assistance.

Provide needed tools, equipment and other work materials.

Lay out the work space and improve the work environment.

Provide needed information and performance reports.

Schedule work hours, days off, vacations, team schedules.

Evaluate performance, give correction and acknowledge success.

Maintain a businesslike atmosphere. Be firm, fair, and consistent in all areas.

Handle disputes, disagreements, misconduct, poor performance and terminations.

## GETTING THE SUPPORT YOU NEED

I make an arbitrary distinction between help and support. Help comes from those you hire for the in-house tasks of the business. In addition, you receive support from a variety of outside professionals: your CPA, attorney, banker, marketing professionals, computer professionals, various consultants, etc.

As your company grows, you may outgrow some relationships. The CPA, the banker or the web designer who provided invaluable support when you were smaller may not be adequate for a larger company. Staying with them becomes a barrier to your growth, profitability, and ease of operation.

The trend is for even good-sized companies to outsource more and more things; not just accounting and legal, but human resources, payroll, parts of their production, design, etc. These same things are increasingly available to smaller companies.

What professional relationships do you need that you never needed before now? Think about support needed in each aspect of your business: administrative, financial, marketing, operations, management, personnel.

Which professional relationships do you need to replace? Use table 6-3 as a checklist.

---

### Table 6-3
### Outside services

| What are your emerging needs? | Whom should you hire or replace? |
|---|---|
| Subcontractors or job shops to whom you farm out work | Outside sales reps, sales rep group |
| Management advisor, mentor, role model, trainer | Mail clerk, shipper |
| Industry expertise | Personnel help: interviewing, screening, training |
| Financial systems, performance tracking reports service | Employee trainer |
| CFO, financial advisor | Personnel policy manager: handbooks, incentives |
| CPA, tax and financial compliance, auditor | Personnel agency: temps, executive search |
| Banker, financier | Retirement fund investment management |
| Payroll service | Communications, telephone, Internet specialist |
| Attorney, legal advisor | |

---

### Table 6-3—Continued
### Outside services

| What are your emerging needs? | Whom should you hire or replace? |
| --- | --- |
| Insurance agent, risk management person | Web site designer and web and e-business strategist |
| Marketing strategist, tactician | Technical and document writer |
| Market researcher | Graphic designer copy writer |
| Merchandiser, facilities designer | Computer systems support |
| Promotion, public relations person | Commercial or industrial leasing agent |
| Distributors | Equipment leasing company |
| | Security |

---

As you grow you may also outgrow vendors or suppliers. What do you need from vendors to spur growth, profitability and ease of operation? For example:

Better terms

Willingness to help you finance your expansion

Volume discounts

Savings through co-op buying

Phone or internet-based ordering or reordering

Leasing of related equipment, systems, and installation

Phased purchase or delivery

Just-in-time delivery

Better policy on returns and restocking

Systems that mesh better with yours

## ASK YOURSELF . . .

1. Who is the highest skilled person you could hire (or delegate more to) to free you up?
2. How much more revenue would your business have to bring in to justify hiring this person?
3. How much more business could you generate if you bit the bullet and hired the person who could take over all the tasks that keep your from focusing on growth?
4. How do your work habits, management style, etc. get in the way of hiring and keeping the quality of person you need?

5. How could any change in your management style, work habits, attitudes or beliefs help your people do a better job for you?

6. What do your employees need from you to be more productive?

7. What outside support would most help you achieve your long-term objectives and overcome your barriers to growth?

8. What professional relationships do you need to hire or replace?

## TO TAKE THIS FURTHER . . .

Several of our workbooks will help you apply the ideas in this chapter to your business. These are co-authored by B.J. Van Horn, Senior Professional in Human Resources. Complete information is in the Book and Resource List.

- *How to Hire Your First Employee.* A step-by-step guide for first-time employers, with forms and templates.

- *Finding and Keeping Good Employees. Part I.* Hire smart so you don't have to manage tough. Guidelines for job descriptions, interviewing, selecting, getting new hires started off right.

- *Finding and Keeping Good Employees. Part II.* Creating a workplace that is firm, fair, and consistent. Retaining good people is cheaper than replacing. Training, grooming, reviewing performance, handling problems. Employment practices, compliance questions.

- *Employer Assertiveness Training.* Changing your management style for a more productive workplace.

## Chapter 7

# Get the Secret Knowledge Out of Your Head

### *The systems and procedures needed for growth*

When you start out in business you do everything in ways that seem natural to you, and it works. Your style might be called "seat of the pants management." You make things up as you need them. Whenever a new situation arises, you figure out a way to address it. When a customer asks for something, you create a deal for them on the spot. With a second customer, you come up with something else to make them happy. When an employee asks about a day off, you make a decision. When a second employee wants time off, you come up with something else.

The impact is that there is little consistency whenever key decisions must be made, you are the only one who can make them. Employees and customers must come to you because you have not set up standardized ways to deal with everyday occurrences.

As your business grows, "seat of the pants management"— which used to work just fine—begins to slow you down. If you do not change, these outmoded ways of doing business become part of the molasses that keeps you from growing further.

"But," you protest, "my special experience (or knowledge/competence/creativity) is what sets us apart and makes us successful." This special knowledge can relate to any part of your business. You notice yourself saying, "Only I can…" or "I have to…"

do estimates on big jobs

decide when to make fund transfers between banks

interact with that customer

tell when the design is complete

reorder merchandise

write up the final formulation

reconcile the discrepancies

monitor cash flow

close the deal

keep us on schedule and within budget

operate that equipment properly

write the ad copy

make that presentation

I'm sure you can add your own "Only I can" items to this list.

This special knowledge is like the "black box" that is part of some high-tech equipment. A black box is a specialized and self-contained piece of equipment that is of critical importance. Things can't happen without it. The black box in your head is the specialized knowledge and information that only you have and is of critical importance to your operation. These critical functions cannot happen unless you are involved, thus you are chained to the business.

"Getting the secret knowledge out of your head" means transferring these things that only you know to procedures manuals, training manuals and checklists so that others can do the task as well as you.

You may object, "I really do have special knowledge and skill. Even if I could transfer it to procedure manuals, which seems unlikely, who else could do this as well as I do?" I often detect an unspoken sentiment here: "If I *could* transfer all my secret knowledge, then what would be special about my business? And maybe they wouldn't really need me any more."

This "black box syndrome" becomes a huge barrier to growth and profitability, whether the special knowledge lies with you or one of your key employees. As your company grows, you just can't hold enough information in your head. Nor can you be available all the time. You need to focus on the strategies for growing the business. The person with black box knowledge is the bottleneck to further growth.

And of course black box thinking is an absolute barrier to operating your business with ease. What happens when you want to get away from the business, or even (gasp!) take a vacation? You can spot the people right away who suffer from black box syndrome: they are the ones whose cell phones and pagers are constantly going off during my seminars, or even when they are on outings with their family.

It's one thing if you work for a big company and your boss insists that you be reachable 24/7. But if *you* are the boss, and you still can't free yourself from the business even for a short while, what does this say about your management style and your priorities?

## BECOME A SYSTEMS-GENERATING WIZARD

The solution to the black box syndrome is to get in the habit of noting what happened, what you did about it, how you did it, and why. This becomes the raw material for manuals, handbooks, checklists, and templates. Before long, others will be able to make decisions you formerly had to make. Routine activities will be done consistently, with fewer pieces dropped out.

You can do this even in the parts of your business where your creativity, design skill, judgment, or problem-solving abilities are most crucial. As you pay attention to what you do, you see things that you must (or want to) hold on to, but you also see parts that you can hand off to others. As you delegate these tasks to others, you are freed to focus on the truly critical things that you are best at, and that give your company its edge.

Let's look at a few examples of how seat of the pants/black box decisions could be replaced by systems and procedures that others can handle—entirely or in part.

| "SEAT OF THE PANTS" APPROACH | SYSTEMATIC APPROACH |
|---|---|
| Whenever you have new office employees, you work with them one-on-one to show them how to do every part of their job. | Your office procedures manual, built up over the last few employee tenures, covers all the basics. You focus your face-to-face training on their special responsibilities. |
| You look at the account balance and decide which bills to pay when; you switch funds among accounts when necessary. | Your cash management protocols and accounts payable schedule allow your bookkeeper to handle all routine transactions, and specify which situations to bring to your attention. |
| The printer breaks down and you drop everything to troubleshoot the problem. After all, nothing can happen without the printer. | The office manager calls the printer maintenance outfit listed in your troubleshooting directory. |
| Your field sales reps give you verbal reports on their progress with various accounts. They often resist being pinned down. | Sales reps must log all their contacts in the computer database, which automatically compiles status reports for you. |
| Your sales manager offers special deals and discounts, and moves favored customers to the head of the production schedule. | Your order entry and scheduling system contains the parameters for all pricing and scheduling decisions. |
| Your counter people take down phone orders on a pad of paper, often forgetting to include key pieces of data. Sometimes these slips of paper are misplaced. | Orders are entered directly into the computer, which prompts users to enter each piece of data, and won't book the order until all data is included. |

You make ad hoc decisions when employees ask you for special times off. This ruffles some feathers: there is muttering about your favoritism.

Your employee manual states your policy on all normal situations; when employees ask questions, you first refer them to the manual.

You look over the shoulders of your designers, and often make last minute design suggestions. Then you complain that they take too long and don't show enough initiative. m

Each project has design reviews at specified stages. The lead designer is responsible for limiting your input to those times. You replace any designers whose work doesn't meet your standards, and trust those whom you retain.

## SYSTEMS VS. PROCEDURES

What is the difference between "systems" and "procedures?"

*The **system** is the thing you use;*
*the **procedures** are the rules for using it.*

Systems are useless without procedures in place that take advantage of them. Suppose you install the latest marketing database system to track contacts with potential customers, but your sales people fail to enter the data as they make calls. Or you install a system to track billable time spent on projects, to compare with estimated hours, but you can't get your people (or yourself) to track time. Or perhaps you have a great system to upgrade your people's field skills through regular training sessions, but you always seem to be too busy to actually perform the training.

There is little point in launching an expensive system without the procedures and commitment to use it properly.

## SYSTEMS ARE THE SPRINGBOARD TO GROWTH

Good systems pay off in many ways:

• **Easier to find people.** The better your systems and procedures, the more tasks that a lower-skilled person can handle, and the higher their productivity. Many business owners who despair of hiring people that meet their job qualifications, have much greater luck when they improve their systems to simplify the jobs. "Our bookkeeper had to be a magician to grasp the convoluted ways our foremen reported job costs. After we adopted an accounting system recommended by our industry association, our invoicing function became almost routine."

• **Easier training.** When someone departs, their replacement can get up to speed much more quickly if you have previously developed a manual covering their responsibilities. Thus you avoid the experience of this company: "It was so disheartening; we just spent several weeks training her, then she left. We had to start all over again with the new woman."

---

**TABLE 7-1**

**Examples of systems and procedures**

Everyday procedures that are specific to your business

    Manuals for your office, shop, or field

    Employee manuals, policies

    Instructions for using or troubleshooting your equipment

    Training programs

    Cash handling, billing, collections

Packaged systems that bigger businesses routinely use that small companies often neglect

    Planning

    Accounting, profit center reports, cost control, cash management

    Budgeting and review

    Scheduling and time tracking

    Point of sale, barcode reader, inventory control

    Project management, operations management

Computer-based systems customized to your needs

    Order entry, job scheduling, customer status

    Invoicing

    Employee performance tracking, reviews

    Marketing contacts database

    Generating estimates or proposals

    Employee incentive programs

---

• **Alignment.** As you standardize things and review them periodically, everyone in your organization will be on the same page. Fewer things will be done incorrectly or fall through the cracks. You have better protection in case there are misunderstandings, including legal protection in the event of a dispute.

• **Consistency**. Procedures enforce consistency on your employees, your customers, your vendors and yourself. They save arguments and misunderstandings. When employees come to you with questions you can say, "Before you and I talk about that, take a look in your employee manual."

Your impetus to codify your policies into an employee manual may be trouble stemming from your previous verbal policies; for example, you and your employee interpret policies differently, or it comes to light that you have made inconsistent agreements with different employees. With a manual, you don't have to explain things all the time. You just say, "On page 17 it says, 'No vacations between Thanksgiving and Christmas.' You signed this."

When customers have a question, you say, "Let's check our written Terms and Conditions." These include such routine items as: How you bill. How you expect payment. When customers get a discount. How soon you can start their job, and when they can expect delivery. What they must do and what your responsibilities are.

While you fear this may been seen as onerous, your customers respect fairness and consistency, and enjoy working with you more. Customers' greatest fears are broken promises, unpleasant surprises, and unexpected charges. If you tell them all these terms up front, so they know what to expect and when, then there is less cause for argument or disappointment later.

• **Profitability.** Your business works more smoothly. Employee productivity increases and costs go down. Work gets done consistently and on schedule, so customers are happier. You focus less on breakdowns and glitches, more on boosting growth and profitability.

## *"Yeah, but . . ."* Why businesses resist systems

Despite the obvious benefits, business owners often resist systematizing tasks. This usually springs from their entrenched habits, beliefs, or fears. Here are some of the biggest ones, along with my response:

• **"The personal touch is what makes us special.** Doing things by the book will take the soul out of our operation."

Good systems free you up to retain your flexibility and personal touch. The owner of a bookstore said, "At first, my employees—and me too—resisted doing things by established procedures. We somehow thought it would constrain our creativity and depersonalize the operation. But it turned out to be liberating! Turning routines into systems freed us up to focus on the fun parts of the business—working with customers and merchandizing."

• **"All our transactions and jobs are so different.** We need to be flexible. Systems just get in the way."

I have never once found this to be true. Of course you need to retain your flexibility. Identify the parts of your jobs that stay consistent and build them into systems. This frees up your flexibility and creativity for the interesting parts.

• **"I prefer to wheel and deal**, and come up with the best decision for each circumstance. So do my employees."

This is a style of business that usually puts a lid on growth. Of course we read about billion dollar wheeler-dealers, but not every small business can pull that off. If you aren't happy with your business size or profitability, then this habit is a good place to look.

• **"My people balk** at adopting productivity-enhancing systems. I have tried to install new ways to do things, but they just wore me down."

So who's in charge? If you keep people around you who prevent you from getting what you want in business, then the problem starts with *you*. Go back to chapter 5 and work on your own beliefs and attitudes.

• **"It's too expensive** and time-consuming to install these systems and procedures."

Yes, it is expensive and time-consuming. But ask yourself, what is the cost of *not* having needed systems and procedures? It is the familiar feeling of wading through the swamp rather than sprinting along the path. Do a simple cost/benefit analysis, using these three questions:

1. How much would it cost you in time and money to make the systems changes you need?

2. What's the total benefit of installing or improving the system or procedure, in terms of increased revenue, reduced costs, saved time (yours and your people's), increased productivity, improved customer service, etc.?

3. What is the ratio of the cost to the benefit? For example, if it would cost you $5,000 and 100 hours to get a new system up and running, but over the first year it would save $50,000 and 1,000 hours of time for you and your people, then the benefit to cost ratio is 10 to 1. You would be crazy not to do it. Not doing it would cost you $45,000!

• **"Only I can do it."**

Ask your people about these special activities of yours. They will say, "That's not so difficult. We could do that. It needs to be simplified anyway. Tell me how you order this kind of merchandise. What is your rule about transferring funds?"

But maybe you really can't tell them, because in truth, you don't know how you do it. It's just a feel, an intuition, you have developed over years. If this is truly so, then you must organize around this activity so that it does not become the ceiling of your growth. You must ruthlessly delegate all the other things you do.

What about the creativity and the problem-solving ability you bring to your work? This truly does set you apart. However, even in these areas, there are parts of each thing you do that can be systematized and delegated. If the way you order merchandise is part of the magic of your business, ask yourself what parts of ordering can be delegated. If clients pay huge bucks for your design genius, how can you maximize your creative input into each project, then turn it over to skilled associates and your business manager?

## *From secret knowledge to duplicating yourself*

Once you begin to describe what you do in a way that others can follow, you immediately see the benefits:

• **Training**. You have a tool to train new people and retrain veterans. You have a quality control tool, which you can use to monitor and evaluate their performance.

• **Marketing**. This material helps you understand what it is you do, so that you can communicate it more effectively to others, and improve your own performance.

• **Leverage**. You can leverage your effort by duplicating yourself, by using your materials to train other employees to provide the same quality service that you do.

• **Protection**. This helps you preserve your intellectual property by specifying what it is that you do in as much detail as needed.

> *Good systems put money into your pocket and hours back into your life.*

• **Turning services into products**. If you describe your core professional activities in this way, it provides the basis for a product you can sell or license. This is extremely important. It provides the basis for you to move from selling time to selling value, described in chapter 11.

## HOW TO DEVELOP SYSTEMS AND PROCEDURES

Everyone acknowledges the importance of employee manuals, written Terms and Conditions for customers, or a marketing database, yet many do not have or use them. They are expensive and time consuming, and they require you to change habitual ways of doing things.

Most of the systems and procedures needed by growing businesses are created in-house, as you need them. But even the computerized, pre-packaged systems that are installed by experts and come with user manuals and training are not complete until you create your own procedures around them, so they can mesh with your operation.

These must be created by someone who observes what happens and writes it down in a way that others can follow. For example, a training manual for your employees it is very difficult to just sit down and write. It often needs to be developed bit by bit over time. Here are some suggestions:

### Who will do it

• Creating systems and procedures often falls to the owner. Write down what needs to be done as best as you can; however, you may not be particularly good at doing this and may need an outside observer.

• As a new person is learning the job, have him/her write up the job manual.

• Have an apprentice or protégé or student intern follow you around, watch what you do, take notes, and write it up. Then go over this together and elaborate.

• Bring in somebody who specializes in creating such manuals, and lead them through all your operations.

### How it will be done

• Are there templates or examples you can use as models? Perhaps from your industry association or from a similar company, or a generic package you purchase. Customize it for your purposes.

• If you start from scratch, outline as much as you can. What are the topics you need to cover? What pieces have you already done as notes?

• Record ideas as they arise. Use either a small tape recorder or index cards.

• Can you delegate this to someone else, such as the person who has to learn the job, a manager, or an outside professional who can observe the process and document it?

### When to do it

• When you hire a new person and are telling them everything verbally, and decide you are tired of going over this same ground with every new hire.

• When one of your existing employees is training someone else. Arrange to get these sessions recorded.

• When you explain something, instruct an employee, or give a regular training session.

• When you've seen somebody mess up and it is fresh in your mind what they should have done.

• When you see someone who is *not* doing something and you realize they should have been given training.

• Any other time you are inspired.

### What it should look like

• Detailed enough, but not too detailed. Don't finalize it till typical users go through it and you are convinced they can follow it.

• Be visual. Use graphs, flow charts, illustrations, check-lists, sample pages and formats, etc.

Here are a few examples showing how these guidelines can be applied:

Matthew cringed whenever he overheard his sales people miss opportunities with customers. During the twice-monthly staff sessions, he would always say, "You should have said . . ." and write selling tips on the flipchart. He had piles of notes from these meetings, but he kept saying the same things over and over again. Finally, while looking for something to keep the summer intern busy, he said, "Here, take all these notes and turn them into training materials." The intern typed and edited and arranged them, then Matthew reviewed and elaborated these into a sales manual called "Talking Points."

Joann, a computer consultant, hired Sarah, an experienced administrative assistant. Sarah's experience enabled her to turn Joann's confusing welter of office tasks into a procedure manual that covered every aspect of the operation, including schedules and instructions for regular tasks, formats and templates, and a troubleshooting guide for all the office equipment. Joann remarked, "Even if I had the time, I could not possibly have done what Sarah has accomplished!" Sarah then trained the next office assistant.

Tom the general contractor purchased an estimating program that was available through the industry association. It was too complicated in some areas and too simplistic in others, but it got them started. Within a year they had customized it so much that the original was scarcely recognizable. Tom was thrilled: "Without that clunky program to get us off the dime, we'd probably still be relying on our old hand-scribbled estimates." Tom remarked, however, that the toughest part was not tweaking the program, but updating the documentation to reflect their changes and making sure his people got up to speed on the program.

Over a period of several months, George the architect (described in chapter 8) kept a log of all the job codes and descriptions he used on various types of jobs. When he felt like he had eighty percent of them (i.e., covering all common situations) he worked with his top two managers to simplify these into a code book, then trained all the project leaders to code their own projects for invoicing. "I used to do this job on evenings and Saturdays," remarked George.

## Caveats

• If you use someone else's model, don't leave in a bunch of material that is extraneous to your operation. Make sure you understand what's in it. If someone asks you, "What does page 17 mean?" you don't want to appear like you're seeing it for the first time.

• Keep it current with a regular schedule of updates.

• Make sure it is real and complete, because you can be held accountable for its contents.

## Overcoming resistance and inertia

For small systems and procedures the inertia comes beforehand. The first step is the toughest. Once it is in place, you and your people will love to use it.

For larger efforts, it becomes a project and generates resistance. How can you minimize the money, time, and hassle of introducing systems? How can you gain acceptance by the users? Look at chapter 14, "The Dreaded Transition Hump" and chapter 12, "Build a Culture of Growth."

For the system to pay off, people—including you—must be motivated to use it and use it correctly.

• The users need training, maybe more than once.

• There must be consequences for not using it, because some people will resist it.

• Plan ahead how you will develop the structure and integrate it into your operation.

• You must have a regular program of identifying and correcting glitches in the system, of troubleshooting and of making improvements and upgrades.

• The information generated by the system must be used. It must be seen to be useful.

• It must be documented. There must be instructions and training for new people who are introduced to the system.

All these procedures must be in place for any system to pay off.

## ASK YOURSELF . . .

Questions to help you spot needed systems and procedures:

1. Where are the black boxes in your operation? What do you do that seems so specialized or complex that no one else can do it right?

2. Where do you make one-of-a-kind or seat-of-the-pants decisions on routine things? Are there customers, vendors, or professional service providers that only you can talk with?

3. What systems that used to work just fine now cause you problems?

4. What systems and procedures would help your people do a better job for you?

5. Where do you or others keep making mistakes, forgetting things and dropping things through the cracks?

6. Where are the bottlenecks? What keeps slowing everything else down? What breaks down the most?

7. What keeps distracting you or pulling you away from more important tasks?

8. Where would you benefit by having policies or procedures spelled out ahead of time, for example, with vendors, employees, or customers?

9. Where should a computer-based system replace something that is now done manually? How could this lead to productivity gains, improved cost control, better use of resources, better customer service, and reduced mistakes?

## Chapter 8

# Promote Yourself to CEO

### *Polish the skills and capabilities you need to boost your growth, ease, and profitability*

The more your company grows, the harder it can be to grow yet further. Why? Because the management practices and habits that worked when your company was smaller are no longer adequate.

You might be the main bottleneck. You may not be "presidential" enough in your management style. You must "promote yourself to CEO"—that is, focus on executive responsibilities and be less of a floor manager and worker.

Easier said than done! While you are trying to keep your focus on the entire forest, many things conspire to keep you stuck in the trees and underbrush.

In our workshops we ask these two questions:

1. How would you describe your management style now?
2. What management style do you need in order to get where you want to go?

In this chapter we will work on upgrading your management style, management practices and management structure—for yourself and for your key people—so that you can take your company where you want it to go.

## HOW NOT TO MANAGE A GROWING BUSINESS

Let's start by looking at some of the most common management styles that hinder the growth, ease, and profitability of growing companies.

**One of the troops.** You come from a working background yourself, and want to keep a hand in the main work. You feel that you have to be able to do everything that your people can do, and work at least as hard as they do. So you are a worker/manager. This creates several problems. You are so busy doing the work, you do not have time to focus on management and strategic issues. You are so close to the other workers that you find it difficult to manage them properly, and to give correction when needed.

**Fire starter.** You seem to get impatient with a smoothly running operation. You are always coming up with new projects, often with overlapping and conflicting demands on your people. Employees have difficulty setting priorities and following things through to completion, because there is always a new thing which must be done right now.

**Open door.** Your door is always open; accessibility is a virtue. Your tacit message is, "I let everyone else set my agenda." However, if you are subject to interruption at any time, it becomes difficult for you to focus on things that require concentrated attention—financial analysis, planning, creating new materials, writing.

**The business is *moi*.** Your actions say that you are the only one who really matters in the business. All the others are appendages. You are afraid that if you rely on your people, they will let you down. The burden this places on you is inexorably wearing you down.

**One big family.** You don't think you need job descriptions or tracking systems. You want to avoid the image of a numbers-driven, impersonal business. The inefficiencies this style breeds stymies your profitability.

### Turn 'em loose vs. Hold 'em tight

Here is a matched pair of management styles. On a spectrum from laissez-faire to micromanaging, some stay in one mode and some jump from one to the other.

**Laissez-faire manager.** On one end of the spectrum you take freedom of action and non-interference to an extreme. You hire a good person, then turn them loose and expect them to learn their own job. You give them inadequate guidance, training, and feedback. Eventually they feel confused, thwarted, frustrated, unappreciated and impatient. You feel that they're not doing the job. They may begin circulating their résumé for a more challenging job.

**Micromanager.** On the opposite end, you interfere and limit freedom of action. You hire good people, but then never let them do their jobs.

Instead of giving enough responsibility and authority, you look over their shoulders and second-guess them. You jump in on tasks you have assigned them. You allow other people—both employees and customers—to go around them and come to you.

Strong workers and managers thus give up taking initiative, and ask you every little thing. You make decisions and solve problems that they should handle. Then you wonder why they don't take any initiative, and why you are still overworked.

**From one to the other.** You may employ both these styles by vacillating between giving people too much freedom and too much guidance. After ignoring them for awhile, you come down hard on them when they make mistakes, and micro-manage for awhile.

You allow things to build up—perhaps for a whole year—then dump all your gripes on them at once. No wonder you hate doing performance reviews! From the employee's perspective, this is the worst manager.

## THE LADDER OF EXECUTIVE CAPABILITIES

In a successful and growing company, the owner is the chief executive and focuses on executive tasks. However, many owners focus too much time on doing the work, and on being manager, supervisor, and administrator. This becomes a barrier to growth. Table 8-1 illustrates this.

People who are running a small business perform tasks at each of the three levels every day. But to *grow* your business, you need to focus increasingly on responsibilities higher up the ladder, and delegate those on the lower rungs to others. You must hire good people and give them increased autonomy over their areas of responsibility. This is true whether you are a one-person company or have fifty employees. You must "climb the ladder of executive capabilities".

Here are some guiding principles for climbing this ladder:

- Learn to spot the differences between worker, manager, and executive in what you do. Select your own responsibilities according to what will achieve your goals.

- You cannot climb the ladder until there is someone ready to step up behind you. You must find someone to fill in behind you and to take over the tasks you wish to move away from. There can be no management vacuum. A vacuum beneath you holds you down.

- The toughest part is not grooming capable people to step up behind you, but working on your own management style—your habits, beliefs, and attitudes that get in the way.

Even a one-person company faces this. If you are a consultant who relies on keeping on top of all the latest technological advances so you can advise your clients, you cannot do that *and* handle all the correspondence and bookkeeping and still have a life. You are always playing catch up. You must be able to delegate such tasks to assistants, whether employees or contractors, full-time or part-time.

Where do you spend your time as executive, as manager or supervisor, and as worker? Keep track of your own time use. Perhaps each day or half-day, think back on what you have done. What tasks fell onto each level of the ladder? In particular, watch for the things you should not be doing (or don't enjoy doing).

How could you reassign such tasks? Let's look at George, who owns an architecture firm with sixteen employees, including five other architects. George called himself "Vice President of Minutiae" and was sick and tired of working evenings and weekends to handle all the work.

I asked George to keep track of how he spent his time for several weeks. (He hated doing this! But he found out some very interesting things.) We made two lists:

| GEORGE SHOULD DO/WANTS TO DO | GEORGE SHOULD DO LESS /STOP DOING |
|---|---|
| run the business | fill in details, correct other architects' drawings |
| develop new projects | |
| select and train new architects | proposals, business licenses |
| design big, challenging projects | dicker with city planning departments |
| oversee and approve other projects | code the invoices for all projects |
| *Work fewer hours!* (emphasis his) | make collection calls |
| | answer the phone while office manager is at lunch |
| | fill in for other staffers when they miss work |

For George to stop doing the things in the right column, someone else would have to do them. And this brought up all of George's fears:

No one but me can do it.

All my other people are so busy.

We will lose control of the detail.

It won't get done right.

Things will drop through the cracks.

They won't watch the numbers like I do.

There will be a lag until I discover their mistakes, and by then it's too late.

If I delegate to him, and then he leaves the company, important know-how will be lost.

. The toughest one was "All my people are so busy." George spent a third of his time doing things the other architects should and could do, but couldn't/didn't because they were all working full tilt as well. We found that the architects spent a quarter of their time doing things that the drafters and support staff should do, but these people were also very busy.

The solution was to add a couple of entry level people—interns and trainees. Then the entire staff got together and jointly decided which tasks to delegate to whom. This approach worked because George had good team players who were committed to doing a good job.

| George |
|:---:|

*delegate to . . .*

| Architects |
|:---:|

*delegate to . . .*

| Drafters and support staff |
|:---:|

*delegate to . . .*

| New interns |
|:---:|

To make this work, they had to apply all the parts of the problem solvent:

- George had to take the time to get the special knowledge out of his head about how to work with particular planning departments, so that the others could do that.

- The architects agreed on conventions they would consistently use so that the drafters could follow their designs accurately.

- The Computer Aided Design expert gave training to the others on how to get the most from these expensive software systems.

- The office manager turned off the phone ringer when she went to lunch so that George wouldn't be tempted to answer it.

## How do you interact with your managers?

There are several different ways, depending on the size of your operation, the number of employees you have, the capability of your managers, and how you view your own role.

1. CEO to executive. You set policy, parameters, and objectives, then let them figure out how to do the job. They take responsibility for producing the desired results.

2. Executive to manager. You set strategy, tell them how you want targets met, then regularly monitor their performance.
3. Manager to supervisor. You give them the pieces they need to meet the targets, then oversee them closely.
4. Supervisor to workers. You roll up your sleeves and help them meet the targets.

As you climb the ladder, if your managers don't climb right up behind you, they keep pulling you back. If you are trying to shift from being a hands-on manager to become an executive of your own company, but your manager still wants detailed guidance from you, then you are not getting the job done that you need. If you are paying this person a top manager's salary, you aren't getting your money's worth.

## Management Capabilities of a Successful Company

In a successful and growing company, the full range of management responsibility is covered by the owner and the management team. But all too often, critical capabilities are ignored, neglected, downplayed, or need to be upgraded.

The skills needed to run a successful business fall into several categories: the professional skills needed to do the work, the management skills needed to run the enterprise, people and communication skills, and self-awareness and self-management skills.

**1. Professional skills.** These are the skills of your business, your profession, and your craft. Know what is special about what you sell; this is unique for every kind of business.

**2. Management skills.** Table 8-2 summarizes management capabilities that need to be covered in any successful company. People have called this list a "job description for a CEO." You needn't have all these skills yourself, of course. Even in a one-person company, you can hire outsiders to help you meet these needs. As your company grows and gets more complex, you must hand off many of these responsibilities even when you *are* good at them.

## TABLE 8-1
## The Ladder of Executive Capabilities

| Responsibilities | Problems and Challenges | It's time to climb to this rung when... |
|---|---|---|
| **3. EXECUTIVE—CEO** | "Queen bee" | |
| • Develop the business. Work *"on the* business, not *in* the business." <br>• Manage from goals of profitability, not just revenue. <br>• Communicate your vision and stay focused on the strategies to achieve it. <br>• Promote or hire skilled people to fill in behind you, to free you up to focus on strategic tasks. <br>• Produce desired results by organizing the efforts of others. <br>• Manage and motivate your managers. <br>• Develop the systems and procedures needed for excellence and productivity. | • Learn to be a visionary and convert vision into actuality. Communicate vision to others. Motivate them with your vision. <br>• Become a strategic thinker: get away from operations and leave it up to your subordinates. <br>• Be willing to bring in people as good or better than yourself. <br>• Take bottom-line responsibility for the direction. | ...management of day-to-day operations prevents you from attending to strategic issues; e.g., growth, positioning, developing new products or services. |
| **2. MANAGER** or **SUPERVISOR** | "Bee keeper" | **It's time to climb when...** |
| • Oversee and organize the work of others. <br>• Delegate, keep the workers on track. <br>• Develop good workers and work habits; hire and fire; evaluate, promote. <br>• Stay motivated to get the task done; be a self-starter. | • Be willing to delegate. <br>• Managing never stops; let up for a minute and productivity diminishes. <br>• It's difficult to find, train, and turn over work to people as good as you are. | ...you can no longer supervise every person working for you—the span of management is just too broad. |
| **1. SINGLE PROFESSIONAL** or **WORKER** | "Worker bee" | **It's time to climb when...** |
| • Do the work. <br>• Produce the results. <br>• Handle the paperwork. <br>• Do the marketing and selling. | • Production is tied to hours worked. A definite ceiling; no work—no revenue. | ...you can no longer do it all yourself. You must hire an administrative assistant or technical support. |

Even in a one-person outfit—where the owner wears all the hats—you need to be on top of these areas. If you neglect areas—say, Profit Management or Cash Management—your company suffers. For your company to succeed and grow, either you have to handle it, or you have to get outside help.

As companies grow in maturity and complexity, the owner naturally spins off more of these functions to other people. There is a natural progression in the way owners handle some functions.

In finances, for example, fledgling home-based companies may start off with "checkbook accounting." The next stage is to upgrade to a computer-based accounting system and hire a part-time bookkeeper. Then you need a CPA to handle your taxes. At a certain stage, you find you need professional advice on managing cash flow and profitability. If you are not a numbers person yourself, you need to hire a CFO. Probably not a full-time, in-house person; rather a "rented CFO" who works with you only as needed. Only when your company has grown well into seven figures is hiring and in-house CFO justified.

**3. People and communication skills.** These overlap somewhat with management skills, but go further:

leadership, decision making, coordinating and directing
charisma, inspiring others
communicating, listening
team building, sizing people up
building *esprit de corps;* shaping the company culture
problem solving
conflict resolution
negotiation
diplomacy

**4. Self-awareness and self-management skills**
knowing your strengths and weaknesses; your values and preferences
understanding how you need to treat yourself; your foibles and warning signals
heeding your personal cycles, e.g., when you perform at your highest and when you need to take a nap

## YOUR GROWTH TEAM

The top team of a successful, growing company includes several distinct teamwork roles. In most small companies, however, some team roles are missing. People are thrust into the wrong roles, and owners insist on taking on inappropriate roles.

## TABLE 8-2

### Management Capabilities. "Job Description for a CEO"

| | |
|---|---|
| **Vision management** | Clarify your vision and keep it always in mind. See the steps to get there. Communicate vision to employees, co-owners, customers and financiers. |
| **Strategic management** | Set the course, keep the company on course, and make course corrections when needed. Keep your antennas out for problems and opportunities. Develop new business, new products and services, new packages and new alliances. Ask how your products or services can be refined to better meet the needs of your customers. |
| **Marketing management** | Know your competitive edge, what sets you apart, how to communicate this to your target audience. Know how to reach your preferred customers. Evaluate your marketing outreach. Know how to close sales and/or be a sales manager. Be famous for your customer service. Train your people in these things. |
| **People management** | Be a master team builder, for both employees and subcontractors. Hire smart rather than manage tough. Keep good people. Delegate, monitor, and hold people accountable. |
| **Profit management** | Be oriented toward making a profit at all times. See profit as the engine of growth. |
| **Cash management** | Set a spending plan. Spend no overhead before its time. Spend money to make money, but get the most from the money you spend. |
| **Operations management** | Make sure your work is done impeccably—by you and your employees—so that customers keep coming back to you. Get work out on time and within budget. Control costs and inventories. |
| **Time management** | Use your time strategically. Guard your priorities and boundaries. |
| **Systems management** | Constantly create systems and procedures to simplify tasks and ease the burdens on yourself and others. Take all the ad hoc and idiosyncratic ways that you and your key people do things and convert them into routines that can be performed well by others. |
| **Resource management** | Get the most from what you have: people, capital, time, physical space and location, equipment, and inventory. |

CEOs of rapidly growing companies are extraordinary team builders. To build your management team, you must find the roles that best complement your strengths.

Several roles must be filled on the optimal management team. As you read this list, ask yourself how well these roles are covered in your company. How many do you personally fill? Who is miscast, that is, cover a role not right for them? What roles are neglected, and how does this hold you back? What team position most needs to be filled to help you achieve your goals?

1. Visionary. Creator. Draws the roadmap. Energizer. Inspires the troops.
2. Driver. Chooses best route on the roadmap. Makes it all happen. Puts all the pieces together.
3. Hard nose. Negotiator, closer. Asks tough questions. Insists. Holds people accountable.
4. Detail person. Factotum. Runs the office, coordinates the operation. Makes sure everything gets done.
5. Marketer. Keeps antennas out for opportunities. Develops marketing plan, builds big relationships.
6. Sales whiz. Sells, sells, sells. Sales manager.
7. Producer. Gets the work done, drives production. Assures quality and productivity.
8. Money watcher. Could be CPA, controller, bookkeeper, or spouse.
9. Sage. Voice of experience. Knows the industry and its foibles.

Notice that there is no role called "Planner." In my experience, the best planning is a collaborative effort drawing on all these roles, but led by the Visionary.

## PLAY TO YOUR STRENGTHS, COMPENSATE FOR YOUR WEAKNESSES

Successful, growing companies are built upon the strengths of their owners and executives. However, these strengths are often hidden or downplayed. Owners are forced to operate from their weaknesses.

You can use table 8-3 to grade yourself and your company. Create a grid and leave enough room to fill in the answers. In Column 1, if other skills make better sense to you, use them. Use Column 2 to rate your own strengths and weaknesses. In Column 3, name the person currently performing this function, whether it is you, someone else, or no one at all. In Column 4, rate how well this function is being done now. In Column 5, rate how important it is to focus on this capability, either now or in the near future.

## TABLE 8-3
## Rate your skills and your company's capabilities

| 1 | 2 Your personal strength or weakness + or − | 3 Name of person doing this now (or no one) | 4 How well is this being done now? (Rate A,B,C,D, or F) | 5 Very important now? ✓ = yes |
|---|---|---|---|---|
| Vision management | | | | |
| Strategic management | | | | |
| Marketing management | | | | |
| People management | | | | |
| Profit management | | | | |
| Cash management | | | | |
| Operations management | | | | |
| Time management | | | | |
| Systems management | | | | |
| Resource management | | | | |

You can create similar tables to rate you and your company's capabilities in these other areas:
- people and communication skills
- self-awareness skills
- team roles

Once you rate yourself in any of these areas, ask yourself these questions:
- What management skills do you bring to the business? How does your business rely on your strengths?
- How are your management strengths hidden or downplayed in your current business?
- How can your business be restructured to take better advantage of your management strengths?

- In terms of running a business, what are your weaknesses? What things are you not particularly good at, don't like doing, or are no longer a challenge?
- As things are structured now, how are you forced to operate from your weaknesses?
- How can your company be structured to compensate for your management weaknesses?

Which areas are very important but not performed well, either by you or others? These of course are your biggest barriers.

- Which lack of capability is the biggest gap in your management repertoire right now?
- What skills do your people most need to improve?
- What capabilities do you need to bring in from outside?

You do not have to be an expert in all of these areas. Some of these responsibilities you should delegate, even if you are an expert.

- What aspect of this area of responsibility must you do?
- What piece can you hand off? To whom?
- What is the highest skilled person you can bring in?
- How will simplifying or upgrading your systems or procedures help?
- What training do you or your people need in order to take on more?

## THE MANAGEMENT GRID

In a successful, growing company, the owner is constantly handing off tasks and responsibilities to others while retaining enough connection and oversight to assure performance.

*Retain key responsibilities while handing off more to your employees.*

However, the owner often has the longest list of tasks, and holds on to far too many things. Other key players may actually have less to do, and are neither challenged nor trusted. The owner feels overwhelmed and burned out.

Here is the challenge for you: How can you retain key responsibilities while handing off more and more to your employees or outside contractors? Use the Management Grid (Table 8-4) to figure out how you can reduce your load by:

- restructuring areas of responsibility
- handing off a piece of every job
- identifying gaps in your management structure
- clarifying how your management team should support each other.

## TABLE 8-4
## The Management Grid

| Areas of Responsibility | President | Operations | Marketing/ Sales | Finance | Admin./ Support |
|---|---|---|---|---|---|
| Guiding the ship | | | | | |
| Setting goals and targets | | | | | |
| Developing new products/services | | | | | |
| Scouting ahead | | | | | |
| Doing the work | | | | | |
| Handling the details | | | | | |
| Managing the team | | | | | |
| Running the operation | | | | | |
| Watching the money | | | | | |
| Troubleshooting problems | | | | | |
| Developing new business | | | | | |
| Doing marketing outreach | | | | | |
| Making sales | | | | | |
| Working with customers | | | | | |

Before sketching your Management Grid, write down what you and each of your key people do. Don't recreate job descriptions; write what people actually do.

**1. Management Grid—Now.** Sketch out the Management Grid format on a large sheet of paper. Across the top write the names and positions of the key people in your organization. Some people—especially you—may fill more than one key position. Some key positions may be vacant, and some positions may be run by more than one person; e.g., a marketing committee.

**Management Grid—Now**

| Areas of Resp | You | Asst. Mgr. | Mktg | Sales | Oper- tions | Finance | Adm. |
|---|---|---|---|---|---|---|---|
| | | | | | | | |
| | | | | | | | |
| | | | | | | | |
| | | | | | | | |
| | | | | | | | |
| | | | | | | | |
| | | | | | | | |
| | | | | | | | |

**Management Grid—Should Be**

| Areas of Resp | You | Gen'l Mgr. | Mktg | Sales | Oper- tions | Finance | Adm. |
|---|---|---|---|---|---|---|---|
| | | | | | | | |
| | | | | | | | |
| | | | | | | | |
| | | | | | | | |
| | | | | | | | |
| | | | | | | | |
| | | | | | | | |
| | | | | | | | |

In Column 1, write in major areas of responsibility in your company. You may have different areas than what I list. In Column 2, write what you do related to each area of responsibility. In the other columns, write what each of your key people does related to each area of responsibility. (Enter different titles if the fit is better.)

If there are partners or more than one owner, list them in the columns next to yours rather than together in one column. This is invaluable for clarifying roles among owners.

When you first do this, you may discover that your list is by far the longest. The first time I did this with a client, his list of responsibilities was as long as all his other managers combined! The purpose of this exercise is to discover how you can delegate a piece of every job that you do to your other key people.

You also discover imbalances in the areas of responsibilities of your key people. In my "Now" example, since there is no marketing manager, all marketing responsibilities are thrust onto the owner and the sales manager.

You may have a manager or worker whose job is too big. "My supervisor works harder than anyone else at the shop." Use the management grid exercise for this person. List everything he or she is doing and see what can be handed off to other people—whether subordinates or administrative support staff. You may discover some resistance on their part to giving up tasks, in which case the supervisor needs to work on his or her own work habits, attitudes, and beliefs, and be willing to take a step up the ladder.

**2. Management Grid—Should Be.** Create a second Management Grid labeled "Should Be." See how much of your own list can be delegated across the management structure. Areas of responsibility should flow from president to each position, so that for each major responsibility of the president, essential tasks are delegated to each key manager.

## THE ORGANIZATION CHART

The organization structure of a successful and growing company facilitates efficient and effective performance and communication.

However, the organization chart of many small businesses has muddled lines of authority, an overly-broad span of management, two heads and dual bosses, or empty boxes. Table 8-5 shows some common organizational glitches, and suggests a remedy or remedies for each.

Sketch your management structure, now and as it should be.

**TABLE 8-5**

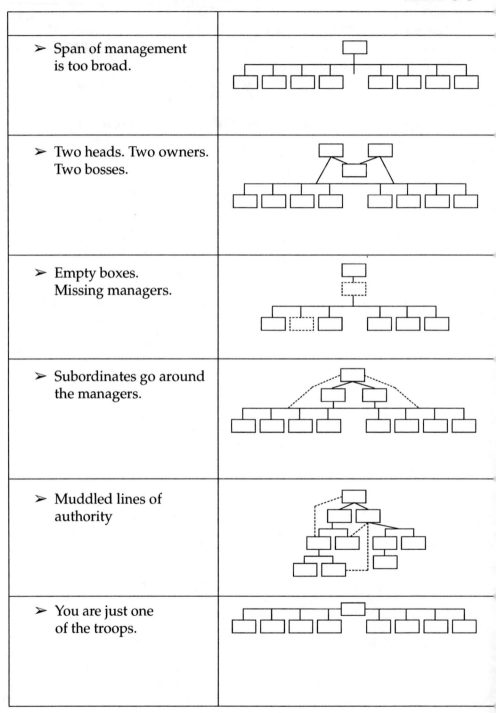

| | |
|---|---|
| ➢ Span of management is too broad. | |
| ➢ Two heads. Two owners. Two bosses. | |
| ➢ Empty boxes. Missing managers. | |
| ➢ Subordinates go around the managers. | |
| ➢ Muddled lines of authority | |
| ➢ You are just one of the troops. | |

## Organizational Structure

| Problem | Remedy |
| --- | --- |
| 1. The span of management is too broad, i.e., too many people report directly to the boss. | Hire a manager, or promote someone to be supervisor, and delegate some of your management duties. |
| 2. Two heads. Two owners, so employees have two bosses. | 1. One of you needs to become CEO. 2. Form a two-person executive committee that makes policy decisions; each of you directs one part of the operation as "vice president." |
| 3. No top manager. You are forced to retain this role, thus you cannot attend to all CEO responsibilities. | Hire or promote a skilled manager. |
| 4. You allow subordinates to go around their managers and come directly to you, thus undermining your managers and misusing your time. | Hold company meetings to spell out lines of reporting and to validate your managers; then refuse to allow subordinates to circumvent the managers. "Don't ask me; ask your manager." |
| 5. Muddled lines of authority. This usually happens when a diffuse team grows and gets more complex. "Joe works for Mary except on special projects; then he reports to me." | If you must have split lines of authority, then spell these out among the managers: "Who does what for whom when? How do we resolve conflicting pulls? |
| 6. You see yourself as just one of the troops, albeit the one who is obliged to sign the paychecks on time. | Either promote yourself to CEO, and hire a general manager, or hire a CEO to run the company, so that you can focus on doing the work you do best. |

## THE "EVERYONE REPORTS TO ME" SYNDROME

The #1 organizational problem faced by small companies: the management span is too wide. The perceived benefit is that it minimizes overhead. You don't have to pay salaries for people who "just manage." But it has a big drawback. You spend so much time being a manager and supervisor and handling small details that you cannot be an effective executive. You work too many hours, you take responsibility for tasks that you are not particularly good at, and you have no backup. If you are not there, performance falls off.

The obvious remedy is to add a layer to your organization chart; for example, a general manager, operations manager, or crew foreman between you and others.

To keep this from being just an overhead position, ask yourself these questions:

- Can this be a working manager who in addition to overseeing the other managers or employees also does a specific job?

- Who among your current managers or supervisors could be promoted to this position? "My $60,000 general manager left. I promoted my $30,000 assistant manager, raised him to $40,000 and improved our systems and training. He's now doing better than the $60,000 guy."

- How could this manager pay for him/herself by:
  a) managing better than you do, so that productivity increases and operating costs go down?

  b) freeing you up to focus on strategic tasks needed to take the business to the next level?

- How much does your business need to grow in order to justify this person's salary? Conversely, how much could your company grow if this person does a great job for you?

- What does it cost you *not* to have this manager? In particular, what are the opportunity costs to you? Filling this position costs you money. Leaving it vacant costs you your focus on strategic affairs, your time off, and enjoyment of your work.

As an exercise, sketch your management structure, now and as it should be.

A. Your current management structure. Which of the structures sketched in table 8-5 do you have?

B. How should your company be organized to accomplish your objectives and allow you to be CEO? How could you straighten out the problems and gaps in your organization?

## BREAKING THROUGH PLATEAUS

As you grow, where do you reach plateaus? "I easily grew up to $1 million per year, but trying to move beyond that has felt like wading through molasses."

Where do you reach the limit of your own skills? In what areas are your personal limits holding the company back? On the other hand, if you focus on your greatest strengths, how far could they take the company?

To break through a plateau, you need to bring in three kinds of capabilities:

- people who bring in skills needed to compensate for your personal weaknesses
- people who complement your strengths, so that you can do even more for your company
- people who can perform the tasks you are ready to move beyond

As owners take on more of an executive outlook, they often say things like this: "I've been holding on to these buying trips I've always done; but now I guess I need to give them up. It's so time consuming. I feel sad about it. Doing the buying is the reason I got into the business in the first place."

You should be wary of giving up the things you most enjoy. You risk taking the joy out of your own business. But how do you square that with the need to climb the ladder of executive capabilities? Remember two things: you're in business to get to do what you want to do, and the business thrives when you do what you're best at.

On the other hand, you may be ready to move beyond responsibilities you have always enjoyed and excelled at, and to take on new executive challenges.

Instead of getting out of things you love doing, look for other things you can delegate. In particular, look for responsibilities you have held on to because they are critical, but give you no particular thrill. These might include financial management, quality control, signing checks, hiring, and firing. How much of such tasks can you hand over, and to whom? To an existing employee or a new hire? Can you outsource these functions? How can you retain the minimum necessary oversight?

For example, suppose your company's success depends on your design genius. Yet you spend a lot of time on the company's financial management. Why? Perhaps you don't really trust your current financial manager to make good decisions. Or perhaps you are reluctant to pay enough to bring in a really skilled person. Maybe you are used to making seat of the pants financial decisions. Ironically, you may say you need to spend less time designing so you can focus more on financial management. But the truth is just the opposite. You need to hire a strong financial manager, put into place needed systems and procedures, and give up making ad hoc, inconsistent decisions.

In hiring this new financial manager, one of your questions to a top candidate should be, "How would you assure that I get just the information I need to maintain oversight of our finances?"

If you're doing mainly what you enjoy but feel a need to expand your duties in order to break through your current plateau, here is another example: Suppose you own a restaurant. You might say to me, "I need to be on the floor. Customers expect to see me, greeting them. If I'm not there, they ask where I am." This attitude is prevalent among people who get into their business because they love customer contact: retailers, restaurateurs, personal service providers. But your customers have you chained to the floor.

If you want to remain the same size, this is fine. But if you need to focus more time on other responsibilities, you have to find ways to cut back on your customer contact without giving it up completely. The answer? Empower your employees. Make sure you have floor managers who are equally capable of inspiring customer loyalty. You may keep a few key customers or accounts for yourself but let others go. You may be on the floor one or two evenings, but not every night.

## BOTTLENECKS AND BARRIERS

The head of a successful and growing company identifies and eliminates bottlenecks, either proactively or as soon as they are discovered. However, bottlenecks have a habit of staying in place, often because they are linked to the owner's management style and practices.

You can identify your bottlenecks and brainstorm how to resolve them, using the problem solvent.

Here are some common bottlenecks. What others are you familiar with?

At some point, every project must go through you or some other key person.

You and/or your key people are developing something new—on top of your regular responsibilities.

A person in a key position is not up to the job. This slows down everyone else.

A key system is no longer up to the job. This slows down every operation.

A key person is missing. Others fill in, but do it poorly.

You are woefully short of space, thus operations are inefficient, slow, and costly.

A key piece of equipment keeps breaking down.

You have expanded and/or acquired a new business; digesting it takes time and attention.

You are short of capital. You are always waiting till you can afford something. You substitute with time and energy, thus things move slowly and with great effort.

You have high turnover, thus you always have to hire new people and bring them up to speed.

Your location is poor; thus you spend a lot of time on travel.

The labor market is tight, so you make do with fewer workers.

Identify the bottlenecks in your operation, and describe how you would like things to be instead. To open up your company's bottleneck, how can you apply the problem solvent?

Get the best help and outside support.

Improve your systems, procedures, and work rules.

Polish your skills and add capabilities.

Make changes in your workplace; add equipment or materials.

And most importantly, how should you change your management style, work habits, attitudes or beliefs?

## HOW TO UPGRADE YOUR SKILLS

Where do you find the time to learn or upgrade skills when you are already busy running a business?

- Focus on eye level problems. New skills are learned best in the context of performing some essential task. You are motivated and have something concrete that helps organize your learning. For example, learn a new software system in the context of doing the job that it is supposed to perform.

- Get a good teacher or expert help—someone who can teach you in the context of getting your job done. For example, you might hire an experienced outsider to come in and provide the capability for you in the short run, then train you and your people over a period of time.

- Timing. Ask yourself, when is the best time for you to focus on learning a new skill?

- Rethink the way you allocate tasks. If you are preparing to focus on mastering some new skill, then perhaps you need to hand off other tasks.
- Go to a seminar. However, you may get excited and loaded up with great ideas, then get swamped upon your return by the demands of running your business. To avoid that:
- Use the buddy system. Two or more people from your company may go through the training together. Then you help each other, say, master the intricacies of an inventory tracking system, or improve the way you conduct employee performance reviews.
- Follow up. Select a training regimen that includes an ongoing forum to help you apply the things you learned and to keep at it.
- Create bite-sized pieces of training. Progress at whatever speed is right for you. Some people master things rapidly, and others take years.
- Set up an accountability program, supported by your business advisor, board member, or key managers. Set goals, time line, milestones, and a mechanism to track your progress. Report progress and problems to your advisors.
- Reward yourself for completion.

### Skills are closely linked to attitudes

As you try to climb this ladder and move from manager to CEO, and to polish your strategic management skills, it becomes apparent that your ability to exercise these skills depends on your attitudes. Your self-confidence and demeanor, the way you present yourself to others, and how you respond to challenges and disputes are as important as your skills. As your recognize deficiencies in these areas, apply the approach in chapter 5, "The Inner Game of Growth."

## HOW TO MANAGE THE EXPERT

How much do you need to know in order to manage a professional who knows a lot more than you do in a particular area? How do you evaluate and direct your CFO, web designer, graphic artist or marketing consultant?

For example, you don't run the press, but you must know how to evaluate the output of the press operator. You are not a bookkeeper, but you must know what you want from the bookkeeper. Your CPA can review the bookkeeper's accuracy. You are not a CPA or CFO, but you must tell them what you need to know to make management decisions. You certainly know whether they are getting reports to you on time and reviewing them with you.

But if you are not known for your number-crunching skills, how do you know what to tell the CFO to do? How do you understand, and act on, what they tell you? How do you know you are getting the straight stuff? If you hire the right person, then he or she can help you answer these questions. The challenge is finding the right person. Draw on your advisors and allies to help you find the right person to hire. Your industry association may be able to help you.

Stick to desired results. Define ahead of time what you want from the experts, and how you will know when you get it. Insist on getting it in a way you can understand. This is a matter of attitude and self-confidence on your part. Don't let yourself feel flummoxed by their expertise. You hired them to make it understandable to you, and if they don't, then they are not right for the task.

## CREATE DEVELOPMENT PROGRAMS FOR KEY PEOPLE

As you move up the ladder, others must be ready to move up behind you. You must either hire someone for his or her proven expertise, or groom a current employee to take on greater responsibilities. Here are guidelines for a management development program for your key people.

- Make sure they are committed to staying with your company, and interested in the position. Discuss with them your vision, your objectives, and the potential role for them. Tell them you want to groom them, but there are no promises unless they show themselves capable and committed.
- Make sure they are qualified for the new responsibilities. Evaluate their strengths and weaknesses, their work habits and attitudes, and compare these to the demands of the job they may move into. First, of course, you must define this new position.
- Identify the specific tasks and responsibilities you want them to master. Assign tasks in these areas so they can gain experience. Set targets for improved performance. Establish the time frame, with milestones along the way.
- Make sure they get training in needed skills via in-house training, outside workshops or seminars, or videotapes and books. Discuss with them what they should gain from these. Check back with them afterwards.
- Mentor them. Teach them by example. Help them think through situations: "What would you do if such-and-such happened?"

- Identify particular job situations, or "laboratories," where they can apply their developing skills. Talk with them beforehand about what they will need to do in these situations. Debrief them afterwards on how they performed.
- Teach them how to avoid problem behavior in managing others, and how to spot it in their subordinates; e.g., behavior that could be construed as sexual harassment.
- When problems arise, back them up. Do not second-guess them—especially in front of others. Do not let employees go around them and come to you.
- Allocate the time, money, and input of knowledge they need to achieve the training goals.
- See what resources they will need to succeed in the position you want them to assume: systems and procedures, work redefinition to enhance productivity, equipment or materials, changes in the workspace, assistance and input from other employees or outside professionals.
- Recognize that this is a trial-and-error process. You must continually monitor and evaluate their progress, and make mid-course corrections as necessary.
- Recognize that this must be done on top of their regular workload. Take this into consideration—either in the time frame or by lightening their regular load.

You can use the *Problem Solvent Worksheet* (table 10-1).

## ASK YOURSELF . . .

1. Which executive skills are most important for you to upgrade to move your company forward?

2. Where do you spend your time on tasks at each level? Track your activities for a week or month; see what you do that falls onto each rung of the ladder?

>Worker
>Manager
>Executive

3. How should responsibilities be reassigned to free you up? What "lower rung" responsibilities should you hand off to someone else?

4. Where should you be focusing your efforts to move your company forward? What are you neglecting?

5. As you climb the ladder, what management vacuum is created behind you? Where do you need to bring in someone else?

6. What management capability should you hire to move your company forward?

## TO TAKE THIS FURTHER . . .

Our companion workbook, *Promote Yourself to CEO*, contains questionnaires, checklists, and templates you can use to apply these ideas to your business, and to work on them with your team.

## Chapter 9

# The Right Tools for the Job

### Workplace, equipment, and materials for growth

*If an army travels on its stomach,*
*then a business grows on its infrastructure.*

As your company grows, you outgrow your infrastructure: the size or layout of your work space, your equipment, fixtures, tools, and software. You also outgrow your marketing materials, packaging, displays, and merchandising. You sometimes fail to recognize how important these items are until you finally change them and see the tremendous difference it makes.

For any barrier to growth, ease, or profitability, you should ask how changing your workplace or your equipment or materials will help you to tackle it. If you neglect these aspects, other expensive changes may be wasted:

- You hire capable new people, install productivity-enhancing systems, yet your work space remains cramped and noisy, thus thwarting their effectiveness.
- Your old computers cannot handle the new software-based productivity systems you have developed.
- Your five-year-old brochure design says, "We're a small, home-based company," thus making it harder to attract the kind of customers you want.

- You've outgrown your location. Your stockroom is crammed so full, your people waste a lot of time searching for things. Your parking space is completely inadequate.
- Your home-based office was great when it was just you and your part-time assistant. Now with the addition of another person, you don't know whether you work out of your home or just sleep in your office.

This clearly goes along with other parts of the Problem Solvent. If you're going to make changes in your behavior, systems, and procedures, and if you're going to change who is working for you and how they are working, you likely need to change workplace, equipment, and materials as well.

## WORKPLACE CHANGES HELP TACKLE BARRIERS TO GROWTH

Changes in your workplace can be essential for supporting the changes in your management that have been discussed in earlier chapters. If one of your barriers has been difficulty in concentrating, then giving yourself a private office with a door that shuts can be essential. Without doing so, you may never be able to make the behavioral change you want. Here are some examples of other barriers and their respective solutions:

> *When he needed privacy, George hid out in his dungeon.*

- George, the owner of an office supply store, has his office just off the sales floor behind a large plate glass window where he can keep an eye on operations, but everyone can see him also. Customers come up and knock on his window and wave to him: "Hiya, George! How are things going?" He loves this, but every time he starts reviewing inventory figures, he gets interrupted. Thus in his slim-margin business, he wasn't watching costs as he should—unless he did it evenings or Sunday.

  His solution: clear out a large closet, install a desk and computer, and retreat to it whenever he needed to concentrate on figures. He calls this his "dungeon," but the concentration this allowed him helped him shave two percentage points off his cost of goods sold within a few months—money that went directly to his bottom line.

- Sharon, the head of a film production company, replaced her clear glass office door with a solid one, and instructed her people when they could and could not interrupt her.
- Jake the consultant moved his office manager one office farther away.

Why? When she was in the adjoining office, he couldn't help straining to overhear who was calling, even though it was her job to screen his calls.

- Anna the print shop owner moved her office out of the shop into a nearby space to prevent her people from popping in to ask questions they should answer for themselves, and to keep her from wandering around interrupting them. Her new office had a live computer connection to the shop.

- Joseph the general contractor works out of his house. His desk is in an ell of the living room. Joe complains that he has no time to himself because he is drawn to his corner office day and night. His solution? He rigged the lighting for his office so it was controlled by an automatic timer mounted in the garage. It switched off at 6:00 PM. Sure, he could override the timer, but the fact that his workspace was dark greatly decreased his temptation to work in the evening.

- Marsha's cramped retail store hadn't had a makeover for close to ten years. She didn't even notice the clutter and the faded paint, but her customers did. She took the courageous step of inviting her business owners group to walk through her place and give her feedback on the appearance through their fresh eyes. Their feedback was tough to hear, but she took it to heart and, over the next few months, made major changes to the store's appearance. A few months later she remarked how sales revenues were climbing, shoplifting losses were down, and she was able to attract better quality salespeople.

- Hansen's Bakery was running at near capacity. They faced the expensive prospect of moving into a larger facility. The employees resisted the idea of a second shift because the outside area was so dark and foreboding in the evening. They installed bright outside lighting on the entryway and parking lot and even got the city to install an additional streetlight. This, along with some additional security measures, made a second shift much more attractive, and was a much less expensive option than moving.

- The new website and online ordering system cost thousands of dollars. The office people joked about how slow it was. But it was no joke to the owner watching them sit there, twiddling their thumbs, waiting for documents to download. Installing a high speed data line was expensive, but she figured it paid for itself within a few months.

- In a tight labor market, the company's growth was stymied by difficulty in finding enough employees to do data entry. Their consultant suggested they hire and train people who were unemployed due to physical disabilities. There was no way however that a disabled person could navigate the steep stairway to the second floor, so they rented a satellite office with a ground floor entrance. They were thus able to expand the available labor pool as they could now hire people that previously couldn't be considered because of the physical limitations of the building.

- The offices for the maintenance firm were in the front corner of the warehouse. There were partitions, but no ceiling except the arched roof twenty feet above. Fumes and noise from the shop regularly invaded. It was so cold, the office staff sometimes wore down vests. The owner finally remodeled the offices, installing drop ceilings, carpeting, brighter lighting, and separate heating and air conditioning. The result? Morale improved, problem employees started smiling, productivity increased, turnover plummeted.

## Yeah, but . . .

You may be reluctant to undertake such changes, despite the apparent value.

**Cost.** New equipment is so expensive! You are concerned about the initial cost, but you also fear committing to a permanent boost in overhead. Maybe you can squeeze just one more season out of the old stuff.

Here though is what you haven't considered: what is the cost of *not* upgrading, of staying the same?

How can you feel comfortable making the needed changes? For example, ask yourself, "you will make the commitment to change when…" i.e. revenue reaches a certain figure. You secure the big contract. You have a six month backlog.

**Habit, inertia.** You are so familiar with things the way they are, you don't even notice the deficiencies. The present way is like an old shoe, worn but comfortable, and while you may not notice the flapping sole, your staff and clients do.

How can you see your situation as others see it? In our Business Groups, sometimes a member hosts a meeting at his or her workplace. One of the benefits is that your group members give you a fresh perspective on the appearance, layout, and workability of your facility. They view it through fresh eyes, and point out things that you overlook. There's nothing like inviting in a bunch of your allies to nit-pick and criticize! But we do this in the spirit of problem solving to achieve the business owner's stated goals.

**Hassle.** You know you need to make the change, but you just keep putting it off till a better time. The "hassle factor" relates to the amount of time and energy you have to put into something that you would rather avoid.

It's a trade-off. When do the niggling everyday inconveniences reach a threshold of annoyance that overcomes your resistance to the change, which will create a major but temporary disruption? Once you make the change, you know you'll say, "Why did we wait so long?!"

## WHAT IS YOUR DREAM WORKPLACE?

Dream a little. Without thinking about how much it costs, sketch out the workplace that would allow you and your people to do the best work, and be the most productive. Ask your people what changes they need in the workplace to do a better job for you. Use table 9-1 to spur your brainstorming. Which of these do you need to add, upgrade, or replace?

*Start by listing what you want, not what you think you can afford.*

Reality will intrude; you won't be able to afford everything you want. But if you start from your ideal, you might surprise yourself how much of it you *can* get. Creative and inexpensive solutions will emerge: you can lease, buy some items used or at liquidation, perhaps receive giveaways from companies with unneeded items.

## HOW CAN YOU AFFORD THESE CHANGES?

How can you upgrade or make needed changes? This stuff costs a lot of money! You can spend twice as many dollars as you have on such things. When you look at the cost of making the needed changes, it is always more than you expect.

What are some creative ways you may be able to make needed changes in this area "on a shoestring" e.g.:

- Farm out some production functions to other companies, rather than doing them in-house.
- Allow some employees to work at home, connected via DSL line or the like.
- Lease expensive equipment rather than buying it
- We furnished our entire office suite at a fraction of the cost for new by buying from two large corporations that were downsizing and moving.
- Form a "virtual company" with different functions performed by different independent units who work together in different combina-

## TABLE 9-1

### Examples of workplace, equipment, and materials changes

What do you need to Add, Upgrade, or Replace?

Existing Workplace

Better workspace layout: your office, other offices, meeting space, reception, cashier

Merchandise area, shop, manufacturing space

Expansion; new space

More space: office, shop, showroom, storage, warehouse

New facility: larger, smaller, different location, different neighbors, near related businesses, near vendors or services

Additional facility. Added location(s)

Storage space, loading, inventory space, shipping, receiving

Parking for customers, employees

Equipment and fixtures

Equipment that would increase productivity and soon pay for itself

New computers, hardware or software upgrades, computer network

Better cash registers, cash drawers, bar code reader tied to inventory

Merchant account to accept credit cards

Office furniture, store fixtures, shop equipment

Phone system, cell phone, high-speed data lines

In-house copier

Computer at home tied to office

Heating, air conditioning, ventilation, lighting

Signs, new paint job, redecoration

Security system

Vehicle

Amenities, e.g., kitchen, break room, bathrooms, wheelchair access

Ergonomic equipment: desks, chairs, keyboards, flooring

Materials

New marketing materials or an update of old look

Identity pieces, brochures, letterhead

Website

Presentation packages, samples, portfolio

Exhibits, displays, merchandising

tions, depending on the job.

For example, a print shop we work with near San Francisco uses an estimator based in Los Angeles and a graphic designer in rural Washington. All are connected by high-speed phone/internet lines because "face time" is not necessary; thus they grow the business without moving to a larger facility.

How can you make small changes that will have a big impact? First you must prioritize, and then determine the least expensive change that will get you started on the new productivity.

Ask yourself how you can make the needed changes in a way that minimizes the cost and hassle. We cover this in chapter 14, "The Dreaded Transition Hump."

Where can you spend money to make the fastest and greatest impact?

Rather than setting your sights on a particular expensive solution, state your goal first and ask what is the least expensive and disruptive change that will achieve your goal.

Such changes often have a long lead time until they begin paying off. The bigger and more complex and expensive the change, the longer the planning cycle. Moving your office or your plant may take a year or two of planning. Where should you put your money early in the process in order to save you more money and headaches later?

How can you identify all the costs involved in getting the system installed and up and running—including training and disruption—and estimate them accurately? How can you estimate the time it will take? Time is often more critical than money, since you can borrow money. You have to run the business while making changes in the way it's run.

How can you obtain the capital needed? Table 15 compares the cost of capital from various sources available to small businesses.

## JUSTIFYING THE COST

How do you justify the cost of making these changes? You face two battling aphorisms here: "You have to spend money to make money" and "Spend no overhead before its time."

Answer these questions:

How much will it cost?

How can I afford to do this?

Can I afford not to make the changes? What is the cost if we continue as we are?

How will it pay for itself? What is its payback period?

How much will it increase profit and cash flow; e.g., increase sales, increase productivity, reduce costs, save time?

Cost must be measured not only in money, but in time, which is often more critical than money. To some extent, time and money are interchangeable. If you have a limited budget (and when do you not!), you can compensate somewhat by putting in more time. If you have limited time, you can compensate by putting in more money.

Be wary of false economies. A client of mine built a centralized production facility. Partly to save money, the owner decided to handle the design, permit, and construction processes. Afterward he admitted that not hiring a general contractor—the outside expert—to handle these responsibilities cost him several months and many thousands of dollars.

Chapter 15, "Calculate the Benefit and Cost," will help you answer these questions. In addition, for major changes, you need to pay attention to how to minimize the cost and disruption of change, as discussed in chapter 14, "The Dreaded Transition Hump."

## APPLY THE PROBLEM SOLVENT

To make these changes in your workplace, equipment, or materials:

- What help do you need from the people working for you?
- What support or expertise do you need from outside professionals?
- What systems or procedures would help?
- What skills should you or your people gain?
- How should you work on your management style, habits, practices, attitudes, or beliefs to make this transition?

## ASK YOURSELF . . .

1. How can you upgrade your workplace, equipment, and materials to help dissolve your barriers to growth? Answer this initially without regard to whether it seems affordable or feasible at the time to make these changes; later you can get practical.
2. How could changing any of your tools or physical surroundings improve productivity and/or reduce distractions and craziness?
3. What items do you need to **Add**, **Upgrade**, or **Replace**?

### Extra credit questions

4. What's the least amount you can spend to make the highest-impact changes?
5. Can you calculate the gain in making these changes in terms of increased revenue, decreased expenditure, increased productivity and efficiency, decrease in lost time, and increase in customer satisfaction?

6. Compare your answers to (4) and (5) to discover the payback period of these changes. (For example, if a workplace change costs $10,000, and saves you $5,000 per year, the payback period is two years. If it saves you $20,000 per year, the payback period is six months. However, if it costs you $50,000 and saves you only $5,000 per year, it may never directly pay for itself.)

## Chapter 10

# Put It All Together

*How to apply the Problem Solvent to your growth barriers*

In the preceding five chapters, we have gone over each element of the Problem Solvent separately. In the examples we used, it was apparent that the various elements need to be applied in concert. So now it is time to put them all together and apply the whole Problem Solvent to some typical barriers to growth, ease, and profitability. I want to demonstrate that this is a general-purpose tool that you should get into the habit of applying to any challenge that arises.

I recommend that, as we go through this chapter, you apply it to one of your challenges. Ask yourself this question: "To move toward my vision of success, and to overcome the barrier (fill in the blank with your toughest barrier to growth), how can I apply each element of the Problem Solvent?"

I'm going to take you through a couple of examples that have been tackled in our business owners' groups, to demonstrate how the solvent unfolds. The group brainstorming is a benefit, but you can do this exercise on your own or working with a partner or coach as well.

Here's the setting: I am working with a group of business owners seated around a boardroom table. One of the people is on the "hot seat," i.e., has bravely volunteered to have his or her problem tackled by the group.

I'm at the flipchart writing it all down. On the white board, I have summarized the Problem Solvent:

To overcome your barrier, ask these five questions:
- What help or outside support do you need?
- What systems or procedures could you upgrade or adopt?
- What skill or capability do you need to gain or improve?
- What materials, equipment, or changes in your workplace do you need?
- How should you work on your management practices, habits, attitudes, and beliefs?

I hand out the sheet shown on table 10.1, Problem Solvent Worksheet, to all the participants. They can fill in their own ideas then hand them to the person on the hot seat. The worksheet helps you rearrange all the ideas into an actionable plan. Here are instructions for using this worksheet:

- Your business goal. Always do this problem-solving in the context of achieving a particular goal.
- The barrier. What hinders you from reaching this goal?
- Desired outcome. What is the concrete measure of success?
- Progress indicators. How will you know you are making progress?
- Apply the Problem Solvent. What are your needs for each category?
- Fill in your M-PHABs, as they are now and as you'd like them to be.
- Activities and milestones. What must be done first, second, etc? What specific events or accomplishments will mark progress?
- By when. How long will different parts take and when should particular milestones be complete?
- Who. Who will do what and when? (Make sure that no single person—particularly yourself—is given too much to do, thus delaying the entire project.)
- Problems, questions, likely bottlenecks. What is likely to delay the process? Where will things most likely get bogged down? Where is the greatest uncertainty in scheduling? What outside events can have the greatest impact?
- Choice points. As you move through this project, where will you make decisions to go in one direction or another?
- Resources needed. Identify the needed expertise, money, time, etc. to accomplish your goal.

## EXAMPLE 1. KELLY'S ARCHITECTURE FIRM

State your barrier in a way that allows you to take action on it. For example...

Kelly's barrier. "I have sole-proprietor mentality. Even though our company has grown and I have several top-quality professionals working

## TABLE 10-1
## Problem solvent worksheet

| Business Goal | Barrier | Desired Outcome | Progress Indicator |
|---|---|---|---|
|  |  |  |  |

Apply the Problem Solvent.

| Help, Outside Support | Systems or Procedures |
|---|---|
| Skills or Capabilities | Workplace Changes, Equipment, Materials |

Work on Yourself. Change your M-PHAB (Management practices, habits, attitudes and beliefs).

| Now | Want it to be |
|---|---|
|  |  |

| Activities/Milestones | By when | Who | Problems, Questions, Choice points |
|---|---|---|---|
| 1 |  |  |  |
| 2 |  |  |  |
| 3 |  |  |  |
| 4 |  |  |  |
| 5 |  |  |  |
| 6 |  |  |  |
| 7 |  |  |  |

Specify resources needed at any stage (money, expertise, information, etc.)

for me, I act as though I am the only one who can make major project decisions, and that I need to be involved in every client contact."

Why this is a problem. "I need to focus more on the big picture by bringing in challenging and lucrative jobs and overseeing financial performance on every job."

Desired solution. "I need to change my attitude and recognize that I have skilled designers. I must allow them to do the job after I set the parameters and let them have primary contact with clients."

How you will know when you are making progress? "Clients will call and ask to speak my project managers, not with me. Plus, I will spend at least 50% of my time bringing in new projects."

## Apply the Problem Solvent

We gave Kelly first chance to talk. He knew most of what he needed to do. I didn't force him to go through the Problem Solvent step-by-step, but just let the ideas flow. Afterwards I went back and labeled them with the category that fit.

- "Sit down with my architects and drafters and tell them how I want to change things and why this is so important to me. I know they will welcome these changes." *Procedures. The way we do things.*
- "Change the way we communicate with our clients. We come across as Kelly and the junior assistants. Communicate that we work as a professional team. Clients get the same top-quality personal attention, regardless of who manages their accounts." *Procedures*
- "Get input from my managers and others on how to make this change work. At what stage is my input the most important? When should I give them a free hand? When should they come to me and when should they work out problems on their own? How should we handle client problems that arise, or clients who ask specifically for me? *Procedures*
- "I should put Reggie in charge of coordinating all the other managers, since he is the most systematic thinker." *Help*
- "Jack should oversee upgrading our design software, and make sure we begin using the project management software that we paid a lot of money for. We may need to improve our computer networking and add another workstation." *Workplace changes*
- "To help with this transition, we must hold regular staff meetings. Reggie will be in charge of these meetings." *Procedures*
- "I need to work with an outside advisor to keep me on target with these changes, because I'm sure my old habits will reassert themselves." *Work on yourself.*

Even though Kelly knew most of the things he needed to do, having the questions and structured format helped him get it all out on a sheet of paper. After he slowed down, others put in their ideas:

- "Maybe you should change your company name. If it's just your name, it might make it harder to project the image of a professional team." *Workplace changes*
- "Make it harder to overhear all the incoming calls. I'll bet you eavesdrop on your managers talking with clients. Keep your office door closed." *Workplace changes, Procedures*
- "But you don't want to lose control of things, or let quality slip. Have a designated period each day when you quickly review project status." *Procedures*
- "Do you and Reggie need to get some training in project management? You could enroll in a university course or bring in a consultant to work with you." *Skills or capabilities, Management style*

The others came up with more excellent suggestions *and* off-the-wall ideas he wanted no part of. (He didn't want to change his company name.)

There's no need to go through these questions in any particular order. Initially, just ask for ideas and write them down however they come. After you generate a lot of ideas, go back and label them by Problem Solvent category. This will help you put them into a project plan, and may help you think of other needed pieces.

After the flow of ideas slows, you can ask the questions to help spark more thinking.

"Can you think of any other changes Kelly should make to the office? What about the equipment or networking? What other help could Kelly use in this? Any outside expertise?" And so on.

Ideas that come up may not fit easily into one of these categories. This doesn't matter. Your goal is to solve the problem, not fit a particular structure.

Remember this:

- Every element of the Problem Solvent will not apply to every problem. Just ask the questions and see what ideas come up.
- No matter which part of the Problem Solvent seems predominant, all the elements may come into play.

Explore the linkages among the different parts of the Problem Solvent. Delegating to Reggie won't work well unless Kelly shifts his own management habits and gets everyone's support on changing the way projects move through the office. Changing the computer network to allow Reggie and Kelly to keep tabs on project status is essential. And so on.

Leave out any piece and the solution suffers. This is especially true for the piece you resist or the question you avoid asking. Repeatedly asking these questions increases the likelihood that you consider all the relevant aspects and don't leave out something crucial.

## EXAMPLE 2. CHRIS'S FINANCIALS
### The problem changes mid-stream

Oftentimes the definition of the problem changes right in the middle of the brainstorming. Chris complained that she's not getting the financial data she needs. Her high-paid financial people are letting her down. The group initially focused on improving her systems and getting better help. We began the brainstorming with the problem statement, "How to make financial data more useful to Chris" by filling in these three columns:

| WHAT CHRIS NEEDS | WHAT GETS IN HER WAY | HOW TO CORRECT THIS PROBLEM |
|---|---|---|
| Accurate, complete, and timely entry of data. | Financials are always late. There are numbers that don't make sense. | Make sure my accountant shares my goal of getting accurate, complete, and timely data. If he can't do it, replace him. |
| Reports that give me just what I need. | I don't know what numbers I need to monitor most closely. | Work with my accountant (or new accountant) to figure out what I need to know about my business performance. |
| The habit of reviewing them regularly. | In the crush of day-to-day, I always relegate reviewing financial statements to the back burner. | Regular appointments with my accountant, on the calendar in ink. |

But the problem shifted when Chris said offhandedly during the brainstorming, "I've always had trouble trusting other people to handle my money. Did you know I still make my own bank deposits?" Chris had now exposed two contradictory attitudes:

- "I don't pay enough attention to the numbers. My attitude is, 'I'm not good at this. I cannot understand financial statements.'"

- "I have a piggybank mentality, not a professional corporation mentality. I keep very close tabs on cash to make sure my employees do not cheat me, but I lose sight of the bigger financial picture. Over the last few years, my best accountants have left before long, and now I'm wondering if I have driven them away."

It became apparent that the system changes would do no good unless Chris worked on these two conflicting attitudes. So the group shifted to apply the Problem Solvent to the attitudes. Since her problem was lack of trust, perhaps some trust-building steps were in order. We asked Chris, "What is one small part of this you could trust someone else to handle for you?" We came up with a sequence of trust-building steps. If one worked, then Chris would allow the next.

Step 1. Someone else could be trusted to take the checks to the bank, as long as Chris reconciled the bank deposits.

Step 2. She could trust someone to make up the bank deposit, if she had an accounting system that double-checked deposits with invoices and collections. The company had the accounting system in place, it just hadn't been used for this.

Step 3. She could hire an accountant to do the reconciliation, and make sure the bookkeeper wasn't making mistakes.

Step 4. Chris could hire a consulting CFO to help her review the monthly financials, focusing on the key indicators of financial performance, and reviewing the checks and balances in the system.

At a later meeting, after Chris had made big progress on these steps, the group again applied the Problem Solvent to the original questions to keep momentum going in the new positive direction.

## USE THE PROBLEM SOLVENT WITH BRAINSTORMING

To brainstorm means to stimulate creative thinking to generate new ideas to solve a specific problem. It relies on spontaneous and unrestrained discussion. "Think outside the box!" you are exhorted continually. "The box" is your self-imposed, habitual, limited thinking, and this comes up a lot with business owners. You need some creative thinking; if your growth barriers were easy to resolve, you would have done so years ago. So our business groups use brainstorming regularly, and the Problem Solvent is a tool for brainstorming. If you feel stuck, or caught in a vicious circle, this may be the best approach to catalyze new solutions to pop out.

*"Think outside the box? Sometimes I have trouble thinking inside the box!"*

We use visualization exercises, role playing, story telling, etc. to get the creative juices flowing and begin thinking out of the box. This generates the bare bones of new ideas, then we use the Problem Solvent to help flesh out the ideas.

If you are on the "hot seat"—i.e., it is your problem people are brainstorming about—here are a few rules:

When you use brainstorming in a group, it's best to have someone other than you be the facilitator. You need someone who can capture ideas as they are thrown out by you and the others. It's very hard for you to talk, listen, and write all at the same time, and you will miss things.

We normally do this in a boardroom setting, with the leader at the flipchart, writing furiously to keep up with all the ideas thrown out. But I also use a small tape recorder so that, if I need to, I can go back and listen to ideas that whizzed by so fast they were missed.

The facilitator should start by writing a brief problem statement on the flipchart. Write the problem in such a way that a solution can emerge. Beneath that, write the desired solution.

Observe these groundrules:

- Avoid doing or saying things that squelch effective brainstorming: "That won't work because…" or "We already tried that."

- Don't explain or justify the way you do it now, or argue with people. Instead, let the ideas emerge, no matter how crazy they sound initially.

- Don't talk too much. Instead, state the problem, then shut up and listen to others.

- Don't let your feelings get hurt by tough critique.

Have the questions of the Problem Solvent written up on another sheet for everybody to refer to.

"Write drunk, edit sober"—a commonly known writer's homily—is excellent advice and applies to brainstorming. Go wild and crazy when the ideas are pouring forth, then go back and soberly review them later. You never know where an idea will come from. Here's an abridged example by people who had previously agreed to these brainstorming guidelines:

George was complaining that he couldn't focus on opening his second facility because his top managers—all very capable people—kept getting into squabbles with each other and he had to come back and restore order.

Joe: "It sounds like a zoo over there." He imitated a monkey screeching.

George, taken aback: "A zoo? No! Things get chaotic sometimes, but it's not a zoo!"

Mary: "Why do we think of a zoo as being so chaotic? All the animals are kept in their own cages."

Barb: "That's why! The animals are locked up in little cages. They have nothing to do but raise a ruckus." She pantomimed an animal in a cage, shaking the bars and grunting. Joe joined in with more screeching.

Joe: "Do you keep your managers locked up in little cages over there?"

George: "Well, of course not...well wait. When Ralph left a couple of months ago, he said he felt he was boxed in at my company."

Dave: "I've seen your organization chart. You say you want people to stay in their own box. Maybe your managers are howling because they feel constrained in their roles."

George was crestfallen: "But I'm afraid I will lose control if I don't keep a tight rein on everyone."

Up to this point, George had defined his problem as an inability to find committed managers. He began to get a glimmer that his management style was partly to blame. Who knows whether he would eventually have seen this without the free-ranging feedback of his advisors, but the brainstorming certainly speeded up the realization.

Now that the group helped him see the problem, it was time to suggest ways to tackle it by applying the Problem Solvent.

## Use the Problem Solvent with project planning

The bane of project planners is leaving out some crucial element, so that people (or you) say afterward, "How could you have forgotten about *that*?" Use the Problem Solvent to help you generate all the things that must be included. This is particularly important for people who are trained or used to thinking mainly one way. For example, an engineer might be very comprehensive on the physical aspects of the project, but more tentative on the human side, while a people person may be just the opposite.

## MAKE A SUMMARY CHART

If you have a cluster of changes to work on, you can use a template like table 10-2 to summarize them. Putting them together helps you see the relationships and overlaps. For example, a tracking system for marketing purposes may also be applicable to your operational needs. Or perhaps you will discover that some of the changes are too condensed and need to be spread out over time. In the bottom row, you can summarize your timeline and milestones.

In the top row in this table I list the different functional parts of your business, but you could label it in different ways, such as different departments, offices, or product lines.

**TABLE 10-2**

## PROBLEM SOLVENT SUMMARY WORKSHEET

| FUNCTIONAL AREAS | MARKETING, SELLING, BUSINESS DEVELOPMENT | OPERATIONS, PRODUCTION, DOING THE WORK | FINANCES, FINANCIAL PRACTICES | HIRING, TRAINING, MANAGING YOUR WORKERS | MANAGING YOUR COMPANY; PLANNING |
|---|---|---|---|---|---|
| Help and support | | | | | |
| Systems and procedures | | | | | |
| Skills and capabilities | | | | | |
| Workplace, equipment, materials | | | | | |
| Work on yourself | | | | | |
| Timeline and Milestones | | | | | |

## CONCLUSION

Get in the habit of using this approach to tackle any of the barriers to growth that you encounter. For that matter, you can use this approach for any business problem.

The Problem Solvent is not a panacea. It is an organized process and set of questions to help guide your thinking into productive channels and to remind you to consider all angles.

You won't necessarily apply every part of the Problem Solvent to every issue. Apply the parts that fit and ignore the rest. You may not be able to figure out how hiring someone or making a workplace change applies to a particular problem, so ask the question and sometimes surprising ideas emerge.

Never overlook the "Work on Yourself" part, to examine needed changes to your own management style, practices, work habits, attitudes, and beliefs.

Once you have generated all of these ideas and labeled them, then it's time to reformulate all this material into a project plan. Use the worksheet on table 10.1 and the accountability templates in chapter 17.

Can problems be totally solved? Some can, some can't. This is like asking if maintenance or housecleaning are ever truly done. Obviously not. You do it now, and you do it again later. The Problem Solvent is a labor-saving device that you apply whenever things arise.

## ASK YOURSELF . . .

1. What problem that you are facing right now could use the Problem Solvent?

2. If you have looked at a problem from one perspective, how could you gain insight by asking all the Problem Solvent questions?

3. Who is on your problem-solving panel? List the people who would be best for brainstorming on your business growth, profitability, and ease.

**Extra credit questions**

4. Develop a timeline for making these changes, showing what has to be done first and the pieces that must proceed simultaneously.

5. Develop a budget for making changes, for both money and time, showing not just your time but your people's time as well.

# Chapter 11

# Recapture Your Time

## *Don't just save your time; invest it*

*"I know I need to focus on my long-term goals, but right now I've got to put out all these fires.*

*"I love my work, but I work way too many hours. The busy work keeps me from taking steps to build my business, and I don't get enough time with my family. But what can I do? If I'm not there at the office, things don't get done."*

*"I feel harried and overworked, and I'm tired of feeling that way.*

"I don't have enough hours in the day!" is one of the most common complaints of business owners. Lack of time ranks far above lack of money in barriers to growth. After all, you can borrow money, but your hours are fixed in number.

What gets in the way of using your time strategically? Sometimes your workday makes you feel like a human pinball. You bounce incessantly from one thing to another: bells ring, lights flash, but do you move closer to your goals? This leaves you with an often unspoken attitude: "I'm not in control of my time, so why pretend that I am?"

Besides this, you may experience resistance to setting a firm goal and sticking to a strategy—perhaps out of fear that you won't get there. You have no plan, and as a result you get buffeted, like a sailboat in a squall with all its sails down.

You may focus on things that are not strategic uses of your time because they are things you do well or feel comfortable with, even if you don't really enjoy them, e.g. bookkeeping or filing.

Your time is gobbled up and frittered away by many small jobs, phone calls, and drop-in visits, by equipment breakdowns and people who show up late for appointments, by employees asking you questions they should answer for themselves, by your looking over the shoulder of someone to whom you've delegated a task, by a sick employee for whom you must fill in, or by a demanding or unhappy customer.

### The business owner's strategic time killers

Take a look at the strategic time killers on table 11-1. These are outgrowths of the ways we run our business: our management style, practices, habits, attitudes, and beliefs. If any of these resonate with you, you surely see that dealing with them effectively requires more than some tricks of time management.

What can you do about these things?
- Interruptions and distractions are unavoidable. How do you minimize their impact?
- The day-to-day work has to get done. How do you carve out the time to focus on longer-term strategic issues?
- Schedules are chock-full and customers want results yesterday. Suppliers are late and things take longer than we expected. How do you deal with the inevitable overbooking?

You say you'd like to do something about it, but are you really committed? Ask yourself, "What are the costs of *not* making the changes in the way I use my time?"
- Your own health, well-being. Burnout, discouragement.
- You lose sight of the bigger picture, and miss seeing oncoming opportunities or hazards.
- Cost to your family, your other interests.

## WHAT'S WRONG WITH TIME MANAGEMENT?

Poor use of your working time is one of the greatest barriers to growth. People say, "I've got to learn to manage my time better!" Thus time management seminars and tools are very popular. In my opinion this puts the emphasis in the wrong place. It treats the symptom, rather than the cause.

## TABLE 11-1

### The business owner's strategic time killers

*How many of these apply?*

- **Go-fer.** You do the low-skilled jobs which don't fall into any employee's job description: delivering materials to the job site, making bank deposits, getting copies made, shopping for office supplies, emptying the trash.
- **Miser.** Save a penny, lose a dollar. You act as your own administrative assistant. To avoid spending $15 an hour, you forego $100 an hour (or whatever your time is worth). You do your own bookkeeping, invoicing, bill paying.
- **Gatekeeper.** Only you can be trusted to open and close each day, so you have the longest hours.
- **Firefighter.** There is always some fire to be put out; and if not, you've been known to start one just to keep things interesting.
- **Leaf in a storm.** You are at the mercy of the winds of business fate. Your schedule is dictated by whatever comes along.
- **Comfort zoner.** You resist doing the things that will take you to the next level, and tend to stay with things you are comfortable with.
- **Worker bee.** You like being crew chief, tending to everyday jobs. It's hard work, but you can see the results right away. It's why you got into the business in the first place.
- **Pinch hitter.** You fill in for everyone. If an employee is absent, you do his or her job.
- **Mr. Accessible.** Your door is always open. You take every phone call. You can be interrupted at any time.
- **Assistant.** You hand over a job to someone. When that person comes back to ask for help you end up doing part of the job you delegated to them.
- **Philanthropist.** You subsidize your clients. You do work for them, but don't charge for all of it. You do this at the expense of your strategic work.
- **Optimist.** Your scheduling is overly optimistic, and things take longer than you expect. This eats into the time you had allocated for other things, and you always feel pressured.
- **Crammer.** You overbook, cramming things into your schedule, which leads to inevitable slippage. Strategic tasks get bumped.
- **Ms. Essential.** Only you can do the task. That means every time it must be done, you must be there—and interrupt whatever else you are doing.
- **Unimportant.** You break appointments with yourself—the most important person in the business—even though you would never break appointments with a client.

You can manage your time very well, and be very productive on a broad range of important tasks, yet they can still be the wrong tasks for you to focus on.

### "Saving time" vs. "investing time"

People also say "time is money," but I disagree. Time is more important than money. Money is replaceable; time is not. Time management helps you *save* time; I want you to focus on *invest-ing* your time.

We all know what it means to invest money: we put some money into something now to get a much greater return later. It's the same with time. Strategic time use means investing your time in activities that give

> *Where can you get the highest return on an hour of your time?*

you a greater return over the long haul. Spending all your time in day-to-day work activities is like spending your entire paycheck on day-to-day living, and investing nothing for the future. If you work constantly, how can you invest time to get a much greater return on your time later? This is the dilemma many business owners face in their daily time crunch.

To recapture your time you must use your time strategically. This means to focus on activities that will best move you toward your goals. Obviously, to do this you must know what your goals are and what strategies will be most likely to achieve them. You must have a strategic plan, and I know from long experience that even mentioning the term "strategic plan" makes many business owners' eyes glaze over. If you don't know or care where you are going, it doesn't matter what path you take. But if you have an objective, it pays to think out the best route, and the most effective use of your time to achieve it. This is what I mean by using your time strategically.

Ask yourself where you can invest your time *now* so that it has a much greater return for you down the line. What will your business be like in a few years if you *don't* invest time now to bring about the types of changes you desire? If you don't ask these things, your business stays the way it is, or wobbles this way and that, or goes off in the wrong direction. These questions point to the core of strategic time use, which underlies recapturing your time and leveraging your efforts.

In this chapter, I will emphasize a handful of principles for using your time strategically, and suggest how you can recapture your time by looking at the root causes of poor time investment.

## *Time management habits of effective business owners*

In contrast to the strategic time killers described above, here are ground rules for effective time use:

1. "Keep your eyes on the prize." Stay focused on your goals and objectives.

2. Emphasize the things you must do to achieve goals and objectives, and minimize time spent on other tasks.

3. Set up your schedule so you can be most productive.

4. Minimize distractions, interruptions, time wasters. Know how to say "no" to demands on your time.

5. Be alert to your own patterns and habits that waste your time. Analyze the dynamics behind time crunches and how to avoid them in the future.

6. Get help staying organized. Have a chief of staff, an organizer, or detail person. Have people to delegate tasks to.

7. Take care of yourself. This is key: pay attention to your health and well-being. Keep up your energy, creativity, and enthusiasm by maintaining the desired balance between business and the rest of your life.

## *How can you use your time strategically?*

To apply these guidelines to your situation, answer these questions:

- To achieve your vision, to achieve the growth you want, to make the changes needed in your company, where should you focus your attention?

- Where are your skills best applied? To answer this, you need to know:

  Your vision of business success

  Your long term objectives, and strategic plan to get there

  Action plan, projects, activities for this year

  Your role and priorities. Your team's role and priorities

- In order for you to focus on these areas, what activities should you give up? What should you hand off to others? What should be on the back burner?

You should have two lists: "Focus on" and "Give up" that might look like this:

| Focus on | Give up |
|---|---|
| Business development (new types of customers, alliances, relationships) | Administrative tasks, everyday routine, data entry, invoicing |
| Looking ahead, keeping your antennas out, learning and researching | Routine management and troubleshooting |
| Financial and operational oversight | Bookkeeping, writing the checks, making the deposits |
| Creating new products or services, or refining existing ones | Supervising every job |
| Working with key customers | |
| Building and managing your team | |
| Developing ways to increase productivity | |

- How can you delegate pieces of jobs you have previously done in entirety, yet retain a minimum amount of creative input, problem solving and oversight?

- Where do you need help? You may need to hire a chief of staff or an assistant to whom you can delegate detail work, or a professional coach or organizer. Another example would be a "factotum," which is an employee who does all kinds of work. ("Factotum" comes from Latin words that mean "does everything.")

- What are the likely crises, urgent situations, interruptions, distractions, or special events that will arise? How you will cope with them?

- What are your habitual time killers? How you will deal with them?

- When you get distracted, how can you get back on track? It often helps to have someone such as a coach, consultant, an advisory board, or board of directors who will notice and remind you, "Hey, it looks like you are getting off track. How can I help you get back on?" (Sometimes your spouse can serve in one of these roles, but I say this with trepidation, because it doesn't work for many couples.)

As you answer these questions for yourself, you will come to understand what strategic time use means for you in your business. But you will still have to recapture enough of your time to focus on these longer-term improvements. Thus we introduce the Three Levels, and the things you can do right now.

## TABLE 11-2

### Start with time triage

Take a three-tiered approach to recapturing your time and using it more strategically:

**Level 1. Triage Your Time.** Generate some "right-now" benefits. How can you stop the time hemorrhaging? Where can you recapture a small amount of time, to give you the space to focus on longer-term improvements in your time use?

**Level 2. Recapture Your Time.** Make some near-term improvements. How can you permanently change the demands on your time, so that you can focus on strategic priorities?

**Level 3. Invest Your Time.** Undertake longer-term restructuring. Over the next year or so, how can you restructure your business to help you make your greatest contribution to its success, have the workstyle you want, and achieve your long-term objectives?

## LEVEL I. TRIAGE YOUR TIME TO STOP THE TIME HEMORRHAGING

### *"I don't have time to improve my time use!"*

It always amazes me how many people sign up for our workshop "Recapture Your Time" and then cancel. I can hear them now: "I am so busy I don't have time to make the changes necessary to use my time strategically." "I was going to attend, but then this crisis came up."

So let's start with some short-term tactics: How can you recapture a little time right away—just enough to give you time and energy to take a strategic approach to all your time?

You can start doing some of these things tomorrow, no matter how busy you are. Pick one or two that could have an immediate payoff for you. To see how to make any of these work for you, run through the Problem Solvent questions recapped on page 156-157.

• How can you guard your time jealously?
  – What is your biggest unwanted distraction, and how can you avoid it?
  – How can you say "no" to a request for your time that pulls you off course?
  – When someone tries to give you back a task you have delegated, how can you say no?

- Where have you crammed too much into your schedule? How can you get more done by **scheduling less**? When should you leave some unscheduled time for the inevitable "right now" things and interruptions?
- What are the **best times** for you to focus on different tasks?
  - What are your high-energy "prime times" vs. low-energy "off times?"
  - When should you make calls so that people are most likely reachable?
  - What task that requires concentration can you schedule so that you won't be interrupted?
- What **non-productive time** could you **reduce** right away, e.g., time spent driving, waiting for somebody, or giving away services you should have sold?
- What part of a time-consuming job could you **hand off** to someone else?
- If you **communicate your schedule** to others, how can they help you stick to it?
- If you **block out time for key activities** (including personal ones) whom should you tell that you aren't available?
- How can you **work more efficiently?** Can you think through a project beforehand and lay out the best sequence of activities?
- What can you do that would conserve your energy or **recharge your batteries**? What tires you out the most, and how can you change that right away?

At the end of the day, ask yourself:

- What did you not have time for? What important priorities got pushed back because of unexpected demands?
- What came up that busted your schedule? How often do such things come up? What can you do about them next time?
- What did you spend time on that someone else could have done? Why do you hold on to this task? Common reasons are: Everyone else is too busy. (Implicit message: The boss's time is less valuable than others'.) Only you can do it.
- What jobs did you do that someone else could have handled a part of? Even if you don't think you can delegate the entire job, what part of it can be delegated?

Business owners often pose a false dilemma: "I've got to do the work, but I also have to do the marketing and selling. I just don't have time to do both!" When you list all the things you spend time on, you may discover you are spending the most time on minutiae that could be dumped, delegated, or delayed. If you cut back on this minutiae, you will have time for both work and marketing. (If it then turns out that you resist doing the marketing, go directly back to chapter 5.)

## LEVEL II. CHANGE THE WAY YOU DO THINGS

### Why do you have a time crunch?

How can you permanently change the demands on your time so that you can focus on strategic priorities? After you begin getting results from time triage, you probably need to make basic changes in the way you run your business.

Better time management will seldom solve your time crunch; too often it is just a band aid. The real causes are deeper and may pervade the way you carry out every aspect of your business. All the situations below have been given by business owners as reasons for time crunches. Do any of these sound familiar to you?

### Marketing and sales

- You don't have the right clients. The clients you have are not profitable.

- You are giving your time away. You are not billing clients for all the work you do. You let them keep adding on things that are not included in the contract.

- Your marketing and selling efforts are not focused. You spend too much time marketing to the wrong people or in the wrong ways. Your message is not focused enough to quickly attract the clients you want. Your marketing approaches are not designed to get you in front of your preferred prospects. You do not qualify prospects quickly enough, so you spend too much time doing pre-sale work for people that you won't end up working with.

- The way you present yourself to customers needs to be changed. You need to sell your customers on the benefits of being served by others in your company, not just by you. You want them to be comfortable working with your associates, and not insist on talking only to you.

### Pricing

- You are priced too low. You offer higher quality for lower price. Thus your work is not very profitable, and you have to work all the harder to make a go of it. You are afraid to raise prices because you might lose business, but perhaps all you would lose are the least profitable clients or customers.

In a chapter on recapturing your time, why are we discussing price increases, improving your change order procedures, etc? How does it fit? If we don't bill for all of our time, or if we leave our prices too low, then we must put in additional hours to bring in the level of revenue we need for our business to run well and to pay ourselves well. Since we're charg-

*Pricing improperly causes poor time use.*

ing a lower rate, we must put in more hours to get the work done. This leaves fewer hours for ourselves and for strategic and executive tasks needed to make our business go where we want it to.

### Planning and vision

- You lack a vision of where you want to go, of what your business can be. Thus you have a "small time operator" mentality and choose your daily activities accordingly.

- Because you are working so hard, you never take time out to plan.

- You do not ensure that each day's activities are those which will keep you on track, moving toward your vision and goal.

### Work habits and attitudes

- Your work habits waste time. You let yourself be distracted and pulled off-course. You are not good at delegating and letting go; you want to hold on to all the tasks. You don't trust others to do a good job.

- You resist some of the tasks that will most advance your business. Instead of developing a profitable business, you do administrative work because it is more comfortable. You act as go-fer to avoid hiring another low-skilled person.

- You schedule too many tasks each day, thus lowering your productivity.

- It is hard for you to set your own schedule and stick to it; you are at the mercy of outside demands. People ask for something and expect you to do it right then.

### Management skills

- You need better management skills. You have good people working for you, but they don't do their best job because you give them too much or too little guidance. They don't do exactly what you want, but you have not told them clearly enough what you do want. Or else you give them too much detail and don't let them use their initiative. You have not used the right incentives to motivate them to do what you most need done.

## Operations

- You could produce the same result for your clients or customers with less time and hassle. You should farm out some of it, add other professionals to your team, or assign parts of it to lower-skilled people.

- You don't tell clients when you are available and not available. You need a policy on when you will drop everything and deal with your clients' requests, and when you will fit them into your schedule.

- You work hard, but not very smart. You work all the time—too many hours, six or seven days a week. You are tired, low energy, unproductive, uncreative; it's drudgery. It's as if you are an employee of a boss who is not giving you enough direction.

## Staffing and teamwork

- You do not select the best people to work with you. Thus they are not very productive and you end up having to work harder at the tasks you are supposedly delegating to them.

- It feels like you are working for your employees—always answering their questions, helping them out with the things you've delegated, and taking care of the tasks they don't really like to do or are not good at. They get paid regularly, and you don't. No wonder you're not motivated!

## Systems and procedures

- You need better management systems and procedures. Too many of the things you do are done inefficiently. You use manual procedures rather than the computer. You have inadequate systems, which you have outgrown and need to upgrade or revamp. Poorly designed systems create more work and headaches for you.

## Apply the Problem Solvent to your time crunch

Do these situations have a familiar ring? Of course! They are just the kinds of things we talked about in Section II on how to apply the Problem Solvent. For any barrier to using your time well, ask these five questions:

- Work on yourself        How can you change your management style, practices, work habits, attitudes, or beliefs to recapture your time and improve strategic use of time?

- Help and Support        Who can you delegate to? What outside support would make the biggest difference? E.g., to keep you organized, get help from a professional organizer.

- Systems and Procedures How can you change the way you do things to boost your productivity and improve time use by both yourself and your people? What secret knowledge can you turn into checklists and procedures?

- Skills and Capabilities What skill would improve time use by you and your people? How can you gain it? How can you be the manager, who produces results by coordinating the efforts of others, and the executive, who focuses on business development and bottom line health?

- Workplace changes; materials or equipment What changes in your workplace, your equipment, or your materials would promote better use of your time?

## LEVEL III. INVEST YOUR TIME, DON'T SPEND IT

To use your time strategically you must apply it where it does the most to advance your business objectives. That is where your contribution has the greatest value, and where you get the greatest return for each hour you put in. Apply these two guiding principles to break the chain between hours worked and revenue earned:

- **Sell value, not time**

- **Leverage your efforts**

### *Get the greatest return from each hour of your time*

A large corporation looks at return on investment (ROI) through cash flow that is generated. However, in a smaller business run by the owner, the most important investment is your own time. You want to maximize the return on the time you put into the business. For every hour you put in, you want to get the most profit back.

You should evaluate whatever you do in your business by "ROT"— return on time. Should you spend your time today stuffing envelopes or developing new business contacts? Bookkeeping or following up on past customers? Delivering supplies to your crews or developing an estimate for a big job? Which gives you the best ROT?

## *Know the value of your time*

What is a working hour of your time worth? How can you find out? Probably the best way is to ask what it would cost to hire someone to do what you do. If you list your major areas of responsibility and put a dollar figure on each task, you quickly discover that all your hours aren't worth the same amount.

> *What is your time worth when you make your greatest contribution?*

In particular, what is your time worth when you are making the greatest contribution to your company?

For example, consider a woman who puts on specialized seminars for large organizations. When we did this exercise together, it was hard for her to even think about how much her time was worth when she designed seminars. Who else could she hire to do this, she wondered. "Are you the only person in the world who can design these seminars?" I asked her. "Well, no," she replied, "but it isn't a common skill. This is why my business succeeds." "So how much would you have to pay?" I insisted. "Could you get someone for $50 an hour? $100? $150?" "No way!" she exclaimed. She figured she would have to pay at least $250 per hour.

So her time is worth at least $250 an hour when she creates or revises seminars. On the other hand, she can hire really competent people to conduct the seminars for less than $100 an hour. Yet her pricing was based on just the opposite premise: she charged clients to conduct the seminars, but threw in the creation or revision almost as an afterthought. When clients asked for a variation of an existing seminar, she always obliged, and spent hours on it without added charge. While she loves developing seminars, she felt the burden of doing this for free.

After our conversation, she resolved to charge for revisions and variations. This had several effects:

1. When faced with a higher price for a special seminar, some clients opted to contract for an entire series of seminars, thus amortizing the development cost over more events—and boosting her revenue per sales effort.
2. She personally led fewer seminars and instead hired and trained others to lead them.
3. She got to focus more of her time on developing seminars—the part of the business she most enjoyed.
4. Her business became much more profitable, she didn't have to work so hard, and she greatly reduced her business travel.

The hardest part of this for her? Getting up the nerve to announce price increases to her clients. Not one of them objected!

Thus did she successfully recapture her time. She used her time strategically to advance her own aims—including bringing in more money, not working so hard, doing things she enjoyed more, and buying a house.

What is your time worth when you are developing business, developing new products or services, developing new strategic alliances, team building, communicating your vision, practicing your profession? Now, how much is your time worth when you are doing your own bookkeeping, running to the post office, filing, or corresponding? How much would it cost you to hire somebody to do those things for you?

Make a list like this of your work activities, and how much you would have to pay someone else to do each job for you:

| Your activities | Hourly rate for someone else to do this |
|---|---|
| A. What you spend the most time on | |
| 1 | $ |
| 2 | $ |
| 3 | $ |
| B. What tasks you enjoy the most | |
| 1 | $ |
| 2 | $ |
| 3 | $ |
| C. Where you have the greatest value to your company | |
| 1 | $ |
| 2 | $ |
| 3 | $ |

Ideally, the tasks you list in A, B, and C are the same! But if they are not, then you can improve the strategic use of your time.

Where do you make the highest economic contribution to your company? How much is that worth? That is the value of an hour of your time. Write this number on a plaque in a prominent place, where you can't help but see it.

**"My time is worth $ _____ each hour."**

Whenever you do tasks that are worth less than this, you are costing your company the difference between this rate and the market value of that other task.

As part of this exercise, ask these questions:

- In what activities of your business are you satisfied with the return to your time?
- Where do you *not* recoup the value of your input?
- How should your services be **priced** to pay you what you are worth?
- How should your work be **reorganized** to recoup the true value of your time?
- How could your company be **restructured** to pay you as much as you want and need—both now and in the future?

This is not to say that you should never stick stamps on envelopes or replace toilet paper rolls. But develop the attitude that such times are the rare exceptions. Guard your time jealously.

It is crystal clear to you that when your $60,000 manager spends time on such tasks, time and money are being wasted. But we, as business *owners*, too often operate as if our own time is free.

Once you know the value of an hour of your time, what can you do with this information?

- Focus on your highest-value contributions. Stop doing $15 an hour work.
- Set priorities for yourself: what you will do and what you will no longer do. Make sure others understand this and give you the needed support.
- Set prices that are based on the value of your time. Apply this rule: "Billing rate = 3 times pay rate." If your desired pay rate is worth $100 per hour, then bill your time to clients at $300 per hour.
- Track how much time you (or your people) can afford to spend on a project, and compare this to your estimates.
- Include your time value on your financial statements, especially as a direct cost of your labor. Only in this way can you know and compare the real profitability of the jobs you work on.

## BREAK THE CHAIN BETWEEN HOURS WORKED AND REVENUE EARNED

This concept is especially important for a service business, where you start out thinking that your hours are what you sell. You must learn to maximize the return (the profit, your pay) for each hour that you work. There are two main ways:

## SELL VALUE, NOT TIME

Move from selling time to selling value. What do I mean by this? Put less emphasis on the time a job takes and more on the value your customer will receive. Here's an example:

**Selling time:** "This job will take 32 hours at $75 per hour."

**Selling value:** "This should save you at least $50,000 the first year, and its cost will be just $3,000."

Suppose you are a graphic designer designing a new logo, brochure, and letterhead for a growing company. Ask your client questions like these: "What do you want these new materials to do for your company? How much will this be worth to your company if it upgrades your image? Will it double your sales? Boost your little company up to be a big company? That could be worth a couple of million dollars, and my design fee is a paltry $5,000." Now you may not say it exactly this way, but that is the attitude you need.

Ask any company that has had a lousy logo design—they know the cost of mediocre design. They know how their company has been held back by not having quality marketing materials.

### The instant impact of selling value, not just time

When you sell value, you focus your client on what they want most: results, e.g., more sales, higher profit, increased exposure and recognition, reduced costs, and greater ease.

When you sell your time, on the other hand, you focus your client on what they dislike: spending money, monitoring your performance, or worrying about getting cheated.

To sell value, you force yourself to ask what value you truly bring your client in concrete dollar terms how you can provide even greater value, and how you can communicate this value to them.

You feel the impacts immediately. Business is more fun. You get to raise prices. You can focus on clients that don't need convincing and to whom you needn't justify what you are selling because they clearly want your product.

What is the value provided to customers by what you sell? Unless you are clear on the value you provide, the benefit you bring to your customer, you cannot emphasize selling value. You are stuck selling your time. You must know the value or benefit you provide to your customers. If you are unclear on what this is, how will you find out? (Hint: Call them and ask: "Why do you do business with me rather than with someone else?")

## *The enemies of selling value*

The enemies of selling value are timidity and inattentiveness:

- "I can't raise prices; my industry is way too competitive." Your customers view your product or service as an interchangeable commodity, because you haven't sold them on your unique qualities.

- The urge to take any business that comes along. If you take on work that is inherently lower-margin, this indicates that the buyer does not particularly value the special features you offer.

- You don't understand the value you provide as seen by your customers. You are too timid, so you don't ask for enough.

- You leave money on the table, i.e., they expect to pay more than you charge. Paradoxically, if you don't charge enough, your customers won't value it. "Hmm. If he's only charging that much, he must not be very good."

- You can't properly estimate the size of the job. Thus you invariably underestimate and end up doing more work for less money.

- You don't emphasize your value. The value of your work may speak for itself; but in addition, you must point out to customers what it is worth to them.

- So-so execution. Leaving out something the customer wants, missed deadlines, blown budgets, inattention, mistakes, poor customer contact.

## LEVERAGE YOUR EFFORT

To leverage your effort means to increase the return to you without using more of your time. For example:

- Increase the return to each hour of your effort. Go after larger, more lucrative projects. Sell bigger chunks. Take on higher margin work, or larger projects. You often find that the cost of selling is just as high for a small job as for a larger one. Suppose it takes you four hours to close a $5,000 job and eight hours to close a $50,000 job. Which gives you a greater return on your selling effort? Likewise—the cost of administration—record keeping, invoicing, collections, etc. will take the same or nearly the same amount of time regardless of the size of the job.

- Increase the profit generated by each dollar of your outlay. The key to leveraging your money is other people's money (OPM). You borrow the money, make a sound investment; the value goes up, you reap the reward, repay the loan, and have a large profit compared to your initial investment. You earn this for having the idea, spotting the opportunity, taking the risk, putting it together, and managing it well. Similarly, to leverage your time, use "OPT"—other people's time. Hire and train others and oversee their efforts.

## The enemies of leverage

- "I have special knowledge" or "only I can do it" mentality. We discussed this in chapter 7. Consultants and professional service providers are notorious for this viewpoint.
- Lost in minutiae. You handle every little thing that comes along, so you lose sight of the desired scale and scope of your business. Opportunities come and go, while you stay stuck in the underbrush.
- Stuck in small thinking; small-operator mentality. What if an investor came to you and said, "You've got a great operation here: I'd like to help you franchise it" and you replied, "Oh, no, that would be way too much work for me." I almost did this myself. A large organization asked if I could design and manage a business support program for their clients. My first impulse was to reply, "Oh, that's way too big for me. I'd better refer you to someone else." Fortunately, that impulse passed in about two seconds. But many of us have this tendency to underrate our own capabilities.
- Penny pincher. "It sounds like a great opportunity, but I just don't want to risk the money." Prudence is a virtue for business owners, but you must also know when to take a prudent leap into the unknown. If you didn't already believe this, you wouldn't be in business anyway.

### MAXIMIZE YOUR ROC (RETURN ON CREATIVITY)

Whenever you create and sell something new—a design, a solution to a problem, or a way of solving problems—how many different ways can you sell it, not just once, but many times over? That is, how can you increase the return from each unit of your creativity?

This is a crucial question for professionals who sell the fruits of their intellectual and creative endeavors. Many creative people despair of ever having an endeavor that generates cash flow without their constant input, or of growing an asset that can ultimately be sold. Yet I review that continuous creative output, and say to them, "Productify!" Turn your creative output into products.

I have done my best to follow this path. I started out consulting with businesses, selling time by the hour or project, creating unique solutions to clients' problems each time. Since then I have climbed a ladder of leverage, with each step increasing the return on my time and creativity:

- Leading seminars and ongoing groups, working with up to a dozen people at a time who face similar problems. They pay less per hour, but my effective rate is much higher than one-on-one consulting. They also benefit by learning from each other as well as from me.

- Training other people to lead groups and seminars for me.

- Writing and selling books that encapsulate my advice. The same material goes into tapes, articles, website content, CD-ROMs, and whatever else comes along.

- License to others the right to use my materials and approach to leading groups.

- Hire someone else to run the operation for me, while I focus on creating new materials from our Hawaii hideaway. (If this works, that's where you can reach me now!)

Here are other examples from people I have worked with:

- The designer of unique kitchens who turned some of his designs into a line of top-end kitchen accessories, which are distributed nationally by major distributors.

- The woman mentioned earlier in this chapter who shifted her emphasis from leading seminars to creating seminars that are led over and over by other people.

> *A Zen master says, "Every day I meditate an hour, no matter how busy I am. Except on those days when the crush of work is overwhelming. Then I meditate two hours."*

- A retailer whose unique store design and merchandise mix grew from one store to a franchise chain.

This takes a lot of work (ask anyone who has written a book!) but you don't have to do it all alone. You can get help both to identify the potential products within your creative output for which there is a likely market, and to help you develop them. Of course once you have identified and developed products, you can get help marketing and selling them.

I coined the terms ROT (return on time) and ROC (return on creativity) to induce you to expand your thinking and view your time and creativity as limited assets for which you should seek the highest return. If you have the opportunity to leverage your creativity, the cost of *not* taking it is the cost of lost revenue, satisfaction, and contribution to your customers.

Once you are committed to using time strategically, time management tools will help you use your time well.

## GUIDELINES TO SCHEDULING SANITY

Lay out your calendar a year in advance.

- Determine your target work week. Which days do you work and how many hours? What hours and days are you not available for work? Block these areas out on your calendar. (E.g., one way to avoid scheduling on weekends is not to put SAT or SUN columns on your calendar.)

- Since you are the most important person in your business, schedule yourself first. Enter vacations, holidays, long weekends, birthdays and anniversaries, family events. Then enter personal time during work hours: exercise, meditation, appointments, etc.

- Enter key business deadlines: tax returns, inventory dates, etc.

- Block out "crunch times:" holiday season, tax season, your annual trade show. Block out "crazy times:" when your employees all go on vacation, your annual open house, when new interns start, when you are remodeling the office, installing new equipment or software systems.

- Enter periodic or non-regular events: Monthly closings, conferences, seminars, exhibitions, training and executive development, presentations to outside organizations; writing and development; of marketing materials, newsletters, product descriptions, articles, etc.

- Don't schedule all your time, because unscheduled things always come up. If you expect to work eight hours a day, then *schedule* only six hours, recognizing that two hours will be needed for other unscheduled activities. If you schedule all eight hours one day, your workday must spill over into the evening, next day, or weekend. If you consistently schedule beyond your limit, you fall behind and miss deadlines.

- Set your priorities. What proportion of your time should you devote to each aspect of your business?

  Doing your regular work for which you get paid

  Executive functions: Planning, strategizing. Developing new products, services, materials; strategic alliances

  Management functions: improving cost effectiveness, cost cutting, training, overseeing, coordination of employees or subcontractors

  Marketing, selling, developing new business, bringing in new clients, making sure customers are happ.

- Schedule your regular activities based on how many hours you need to spend on each.

- Track how much non-productive time you spend: driving, waiting for somebody else, giving away services you should have sold and time you just can't account for.

## CARVE OUT TIME FOR DEVELOPMENT

To help you leverage your creativity, here are guidelines for carving out time for special projects, such as writing, creating, or designing.

- Principle #1: Make it a priority, instead of a perpetual back-burner activity that you attend to if you don't have something else to do and aren't too tired.

- Block out your development time on your calendar in ink. (Too bad there are no indelible entries on your computer calendar.)

- Don't schedule development time during your crunch times, and avoid scheduling over your personal time.

- Beware the "24/7" syndrome, i.e., doing it evenings and weekends. (I wish I could follow this advice myself.)

- Learn to capture creativity quickly when it bursts forth: Keep a notebook or index cards with you. I am never without my microcassette recorder. I turn it on when I am explaining something, and I record all my seminars and presentations. I mutter into it while driving, walking in the hills or when I wake up in the wee hours. This works because someone else transcribes my dictation. (Note: Transcribing a rambling conversation is next to impossible, so I often listen to the tape of this conversation on one tape recorder while dictating an edited version into a second recorder for the transcriber. This requires good ear/mouth coordination!)

*If your business thrives on your creativity, then schedule your creative time first—in ink.*

- Plan out and prioritize what's needed to complete these projects. Divide them into bite-sized pieces, or even nibbles.

- Produce some quick results right away. This generates more energy.

- If you lack an imposed deadline, create an arbitrary one, e.g., promise a presentation to a group in two weeks.

Know the answers to these questions:

- When is your "good thinking" time? What times should you avoid?

- How long should a block of development time be? Hours, part of a day, a brief retreat, or an extended sabbatical? Some people do fine with bits of time here and there, while I need at least several hours, and really get rolling if I can block out a week.

- Where? Home, office, library, or away at a retreat? I can't focus on writing at the office; I work best at home where I can spread papers all over the dining room table. My wife is somewhat resigned to this.

- What is the best catalyst? What releases the creativity floodgates? A problem to solve? A contract and deadline? Talking it through? Most of the ideas in this book came while I was standing at the flipchart with a marker, trying to explain in simple terms how someone should tackle a problem.

- What atmosphere is best? Quiet with no distractions, or music? No windows, or plenty of sunshine? During college, I could study much more effectively in the hubbub of the student union with the smell of french fries, than in the hushed windowless library smelling of musty books.

- What help and support do you need? Sounding board or editor? Someone to whom you report your schedule and results? A ghostwriter? Some people are lone creators, others need collaborators. I constantly talk my ideas over with others, and use my talks and workshops to test ideas and flesh them out.

## ASK YOURSELF . . .

1. To achieve your vision of success, what tasks should you focus your attention on?

2. What is your biggest time killer? What keeps you from giving it up? To give it up, what do you need? How should you change the way you do things?

3. What are your biggest schedule busters? What can you do to reduce them?

4. What is an hour of your time worth? How can you increase the return on each hour of your time?

5. How can you move from selling time to selling value?

6. How can you leverage your effort, or increase the return on a unit of your creativity?

## Chapter 12

# Build a Culture of Growth

I n chapter 1 we described a Culture of Smallness, using these examples:

- The lack of controls, systems, routines, written policy or documentation. "We make it up as we go along."

- "We are all one big family." "We all do many jobs." A dislike of hierarchical structure; no job descriptions or boundaries.

- "My door is always open" (meaning "You may interrupt me at any time").

- Hippie entrepreneurs who have never quite grown up. Profit is suspect.

- All profit is shielded, hidden: "Life is a write-off." When you earn extra money, you spend it. In your drive to minimize taxes, you avoid profitability as well.

- "We're in a muddle. We don't know what is profitable or unprofitable. We don't know which employees are most productive and which are just making excuses. We know we're not billing for all the work. We're losing out on good jobs because we're not organized to handle them."

## *What is a business culture?*

Your company's business culture grows out of accepted behaviors and work habits, the ways people interact, and the attitudes and beliefs of all the people in the company: the owner(s), employees, subcontractors, customers and vendors and perhaps even family members.

The company culture is often at odds with what the owner proclaims and with mission statements and posted company policy.

In a culture of smallness, the way the business owners think and interact with employees and the way the work is done limits growth and keeps the company small. Perhaps it worked previously, but it is not working now and is a big barrier to further growth.

In a "culture of growth" the attitudes, work habits, and interactions of all the people support the growth of the company

In what ways do you and your people "think small"? How can you transform a culture of smallness into a culture of growth? For example:

| A CULTURE OF SMALLNESS | A CULTURE OF GROWTH |
| --- | --- |
| It's a family business. Family drama plays out in the workplace. | It's a team. The owner is the coach who calls the plays. Everyone must fulfill his/her role, or get off the team. |
| You treat employees like family—often a dysfunctional family. "My employees are like kids, and they rule the roost." | You treat employees with firmness, fairness, and consistency, based on job descriptions and performance standards. |
| You interact with customers and suppliers in a very casual way. "Need a rush job? Sure, I can bump other people; or I'll come in on the weekend to get it done." Change orders are verbal. You often don't charge for the extra work. You are so busy doing the work you don't take time to send out invoices. | You run a people-oriented company, and give your customers excellent service. Your consistent policies on scheduling, pricing and billing allow you to be competitive yet profitable. Your customers always know where they stand with you. |
| When customers come in, they expect to see you. You must always interrupt what you are doing to put in face time with them. | Even though you are the driving force, your key people are capable and trusted, and are respected by your customers. |
| You and your managers get together after hours to work things out for the next day. | Your management team holds regular meetings to review progress toward posted targets. These meetings are held even when you are not there. |

Your business culture shifts at each stage of growth. One company may go through successive shifts. For example:

| FROM | TO |
|---|---|
| Free-lancer, part-timer | a professional practice that is a "real company" |
| One person: "I wear all the hats." | hire an assistant and delegate |
| Leaderless group of associates: "No titles here." | team with a coach, systems and procedures |
| You are the driving force and are involved in everything. | You build a skilled and committed team; some are better than you are. |

How do you know what your business culture is now and what it needs to be? Perhaps you should let go of some of your habitual ways of doing things, yet others are wisdom. How do you tell which are which? What should change and what should stay the same?

Ask yourself: to get where you want to go, what does you business culture need to be?

To attract the customers you want to reach? What do they expect from a prospective vendor such as your company? How will you as owner be expected to do your work? How does your company need to look?

To attract the caliber of employees you need?

To achieve your desired scale and productivity of operation? To be profitable, yet competitive and cost-efficient? To utilize your growing workforce? To allow you to climb the ladder of executive capability? How do you and your people need to interact?

To free you up to concentrate on strategic issues and determine the company's focus and approach? To set a reasonable plan and carry out that plan?

*How do you and your people "think small?"*

This does not mean putting forth a glitzy exterior or putting on a special effort to impress people. It means coming across as solid, professional, businesslike, reliable, friendly, and so on. You should list the things your customers want from you. Not just the customers you have now, but the customers you want to have.

Here's an example: Suppose you are a general contractor. You have gotten this far by being diligent and reliable, working very hard, keeping close rein on your two crews. Your pickup truck is your office; dirty jeans your uniform. You sketch out designs on a yellow pad and do estimates on the back of an envelope. This approach has worked well for you.

But now you want to take on larger, more lucrative projects, yet such prospects don't seem to take you seriously. You also want to get paid for the design work you do—after all, you spend a lot of time on that—but customers resist being billed for rough sketches. Furthermore, your crews can only go so far relying on your rough sketches. You spend your days flitting from job to job, giving them detailed instructions. Since you have so much of it in your head, you are the only one who can discuss details with clients.

> *What does your company culture need to be to get you where you want to go?*

You look at another general contractor who operates at the level you aspire to. His rough design sketches are never given to clients. They are turned into drawings by a draftsman, with enough detail that his crew foremen and sub-contractors can follow them with few questions. Crew foremen are involved in client meetings from the beginning, and can handle most inter-actions with clients. He dresses as a professional for client meetings, not as a worker. His vehicles are clean and uncluttered. He has an administrative assistant who answers the phone, coordinates the schedules, collects all the time and materials data, and produces invoices on the computer.

Even though his overhead is higher, he is still making more money than you are, because he gets bigger jobs, and because he bills for all the work he does.

Ask yourself the same thing: what works for you and what should be changed? There's no proper culture for growth; it depends completely on what produces the desired results. Use the questions on table 12-1 to describe your current business culture, and what you want it to be. To do this, you need to answer each question twice: First, how is it now? Then, how should it be?

## RESISTANCE TO CHANGING CULTURE

No matter how important it is to change the ways they do things, business owners resist doing so, for fear of upsetting their comfortable company culture. Do you find yourself dreading and putting off changes in procedures, personnel or management style? You're not alone.

"Why change?" you might ask. "We've always done it this way. Look how far it has gotten us." Indeed, if you are satisfied, why change? However, if you are held down by the current culture, then it's worth the effort to make the change.

What are you afraid your business culture might become? I often hear plaints like these:

"The way we have been doing things is what makes us special. We hold on to our bumbling, anything-goes style for fear of becoming an impersonal, heartless company, run by the book and by the numbers."

"If we adopt a bunch of systems and procedures, our employees will not like working here any more, and neither will I."

"Insisting that we do everything by procedure will probably drive away all our customers."

"Just the thought of trying to change the way all these people do things gives me a headache."

People use such concerns to avoid making any change. The challenge is, how can you hold on to the positive qualities that make you attractive and distinctive—both to customers and employees—while moving past those negative qualities that are holding you back?

Here are some before-and-after statements from business owners with whom I have worked. In each case, the anticipation of changing long-entrenched ways was much worse than the actuality. Despite misgivings, they persevered and made the changes. Afterwards, they were universally pleased that they had done so. They liked the outcome, and so did employees, their customers and vendors.

## Before . . . after

Bookstore owner on putting in inventory tracking and ordering systems: "We'll lose the human touch if we begin doing everything by the book. My people don't know how to use computers."

> "Using the system to handle routine stuff frees us up to focus on the creative part of our work. Customers love it."

Print shop owner on managing jobs by checklists. "Every job is different. Customers want things that aren't on the checklist. Having to write all this stuff down cuts my productivity."

> "Our production manager, who hated the system at first, ended up coming in on weekends to teach himself the system, and now he's the strongest advocate. By the way, his performance bonus took a huge leap."

Family members hold key positions, and don't always do a good job. "After all, it's my family. They drive me nuts sometimes, but I've got to stay loyal to them."

> "I found that my managers who *weren't* family were really fed up. When I started treating everyone the same, the team really kicked into high gear. Now they brag about our professionalism."

## TABLE 12-1

### What is your company's culture?

- What anecdotes and stories do you tell about your people or your business? Who do you use as good examples, as bad examples, and why? Who are your favorites? Who is a "typical" employee, and why? What do these things say about your business culture?
- How demanding and stressful is the workplace?
- What are your people's attitudes toward the mission of your company, toward doing their work consistently, keeping track of their work activities and keeping others informed?
- What is the attitude of your people toward your customers and toward vendors?
- What is their attitude toward taking responsibility? Stepping up to the challenge? Making independent decisions?
- How do you nurture creative, risk-taking behavior by your employees? How do you reward spontaneity, flexibility, initiative and quick reaction?
- Who controls the pace of work? Who sets performance standards?
- What is the level of formality? How do you and your top people expect to be addressed? What are your norms about dress and appearance?
- What are your typical work schedules? How tightly do you adhere to them? Punch clock or in-and-out at all hours? 8 to 5 or flextime?
- What is the balance between focusing on work and dealing with personal situations, e.g. workplace relationships or outside relationships?
- How do people communicate within your company? Between people on the same level, between supervisor and subordinate, between you and your supervisors, between you and the workers? What is the quality of teamwork?
- How do your employees get feedback on their performance from you and their supervisors?
- How do you communicate policy and policy changes with your employees?
- How open are you with your employees about how your company is doing and its financial performance? Do you encourage employees to learn more about the company?
- How does your company determine raises and promotions?
- Is your company more likely to promote from within or hire new managers? How do you train and cross-train?
- How does your company deal with poor performance, violations of policy, etc.?
- How are problems, disagreements and disputes handled?
- What is the position of your company in the community? How supportive is it of community events or causes that don't have a direct impact on your workplace?

A consultant resisted hiring an employee and handing off stuff. "I don't want employees. They are too darn much trouble."

"I've shifted from being 'Ms. Lone Wolf' to being a real company. Hiring Nancy was such a great move for me. I now have three part-timers. It has increased my billable time by 50%."

An architect continually fiddled in the projects he had delegated to other designers, throwing everything behind schedule and over budget.

"I promoted one designer to project manager and made everyone responsible to her, including myself. She keeps people on track and I stick with design and customer schmoozing."

The head of an advertising firm let account managers tell him how much time they needed to spend on jobs—estimates that kept expanding over time.

"By putting in these project management procedures, our designers became a lot more productive and conscious of budgets and timelines. This had a huge payoff getting our customers' work done on time. We now use these procedures as an effective sales tool. My managers who resisted them so much now brag about them. New clients are attracted to us because of this shift in the way we do things."

Let's look now at how to cultivate a culture of growth, of ease, and of satisfaction. Profitability gets its own chapter.

## BUILD A CULTURE OF GROWTH

How fast do you want your company to grow (see chapter 2)? Your business culture can hinder growth or allow growth. It can encourage steady growth or force rapid growth.

Let's use an analogy with growing flowers in your garden. Level 1: Stop stunting your plants. Stop withholding needed water, sun and fertilizer. Level 2: Nurture the growth of your plants with extra fertilizer and pruning. Level 3: Force their growth with the constant application of super nutrients. Provide hothouse conditions. I presume this is the way farmers grow 600-pound pumpkins.

It is the same with business. First, stop doing things that stunt the growth of your business. Allow it to be healthy. Second, give it the resources, systems, and expertise it needs to grow naturally. Third, if you wish, boost it to super-growth through the application of venture capital and special expertise.

Level 1: Much of this book is about Level 1—removing the barriers to growth. Just as you can turn a stunted plant into a healthy one, so also you can grow your business just by tackling the barriers to growth, and giving it the resources it needs. You can accomplish this by repeated applications of the Problem-Solvent. If I could, I'd put it in a can and sell it as Miracle Biz Grow. I'd be swimming in money!

Level 2: Healthy business growth springs from a desire to grow your business, a vision of how it should look, a plan, a strategy. Level 3 looks a lot like Level 2, but even more so. Prepare for desired growth and lay the groundwork. Identify your growth engines: people, package of services, etc. Attract needed capital by demonstrating the potential for profitable growth and healthy return on investment. Put together the growth team. Find role models for growth. Develop the infrastructure for growth: plant and equipment, productive capacity, professional support services and vendors.

Not everyone is interested in Level 3, but every business owner should want Level 1, and most of us want Level 2.

Sometimes, despite the desires and best efforts of the owner, a business fails to grow because the business model is not right. In this case, you need to change the model and come up with a different way of conducting your business that will allow the growth you want.

But how long does it take you to recognize that your current business model is not working? And are you then willing to change it? How long will it take to change your business model once you have started in a better direction? The answers to these questions depend on your own courage, vision, and expertise, the capital available and—of course—luck. There is nothing like being in the right place at the right time, but you help create your own luck and you can certainly stop getting in the way of your luck.

### Are you all on the same page?

You and your key people—owners, partners, managers—need to be in general alignment in several areas:
- Goals. You can't expect employees to have the same goals you have as owners, but their goals must be in alignment with yours. You must be pursuing the same mission. That is to say, the way in which you pursue your respective goals must be mutually supportive.
- Level of commitment. Your employees may not have the same level of commitment you do, but it must be strong enough for them to make the needed contribution to your mission.
- Energy level. A team in which some members are high energy and others are lower can create a problem, even if all are equally skilled and dedicated, and are doing a good job. Taking people from a laid-back office and putting them in a frenetic one often leads to a clash of energies. This is one reason many mergers fail.

- Level of comfort with rapid change, newness, uncertainty, confusion, multi-tasking
- Style. In business style, there's no necessary right or wrong way, but if there's a clash within the company, productivity is hurt.

   Dress and personal presentation, e.g., preppie/button down vs. casual vs. nerd grunge

   Mode of address: Dr./Mr./Ms.; first names, nicknames

   Assumptions about how communication is handled, problems are addressed, feelings are aired, disputes are resolved

   Work ethic and work schedules, e.g., 8 to 5 vs. flextime

   Sober and politically correct vs. joking, ribbing and kidding

   Level of tolerance for diversity; willingness to work with people who aren't on the same page in all these ways

## A culture of growth depends on generating surpluses

Companies that fail to grow as much as the owner wants seem like they are short of everything; they just scrape by. A scarcity mentality is a key component of a culture of smallness. In contrast, growing companies have surpluses of several different types:

- Ideas, creativity. A few big ideas plus many smaller ideas. Knowledge, technology or patents that are protectible.
- Expertise and experience beyond what is needed right now
- Energy. Surplus energy grows out of an ease of operation, satisfaction, having the right people.
- Resilience. Surplus energy gives you the ability to bounce back.
- Time. Your mode of operation must free you to focus on growing the business.
- Opportunity. Chances are best if you are not limited to a single uncertain opportunity, and have backup plans.
- Profitability, cash flow. The potential for a return on investment is amply demonstrated.
- Extra capacity. If you manufacture products, this means unused productive capacity, or the ability to mobilize productive resources. If you sell services, it means the possibility of leveraging your effort, i.e., increasing the return to you for each hour of effort you put in.
- Credit. Sources of capital you can tap when needed.

## TABLE 12-2
# Requirements for a culture of growth

| You | Your people |
|---|---|
| want to grow | want to grow with the company |
| have a vision | are aligned with your vision and mission |
| are energetic, have drive | are dedicated, hard working |
| are good team builder; attract top people | are independent, but team players |
| have an instinct for providing value to customers | focus on providing value |
| have respect for business basics | are competent, top quality |
| keep antennas out for opportunity and challenge; stay proactive | see what needs to be done and take charge of tasks |
| have an eye for strategy; are a planner, organizer | will stick with the game plan |
| have an eye for profit | take responsibility for meeting your revenue targets, budget, and time lines. |
| get needed advice, listen, and learn | are willing to learn, and to mentor others |
| are decisive | can take charge and make decisions within policy parameters. Use good judgment |
| mobilize and organize resources: people, money, expertise, plant and equipment | do the best with resources available |
| are not afraid of failure and are willing to take a risk, go for it all | will follow you into battle |

These qualities go beyond how good your product or services are, how well capitalized you are, or how lucky you are. But these qualities help you create your own luck. In the best of economic times, companies lacking some of these qualities may thrive. In tough times, companies that exhibit these qualities do better, rise to the top, and are poised to move forward when fortunes improve.

When people with these qualities fail, they get back up on their feet and try again. This is why many venture capitalists prefer working with an entrepreneur who has failed a couple of times.

When I started this list, profit and cash flow were at the top. But when I thought about which were really most important, others moved up the list. In my experience creativity, expertise, and energy will draw forth cash flow; while the opposite is far from assured. While it is true that lack of capital can stunt growth, lack of money is more often a symptom than a cause of company problems.

A culture of growth also implies ease of operation and satisfaction, as well as profitability.

## BUILD A CULTURE OF SATISFACTION

We are in business to get to do what we want to do. Otherwise, why not work for a big company and avoid the headaches of company ownership? If your work is not satisfying, why are you doing it that way? Does your business success depend on your energy and vision and drive? If it does, and you don't derive satisfaction from your efforts, these suffer.

*You are in business to get to do what you want to do. Otherwise, why bother?*

Being satisfied does not mean resting on your laurels; rather, it means gaining satisfaction from your effort and the results, and from your interactions with others.

Is it important that your people derive satisfaction from their work? Some would say no: "Just come to work, do your job; you don't have to love it, just do it!" However, this approach does not work well for many small businesses. If your competitive advantage rests on the quality of the work performed and the customer service by your people, then your employees' satisfaction is very important to you. For knowledge workers and service workers to perform at their best, they need to be satisfied with their work and their work situation. Satisfied workers lead to growth, profitability and ease of operation.

The result: higher productivity, greater commitment, loyalty, longevity and lower turnover. Your people put in extra effort for you and uphold your quality standards. They take pride in their work and have better teamwork. They learn more readily and move up to take on greater challenges. They help you recruit other good employees.

This is true for low-skilled as well as high-skilled workers. I have seen this even with restaurant employees and construction crews—notoriously high-turnover occupations. The loyalty and longevity of satisfied workers provides the company a substantial boost—in both customer satisfaction and the diminished cost of employee turnover.

Let's put this the other way: for small business, several of the highest-cost problems are caused by low employee satisfaction, including cost of replacing employees, the cost of replacing lost knowledge when skilled people leave, and greatest of all, the cost of replacing customers driven away by poor service. Surveys of employees suggest that the number one reason they start looking for another job is dissatisfaction with their bosses.

> *A culture of ease does not block growth – it promotes it.*

How can you build a culture of satisfaction among your employees? Make sure that your workplace has these qualities:

- An employment environment that is firm, fair and consistent. People see that everyone is treated the same.
- The boss is satisfied. Your energy and inspiration sets an example.
- You have the right people on board. Good people like being part of your team.
- The work situation is productive. Your people have the needed training, tools and coordination.
- Your management style is working. People know what they are supposed to do. They have clear and consistent direction, feedback, acknowledgement and correction.
- People see positive results from their effort.
- Your people feel respected. They experience ethical and honest treatment.

If you do not have this culture of satisfaction in your workplace you can create it. In my experience, people of integrity want to work the way I have just described. If you have people who do not want to work this way, then they are not the right people for you.

However, nobody is perfect. There are glitches in the system that hinder people from doing the best job they can, even when they want to. How can you elicit their best performance and minimize their negative behaviors? Ask this the other way: what situations or behaviors in your workplace thwart people from doing the best job they can or from having the best attitude about their work?

How can your systems and procedures and checks and balances get the best out of your people?

## BUILD A CULTURE OF EASE

Profitability is a key measure of how well a company works. The degree of ease is another.

A business culture of ease and a one of satisfaction are closely related. Together, ease and satisfaction are the foundations on which growth and profitability are built.

| **Growth. Profitability** |
| :---: |

▲

| Happy customers. Strong reputation. | Higher quality products and services. | Lower costs Strong competitive position |
| --- | --- | --- |

▲

| Quality service. | Innovation. Skills and strengths are well-used. | High productivity. |
| --- | --- | --- |

▲

| Low turnover. Knowledge is retained. Extra effort. Responsibility. Satisfied, challenged employees. |
| --- |

▲

| **Workplace culture of ease and satisfaction.** |
| :---: |

This creates a full cycle. (The arrow goes from the top back to the bottom.) Growth and profitability feed back to increase satisfaction and ease of operation.

| EASE KILLERS | EASE BUILDERS |
| --- | --- |
| Just plunge in and slog away. There's no time to stop, reflect, consider or plan. | Work smart. Step back regularly, take the long view, get advice, set goals. |
| You believe in hard work. Hard work is a virtue. Your work is your life. | Life comes first; work must fit in. |
| You have to set the example for the others by working the hardest. | You set the example by being productive, focused on results, working, then playing. |
| You can't take time off. Your people will lose respect for you. Things will fall apart. | People respect you because you do a good job, and you sign their paychecks. |
| You've got to make sure everything is done correctly. | You can trust the others, let go. |

## HOW TO CHANGE YOUR BUSINESS CULTURE

Developing a culture of growth is like applying the "work on yourself" idea of chapter 5 to your entire workforce. As business owner, you must start with your own management practices, habits and attitudes in order to shift the culture of your company. You must lead the way. You cannot get your team to change unless you do.

Start by answering these two questions:

- How do you have a culture of smallness in your organization now?
- How does the culture need to be shifted to get where you want to go?

First, apply the Problem Solvent, as we described in chapter 10. Once you identify the specific changes you want, ask how you can accomplish them by changing your systems or procedures, upgrading people's skills, making changes in your workplace, changing people's job descriptions or bringing in new people, and of course, working on your own management style. Reread the "before and after" section just above, and you see how such changes were the tool for culture change.

Secondly, take advantage of special circumstances that can catalyze change in your organization. If you watch small companies over time, you notice that certain things happen that causes their culture to evolve or jolts it into changing.

**Shock, necessity.** Inroads by a powerful competitor. Business downturn. Loss of a major customer. Such threats to survival focus the attention and increase people's willingness to change. (If it doesn't, they should be helped out the door.)

**New ideas or energy.** An enthusiastic new person comes in, perhaps replacing someone who resisted change. Or perhaps you or your key people attend a seminar and come away with a new commitment to making changes.

**New technology.** The new computers or shop equipment make a huge difference and open people to expanded possibilities.

**Big opportunity.** You—and your people—see that unless you make major changes in the way you do things, this big one will get away.

**New work rules.** Could be hardheaded rules: "Those who get to work on time every day will continue to receive a paycheck." Could be inspirational: "If you work with me to make this new system work, then as soon as we achieve a 90% on-time rate, I'm throwing a party for all of us."

You can take advantage of such circumstances to move your company culture in the direction you wish. Use them as symbols to underscore the importance for change, and then put forth your plan as you outlined above.

Even so, people will resist the change, and so will you, no matter how strong the impetus.

### Business culture is a hard thing to change

The way to get from one to the other is to apply the Problem Solvent.

Here are several keys to changing your business culture:
- You must know what you want it to become and why this is crucial.
- You must convincingly communicate the necessity and the direction of change to others—and to yourself. Communicate your vision of how you want it to be, your expectations and your enthusiasm.
- Change your business infrastructure to support the culture change: systems and procedures, workplace and equipment, etc.
- Address the concerns of your people, employees, customers, and vendors. Get their help, make it a team endeavor.

> *The culture is carried by all the people in your company. Only you are the impetus to change.*

- Be positive. It is not that the way you have been doing it is wrong, just that it is now time to move on to the new thing, and it is in everyone's interest.
- Make sure you have the right people. Give your people needed training; promote those who can take a leading role in bringing about your desired changes. If you bring in new people, hire those who already embody the new culture.
- You may need to let some people go, including long timers. Not just employees, but perhaps also customers, vendors, service providers. For example, your banker or accountant may find it very difficult to interact with you in the way you need.
- Get help. Business owners often bring in an outsider to communicate the change, to mark the change as something special, and to follow up. Bringing in the outsider helps you introduce needed changes in a way that does not raise so much resistance. It also helps mark the event as something special. "Our business has reached a stage where we need to make changes to go on to the next level. This pertains to me as much as it does to you. I am bringing in my business advisor to help us all make this transition."
- Be patient. This process takes time. All change is resisted. Behavior changes are resisted the most. Be persistent. Perseverance pays off.
- Provide on-going support. I often work with business owners and their employees over an extended period of time until the transition to the new way of doing things is firmly entrenched.

• As business owner, you are central to any shift in business culture. It starts with you and flows from you. You set the example and keep people on track. You resist their resistance and persevere.

As you start to make these changes, some people will enthusiastically climb on the bandwagon. Work with them first to produce some results. Others will hold back and be doubtful, but when they see good results, they also will climb on board.

Yet others continue to drag their feet. In some cases, you must replace these people or put them into a lesser position. Sometimes companies are reluctant to do this. They allow the foot dragger to hold back the whole company. Because old Jim has been loyal to the company, we cannot force him to change. Except that Jim is not loyal to the company anymore because he won't go where you want to lead. Also, he's probably miserable, because he recognizes—even though he's not saying so—that he cannot keep up.

Of first importance is communicating your vision of how you want it to be, your expectations and your enthusiasm.

## ASK YOURSELF . . .

1. Where does your company have a culture of smallness? How does this hamper you?

2. What do you want to accomplish that impels you to change your company culture?

3. Describe your desired culture of growth, ease, and satisfaction.

4. As you change, where will you encounter resistance?

5. How can you apply the Problem Solvent to change your company's culture?

## Chapter 13

# Build a Culture of Profitability

## When profitability is no longer optional

*"We had record-setting revenue last month, but even so, I had to loan money to the business rather than writing myself a paycheck," complained the business owner. "That did it! I decided right then that profit could no longer be optional; we have to be profitable! I will still provide excellent service and make our customers very happy, but not at the expense of profits."*

When your new business is starting up, you are often more concerned about getting any business in the door than in making a profit. You want to build awareness of your business, to build market share, to plow money back into growth and marketing. You will take any customer—profitable or not. Even high-tech companies who are funded by outside investors often put profitability far down on their list of priorities in the early going.

Furthermore, you *expect* your business to operate without profit. Business gurus tell you, "Don't count on becoming profitable during the first six months of operation...first year...first two years." In the early going, you may not pay yourself a salary. You live off savings, credit cards, your spouse, or your day job. Profit is optional! You just want to survive.

When you do pay attention to money, you focus on building your revenue. You measure business growth by revenue growth.

This may be an essential stage in the life cycle of a new business. (However, it is true that many businesses are profitable from the very beginning.) Yet, as your business grows and becomes established, this mentality no longer serves you. This realization may hit at different times, for example:

- You need a bank loan and the bank won't lend you money because you don't show any profit on your books.
- You are tired of working so hard and seeing so little money in your pocket.
- You want to pay yourself better so you can build up your wealth, put your kids through college, provide for your retirement. You realize you won't be able to do this working at minimum wage.
- You want to get a return on your investment of both time and money.
- You decide it is high time to build up the financial strength of your business for expansion, to weather business ups and downs, or to acquire another company.

When these things happen, you get to a point where you say, "Profitability is no longer optional for me!" You vow that from that point on, everything you sell must make a profit. Everything you purchase must pay for itself and allow a return on investment. Everyone you hire must contribute to the financial well-being of the company.

This is a key transition to becoming a "grown up" company.

Even after you take this vow of profitability, you may find it's hard to change old habits, some dating back to Day 1 of your business or even before. These attitudes and habits are the profitability killers for small companies.

### Profitability killers of small business

Here are money management habits and attitudes that thwart profitability:

- "If we earn a profit, it all goes to taxes anyway, so let's spend it."
- "When extra cash comes in, I go to BizToys Are Us."
- "Since my books are always way behind, I couldn't track expenses if I wanted to."
- "Times have been good. So we've hired a few extra people, bought new computers . . ."

- "Budget? I think I heard that word once."
- "With a home office, I merge business and personal expenditures. I have no idea which are which really."
- "Ask my bookkeeper."
- "We're a bit short of cash, so just charge it."
- "There's a part of me that still thinks making a big profit is somehow immoral."

Many of the other barriers we described in Section II make it much harder for you to operate profitably:

- You don't have enough help, so you wear all the hats. Thus you cannot focus on the most profitable use of your time.
- You have inadequate systems and procedures, so you operate inefficiently. You don't know what is profitable and what isn't; which employees are carrying their weight and which aren't.
- You have poor skills and capabilities for money management, people management, cost control.

*Lack of money is usually a symptom— not the cause— of problems faced by small business.*

- Your workplace and your equipment hold you back and limit your productivity and profitability.

To dislodge these old habits and make good on your vow of profitability, begin to put in place the twelve principles of small business profitability.

## TABLE 13-1
### Twelve principles of small business profitability

Go for break-out, not just break-even revenue.

Pay yourself first.

Spend no overhead before its time.

Know when you must spend money to make money.

Price for profitability.

Know the profitability of your next sale.

Hire a CFO, not just a CPA.

Create financial statements that serve you.

Set a spending plan and review performance regularly.

Watch costs like a hawk even when times are good.

Borrow money when you don't need it.

Keep your eye on the balance sheet.

## TWELVE PRINCIPLES OF SMALL BUSINESS PROFITABILITY

### 1. Go for break-out, not just break-even revenue

Instead of focusing on the *break-even* level needed to *survive*, calculate the *break-out* revenue needed for your business to *thrive*. To get from break-even to break-out revenue, add in the following amounts:

• The full market value of your contribution to your own company.
• A fair rate of return on the investment (both time and money) you have made in your company.
• Funds to cover the cost of expansion, replacement and maintenance, employee bonuses and incentives, and debt repayment.
• Funds for your special long-term needs, such as retirement and living the lifestyle you want. These items must be covered by the cash flow generated by your business.

*Break-even revenue + what you want and need = Break-out revenue.*

After you calculate the break-out revenue your business must earn to cover these needs, post your monthly or daily revenue target where you can see it every day.

### Plan for profit and cash flow

To operate at break-out, adopt a profit orientation, not just a revenue orientation. When you set your annual revenue goals include the amount of profit you need and want. Then use that figure to project the amount of business you need. Use your target rate of profitability to set prices, to make estimates and submit proposals.

In our annual plan workshops we have people turn their profit and loss statement upside down, putting the bottom line on top. You start with the amount you need for your bottom line then work backwards to determine the needed revenue from your business, and the number of customers or jobs.

How much profit do you need? Profit for a small business must cover these things:

• Your pay if you are a sole proprietor or have a partnership
• Debt repayment
• Your personal income taxes
• A fund for growth and a cushion for adversity

In addition to these items you must generate profit from your regular business operations to cover items that become business expenses once they are paid. For example:

### TABLE 13-2

| **Make the Business "Bottom Line" Your "Top Line"** | | |
|---|---|---|
| Turn your P&L upside down, so that the *bottom line*, or net profit, becomes the *top line*; i.e., the first thing you consider. | | |
| **How your P&L normally looks.** | | |
| Gross sales revenue | $1,000,000 | 100% |
| − Cost of goods sold, direct costs | 450,000 | 45% |
| = Gross profit | 550,000 | |
| Gross margin | | |
| (gross profit ÷ revenue) | | 55% |
| − Overhead, fixed costs | 350,000 | 35% |
| = Net profit (before your pay) | $200,000 | 20% |
| **Make the "bottom line" the "top line."** | | |
| Your paycheck (including taxes) | $120,000 | |
| + Overhead | 350,000 | |
| = Needed gross profit | 470,000 | |
| ÷ Gross margin | | |
| (known from prior operation) | 55% | |
| = Break even revenue | $855,000 | |
| Note that this business is larger than necessary to pay you what you need. A business breaks even when the Gross Profit = Overhead + Your Pay. | | |

- Bonuses and profit sharing for your employees
- Funds to cover needed upgrades, deferred maintenance, desired increases and staffing, increased benefits or raises

Your accountant will insist that these are all expenses, not profit, and this is true—after the fact. However, too many small business owners fail to anticipate these items when they project needed revenue, set prices, and make estimates. Your business may cover all your regular operating costs yet not produce enough surplus from operations to cover these added items—unless you plan for it!

For example, suppose you own a general contracting firm. Whenever you submit a bid for a job you of course make sure that you cover all the materials, labor and subcontractors and also cover a portion of your operating overhead. You know these costs from experience. But unless you consciously plan for it you may not include in your estimates enough to cover other outlays you want to make, such as giving year-end bonuses to your people, contributing to their profit sharing, or buying better tools for your crews. If you fail to do this you will never have enough at the end of the year.

A profit orientation also requires the following:
- You compare different types of work, different product lines or projects, etc., according to how much gross margin they will bring in, not just how much revenue. When we are small, we go after everything, including jobs that are not very profitable. Profit orientation means you are focused on those jobs, customers and products that are most profitable for you.
- You learn to compare the different parts of your business and different options based on the gross profit margin. "If I increase sales of A by 25%, how much profit will be generated?" "Over the next year, I could focus my efforts on doubling the sales of B, or doubling the sales of C. Which will be more profitable for me?"
- You find the activities that give you the greatest return on your time, especially if you are in a service business.

## 2. Pay yourself first

During the early stages of your business, your attitude may be, "I'll pay all the other obligations, and if there's anything left, I'll pay myself." This is a bad habit to get into. You are your company's most important employee. Why should you treat yourself worse than other workers? I recommend that you pay yourself a regular paycheck, even when you don't have the money to do so.

Figure out your paycheck: How much you need and want for current living cost, desired lifestyle, and long-term financial needs. Pay yourself this amount on a regular monthly basis. If you cannot do this now, how soon can you do it? If you don't see how you can ever pay yourself that amount then it is time to rethink your business. Why stay in a business indefinitely that does not pay you the amount you want and need?

Of course you take into account funds available from other sources: your spouse, investments, inheritance, pensions, etc. However, if your business does not provide you with a good return for your time over an extended period then it is really a hobby or a charity you run for your customers.

The amount you want and need should be the minimum amount you receive from your business. Cultivate the attitude that your business should provide you with a lot of money—much more than if you put the same amount of effort into working for another company. After all, you're taking the risk and putting in the entrepreneurial energy. You deserve to get paid for that.

Your pay to yourself should include:
- A return on your investment, time and money in the early stages of your business

• A premium for taking entrepreneurial risks. Some owners pay their employees better and more regularly than themselves. The employees receive more benefits and their pay is guaranteed. This is just the opposite of what it should be.

*Your earnings should be higher than your salary would be from another company.*

• A cushion to hedge against possible future downturns and adversity.

My book, *Pay Yourself First*, helps you calculate your paycheck and then figure out how large your business needs to be in order to pay yourself that amount.

## 3. Spend no overhead before its time

Fledgling small businesses often invest in office equipment, brochures and a staff before a cent is made. My advice: prove that you can make some money first before committing to big expenditures. I live near Silicon Valley, recently populated by high tech dot-commers funded by venture capital. It made my jaw drop seeing how fast these companies spent their investors' money. They called it the "burn rate." The business owners I deal with are spending their own money and do not have that luxury.

What is the smallest amount you can spend to produce the desired result? If you are not sure of the outcome, how can you test it by spending a little bit at a time before committing a huge amount on an untested program? For example, I have seen people spend thousands of dollars on slick new brochures, then discover that the way they were describing their business wasn't very effective. Why not use letters and less-expensive marketing pieces until you are clear on the most effective ways to present your business?

I have seen businesses commit to expensive new offices and tenant improvements on the strength of one big contract and then discover that their high monthly overhead crippled them during subsequent lean times.

## The blessing and curse of outside capital

It is often said that lack of adequate capital is the number one cause of new business failure. So having a significant sum of outside money—from savings, golden parachute, inheritance, trust fund, spouse, money from your family, venture capital, etc.—is a real blessing. It lets you get started. It gives you breathing room to develop the business.

At the same time, it can also be a curse. With this initial money, you get complacent. You spend too much on non-essential items. You go on too long without insisting on profitability. You take on jobs that are not profitable, so despite your initial capital you run up debt.

When your capital runs out you may not have developed the discipline of insisting on a profitable business, nor the skills for doing so. You may have committed to a level of overhead that is not justified by the business you are developing. Despite your initial nest egg, you go under.

## 4. Know when you must spend money to make money

You must know how to balance this principle with No. 3. You must have an appropriate workplace, needed help, and marketing materials that will impress your desired customers. The rule here is: spend money on things that will pay off.

- Get the most bang for your buck. What's the least amount you can spend to get the biggest result?
- Know how to calculate the likely payback period and how you can compare the payback of different options. We cover this in Chapter 15. For example, should you hire a PR firm or run an advertising campaign? Should you upgrade your old equipment or install new? Should you do the work in-house or farm it out?
- When you need to spend money, spend it. For example, a small manufacturer of unique household products got outside capital to market his products nationwide. He was scrupulously staying on his spending plan, but his financial backer said, "The heck with the spending plan, spend the money you need to produce the result right now. You have a limited window of opportunity and if you miss it our investment is lost."

## 5. Price for profitability

Once you plan for profitability, as we discussed above, then set your prices to assure this. Many small businesses under-price, often on the belief that they must provide more for a smaller price than their larger, better-capitalized competitors. This is the route to bankruptcy.

**Profitability in the face of competition.** Given the fact that you have low-ball competitors, how do you organize your business so that you can be wildly profitable even so? You must know what sets you apart from your competitors, know why your preferred customers do business with you rather than with someone else, and know how to communicate this to those you want to reach. This allows you to rise above "mere commodity" status to offer a specialty product or service, and to price accordingly.

If people don't see the unique benefit of what you offer them, they aren't willing to pay your price. If you can't get your price, you can't get the profit either. You cannot afford the help that frees you up to focus on achieving your vision.

Set your prices using two different approaches:

**A. Cost-based pricing.** What price will cover all your direct costs plus your overhead, your needed profit and your pay to yourself?

**B. Market-based pricing.** What is the highest price the market will allow you to charge?

If B is greater than A, charge B. If A is greater than B, go back to the drawing board:

- Re-engineer your product or service so that the cost of providing it—including contribution to overhead and needed profit—is no greater than the market price. Find ways to cut either direct costs or overhead.

Or

- Communicate the value to your customers so that they will be willing to pay more.

Imagine that you are an automobile dealer. Since you are new and want to build up your reputation, you are going to sell Cadillacs but only charge Chevrolet prices. Can you make a go of this business? Of course not.

*If customers balk at your price, you haven't communicated the value.*

Business owners complain to me that even though the quality they provide is what their customers want, the customers nevertheless ask for a price break. Imagine going into the Cadillac dealer and saying, "I really want a Cadillac but I only want to pay a Chevrolet price." What is the response of the Cadillac dealer?

If you are selling a high quality product or service and prospective customers balk at the price, then either you have not adequately communicated the value to them, or else they don't really want what you offer, in which case they are not a qualified customer for you.

## 6. Know the profitability of your next sale

This is one of those things that sounds obvious yet many business owners have trouble with it. You must know your Gross Margin, which is one of the most important numbers in your business. Here's how gross margin is calculated:

| | |
|---|---|
| **Gross revenue** | Total receipts from sales (based on history or projection) |
| **– Cost of sales** | Expenses you must incur in order to make particular sales |

| **= Gross profit** | What's left from gross revenue after you pay the cost of sales, but before you pay your overhead and yourself |
|---|---|
| **Gross margin = Gross profit ÷ Revenue** | Gross margin is the percentage of revenue left after covering cost of sales |

While simple in concept, many businesses have trouble with this calculation because they do not properly allocate costs between Direct Costs and Overhead—especially labor. Consider these examples where employees' time is split among different tasks:

| | **Direct labor tasks** | **Overhead labor tasks** |
|---|---|---|
| Hair salon stylist | Work with clients for hourly pay plus commission | Inventory work, clean up, open and close |
| Contractor's foreman | Oversee field crews | Talk with clients about additional work, submit time sheets for crew, travel time between jobs |
| Administrative assistant for consultant | Type up and edit reports for the consultant's projects | Bookkeeping, mailings, follow up calls, pay bills |

The path of least resistance is to allocate all this labor to one account; however, this practice prevents you from knowing the true costs—and thus profitability—of any of this work. You cannot accurately answer questions such as these: "When can we profitably hire another stylist?" "Did we complete that remodel project within budget?" "Which type of consulting project is most profitable?"

The biggest barrier to allocating labor properly is the necessity of tracking time use. Small businesses—both owners and employees—are notoriously resistant to this. But to have a profit orientation, there is no option.

## 7. Hire a CFO, not just a CPA

Most businesses have a CPA to help with tax returns. However, many small businesses have no one to fill the CFO (chief financial officer) function. You may be good at this role yourself but many small business owners are not, and rely on their CPA. But CFO and CPA have different financial functions. Many CPAs are not well suited for the CFO role, even if they think they are. Table 13-3 summarizes the difference between CPA and CFO:

## TABLE 13-3

## The difference between a CPA and a CFO*

| CPA | CFO |
|---|---|
| Reports on historical financial statements. Emphasis on verification and attestation of what has already transpired. | Helps manage current and future financial growth, and influences events to create and assure financial success. |
| Focuses on compliance matters: federal and state taxes. Audits. Occasional tax planning. | Anticipates. Plans and implements financial strategies to complement the business objectives of the company. |
| Adheres to conventions, requirements, and form over substance. Sometimes unwarranted emphasis on exactness. | Is generally more flexible. Considers alternatives without dogmatic constraint. Emphasizes displaying data to best support management and financial decisions. |
| Is responsible to a client vis-a-vis tax cycles: especially year-end. | Recognizes that events occur continuously, rather than at discreet moments. For example, your CFO may focus on your holiday season—October, November, December, and January—which spans two calendar years. |

*Adapted from *Increase Your Cash Flow*, by David Levinson, CPA, and Mike Van Horn

If you are relying on your CPA, use this list to size her or him up.

**What a CFO should do for you:**

1. Prepare financial statements.
2. Analyze financial statements and make them more meaningful. Catch blips and trends immediately.
3. Focus on generating cash flow.
4. Analyze profitability by product or market.
5. Cash flow projections
6. Inventory management
7. Help business owners create assets and income outside their business.
8. Assist in bank financing.
9. Stay responsible to you vis-à-vis tax cycles.

I recommend that you hire a professional to handle your CFO function even if you are good at it yourself. It is worthwhile for you to gain an outside perspective. You don't know it all. You can overlook things or fool yourself, and it is probably not a good use of your time.

For a small company, a CFO is probably not a full-time position. Hire a professional as needed, just as you do your CPA. This person may or may not be a CPA.

### 8. Create financial statements that serve you

Many small business owners are not financial wizards. If you feel intimidated by financial statements, you are not alone. Suppose you and I are going over your financials to see why your financial performance is not up to your expectations. As I review your statements I ask you some questions:

- How much are you spending on marketing? What are marketing expenditures as a percentage of your revenue?
- What is your total labor cost?
- What is the most profitable part of your business over the past year?

You peer at your financial statements, but we quickly determine that none of those questions can be readily answered by looking at them. Why not?

- Marketing costs are buried in such things as printing, advertising, postage, professional memberships, travel, and professional services.
- Labor cost is difficult to pinpoint because it combines salaries, payroll taxes, insurance, bonuses, and employment agency fees.
- You can't tell which part of your business is most profitable because you don't allocate labor costs that way, and you don't know how much time your people spend on different parts of the business.

*If your accountant won't give you the financial formats you want, fire him.*

These can be crippling deficiencies. If you don't have a financial background, you may throw up your hands in despair at the difficulty of getting needed financial information, and stop looking at your financial statements altogether. You may feel that it is your fault that you are not able to comprehend the statements produced by your bookkeeper or accountant, when instead you should say to them in no uncertain terms, "Prepare statements for me that I can understand and use or I will replace you!"

**Customize your financial reports** to give you just the information you need, and nothing else, to help you make better financial and management decisions. For example:

- Reorder and recombine numbers. For example, group together all the costs that relate to labor or to marketing.

- Split cost items and allocate to two different categories. For example, such items as printing, postage, or telephone may be part marketing expense and part administrative. If these are significant costs then divide them.

- Put the labels in the middle, so you don't have to trace your finger across a dozen columns of fine print.

Here is a statement that illustrates other ways you can customize:

| | Nov | Dec | Jan | 3-mo. Average | Year to date |
|---|---|---|---|---|---|
| Revenue received | | | | | |
| Billed work | | | | | |
| Cash on hand, 15th of month | | | | | |
| Line of credit balance, 15th of month | | | | | |
| Direct labor as % of billings | | | | | |
| Receivables over 60 days, 15th | | | | | |
| Contract backlog | | | | | |
| Sales per employee | | | | | |
| On-time completion rate (% of jobs completed by Promise Date) | | | | | |

- Pick the top six financial numbers you need to track on a regular basis, and create a statement that shows only these items. Mix and match items from your profit and loss statement and your balance sheet. Include items that are not on your financial statements.

- Bridge two years. Most tax returns require statements from January to December. But as a guide to management, statements that go across years may be more useful—especially if that encompasses your busy season.

- Use moving averages. There's nothing magical about monthly reports, especially if there is so much variation in your revenue and expenses that monthly figures make little sense. You may get more useful information by averaging the most recent three months, thus smoothing out large fluctuations that mean nothing. In January look at the average of October, November, December; then in February look at November, December, and January. Compare this with the average of the same three months the previous year.

• Calculate ratios. For example, track direct labor cost as a percentage of cost of good sold, or direct labor compared to overhead labor, or marketing contacts two quarters ago compared to sales this quarter. Watch for changes in these ratios over time. Many financial statements show each item as a percentage of gross revenue. This gives you a lot of superfluous data, for example, that bank charges equal 0.16 % of revenue. This may hide figures that should jump off the page and shout at you; for example, that your cost of goods sold has edged up from 45% to 47%.

Here's a simple measure that many small businesses use to calculate how much they will have available for special purposes. It often gets used to figure out "What bills can I afford to pay now?"

     Cash on hand

+   Expected cash receipts. This includes accounts receivable you are likely to collect within fifteen days, expected cash sales, prepaid deposits, etc.

−   Expected cash outlays (even if not on the books), accounts payable for this month, regular obligations such as rent, payroll, and paying yourself.

=   Likely amount available for unbudgeted expenditures.

Some would be satisfied with Cash + A/R − A/P. To this I add expected receipts and outlays that do not show up in Accounts Receivable or Payable.

Graph them—in color if need be. Do this not only for yourself but also for your key people who need to see financial performance data. I worked with the owner of a flower shop who could never get her people to price special arrangements to assure the proper margin. They seemed oblivious to the numbers. Finally, she graphed just two numbers: A) selling price, and B) cost plus needed mark-up. When A was greater than B the graph was green; when B was greater, it was red. She said, "When the chart is in the green, you get your bonus; when it's in the red, you don't." Within two months, there was hardly ever a dip into the red.

This takes a profound shift in your attitude, from, "How can I understand these statements my accountant gives me?" to "What specific financial data do I need to review, and how should it be displayed so it makes the most sense to me?" This approach is heresy to many accountants, so here's where you separate the CFOs from the CPAs.

Your bookkeeper may be the biggest culprit. I worked with the owner of a small jewelry maker who divided his time between running the business and producing jewelry. I told him he could not know the real profitability of different product lines unless he treated his own production time as a cost of goods sold. I developed a spreadsheet to demonstrate this. His bookkeeper got in a real huff: "You can't do it this way," she insisted. "He's a sole proprietorship. It's against the rules to treat his pay as a cost of business!"

The most implacable barriers may come from the computerized accounting systems most commonly used by smaller businesses. Just try customizing your statements the way I have proposed!

Accounting programs and generally accepted accounting practices are designed for the purpose of calculating taxable income, auditing, and comparing one company with another. To get statements that help you make better management decisions, you must supplement your official statements with ones that you—or your CFO—design for your needs. To get the flexibility you want, use a spreadsheet program. Design it so that it imports from your accounting program just the data you want, then arranges and displays it so that it makes the most sense to you and your key people.

> *Financial statements look backwards. You need forward-looking statements.*

Finally, get your statements done on time! Here is something that happens all the time. During my July meeting with a business owner I ask, "How was your June performance?" The response: "I'm still waiting on our May figures." This is inexcusable. It's like driving on the freeway while looking only in the rearview mirror. This man, while waiting two months for his elaborate computerized financial statements, pencils out on the back of an envelope the "real figures" he needs to make decisions right now.

## 9. Set a spending plan and review performance regularly

Don't just review financial statements one month at a time. Compare periods. Print out statements for all the months of the year on a spreadsheet. As you run your finger along one line item, you see how it changes over the year. A blip upward or downward instantly gets your attention; whereas viewing one month at a time may not.

Compare this year's statements to the same period for last year, or if you can, with the last several years. Pick the comparison that makes the most sense for you. This year with last year, this season with same season last year, the actual compared to projections.

Use your accountant, CFO, or other advisor for regular reviews to make sure you ask the tough questions and take any needed corrective action.

## 10. Watch costs like a hawk

Business growth often seems to conflict with business profitability. Growth requires spending up-front and often places huge stress on cash flow. But if you anticipate growth, you can make changes in your financial management that will make it easier to finance growth as it occurs.

Build cash flow discipline in anticipation of growth. Operate lean and mean even when times are good. Many companies get lulled into sloppy operations by growing sales. They get soft and flabby. They stop enforcing cost control disciplines.

**The money freed up by cost cutting goes directly to the bottom line.** Where can you save money? What overhead or direct cost items offer opportunity to spend less, and thus put more money right into your pocket?

The best way to explore this is to go through your Profit and Loss statement line by line. Look at each line and ask, "How could I squeeze some hard cash out of this expenditure in the coming year?"

It's best to print out your P&L and Balance Sheet in spreadsheet fashion, with a column for each month, plus the annual total. As you look at one line item across the columns, strange blips or dips jump out at you. (Often, you discover all the ways expenses have been recorded in the wrong general ledger account. I keep finding mystery numbers called "unallocated expenses." These need to be corrected before you can even answer these questions.)

Start with the largest, most variable items, wherein lie the greatest potential for savings: Marketing. Telephone. Labor. Insurance. Printing. Leases. Purchases for inventory.

You will probably need to spend more money and trim expenses at the same time. Trimming waste frees up funds for growth expenditures (or for trips to Maui).

| Line item that is ripe for pruning | Last year's amount | Potential % savings | This year's budget | How the savings will be made |
|---|---|---|---|---|
|  |  |  |  |  |

## 11. Borrow money when you don't need it

Your banker will confirm that it is tougher to borrow money when you need it desperately than when you don't need it. So plan ahead. Here's one way: Gain approval for a line of credit from your bank, then borrow a small amount of money, whether you need it or not. In a month or so, pay it back. Then borrow a little more, and pay it back. As you do this a few times, you build up a repayment record with your bank. Your line of credit limit will probably be raised. If you take other steps to protect your credit record, then when you need the money, you will already be approved.

As your company grows, sometimes you outgrow your bank. A bank that was comfortable giving you a $100,000 line of credit may balk when you need $250,000 to build out your expanded production facility. It is time to shop around for a new bank. See how they respond to this approach: "We would be interested in bringing our banking business to you if we can obtain a term loan for plant and equipment, plus working capital for expanded production."

## 12. Keep your eye on the balance sheet

Many small companies virtually ignore their balance sheet. For a cash-based service business, this may be understandable. But many companies with substantial inventory and fixed assets neglect their balance sheet. They may categorize outlays for new equipment, tenant improvements, or inventory increases as regular expenses on their profit and loss statement, rather than as changes in asset levels on the balance sheet. If you do this, it distorts your income for tax purposes, but it also makes it impossible for you to know how profitable your operations have been. Without reliable and consistent data on regular costs and revenues, how can you expect to have a culture of profitability?

To sum up: You need a combination of adequate financial systems, report formats designed to give you exactly what you need and no more, procedures to enter data quickly and accurately, competent people committed to producing timely reports, the will on your part to insist on this, and the commitment to use the reports when you get them.

### ASK YOURSELF . . .

1. What are your barriers to profitability? What keeps you from the profitability you want? How have you been complacent about profitability?

2. What parts of your business are least profitable? Why do you hold onto them?

3. What are your profitability dilemmas and sticking points?

4. How can you apply the Problem Solvent to build a culture of profitability, and become more profitable?

5. What numbers do you wish you could get to make better management decisions?

6. Sketch a financial statement that would give you the information you most need.

## Chapter 14

# The Dreaded Transition Hump

## *I. How to Minimize the Disruption of Change*

> *"A year ago, this point of sale and inventory control sys-*
> *tem looked like a sure thing. We would get it up and run-*
> *ning in a couple of months and it would pay for itself*
> *within a year. Where did I get the idea that I could delegate*
> *it all to my manager, and that it wouldn't disrupt our oper-*
> *ations? Wow! It took us six months and triple the budget to*
> *train people and tie it to our other system. It's paying off*
> *tremendously now, but boy, it took a year and untold hours*
> *of my time."*

To make any major change, you must cross over the "transition hump." Here's the way it works: You are now at Point A and wish to get to Point B. At Point A, you are already working as hard as you can. To make the changes needed to get to Point B, you must continue working full speed—and do more besides. The transition hump consists of the additional money and time you must expend in order to make the transition.

For example: Suppose you are now working sixty hours a week and would like to get it down to forty. You can do this in a variety of ways: training new people, installing better systems, bringing in better qualified people, delegating, etc. However, each of these may require you to increase from sixty hours up to seventy or even eighty hours initially before you get down to forty later.

## Your wish

You wish you could proceed smoothly from Point A to Point B.

 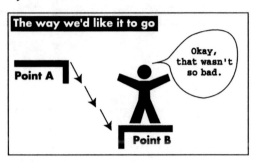

**Point A**—where you are now— is a difficult place to be in. Workload too heavy, not enough money, not enough help, confusion, lack of organization.

**Point B**—where you would like to be— is less stressful. Workload under control, more and better help, better systems, better organization, greater productivity, better cash flow. **Point A** is frantic. **Point B** is operating with ease.

## The reality

Transitions don't usually proceed smoothly. The transition hump implies greater effort, greater attention, more money spent in order to solve the problem. It gets worse before it gets better.

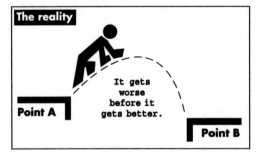

### Your fear

Your fear is that you will get up on the hump of seventy hours a week and stay there; it will never go back down.

The transition hump affects not only you but your people as well. Have you faced this phenomenon? Are you in the midst of it now? Are you reluctant to make a change because you can see it coming?

## Your goal

Your goal is to find the "path of least resistance" from A to B. To minimize the height, difficulty, and bumpiness of the transition hump, how can you minimize the impact of the transition?

Many of the changes we talk about in this book will include a transition hump. Here are typical examples of transitions, including some unanticipated consequences:

- A custom manufacturer installed software for logging sales, tracking orders and inventory, and scheduling production. *Transition hump:* It slowed things down at first because the sales people sought ways to get around it so they could grant favors to top customers.
- An architecture firm changed business culture. The owner decided to delegate job oversight to the project manager and henceforth stick to design and marketing. *Transition hump:* The owner had to educate his customers to trust the new arrangement. Initially he let the designers go around the project manager and come to him, thus undercutting her.
- A training business launched an e-commerce component on top of the regular business. *Transition hump:* The website with e-commerce capability took several iterations before it worked well.
- A consultant hired her first employee, requiring a new work station and change in her work style. *Transition hump:* She spent several weeks training; then the new woman left, so she had to hire a second one (this time with the help of a professional interviewer) and train her.
- A restaurant built an expansion next door, doubling available seating. *Transition hump:* The six-month project dragged out over a year, largely due to additional demands by the city during the project.
- A florist introduced a performance-based incentive system. *Transition hump:* The guaranteed easy-to-use software gave them fits, and initially the sales clerks manipulated sales dates to increase their incentives.
- A bakery hired a new manager from outside. Previously, people had always been promoted from within. *Transition hump:* Long-time employees resented the new man, and the owners didn't support him strongly at first.
- A specialty manufacturer farmed out a type of assembly it had previously done in-house. *Transition hump:* Rather than lay off the displaced workers, the company decided to retrain them for other production tasks.
- A professional partnership split up, each partner taking over part of the operation and some of the employees. They both moved to new locations. *Transition hump:* Each new entity missed the capabilities of the departed partner, and had to replace them.
- The founder retired, turning over the presidency to his daughter, who had worked there for ten years, and had recently received her MBA in an executive program. *Transition hump:* She made big policy changes; then two long-time managers left and she fired a third.

- The shop manager bought the company from the estate of the founder, who had died of a hearth attack. *Transition hump:* It took awhile for the other workers to accept a former co-worker as boss. Took him awhile to get used to holding people accountable. He still wanted to be liked as one of the guys.

I am describing a limited transition or project, rather than a lifelong undertaking. It has a beginning, middle, and end, even though sometimes it's hard to see the end when you are in the thick of it.

## Transition traps and horror stories

We all know horror stories where the transition hump becomes a "transition mountain," with a seemingly infinite increase in effort and frustration. Here are some typical ones:

"We underestimated the learning curve, how long it would take our people to become productive using the new systems."

"We failed to anticipate the difficulty in getting the vendor and the consultant to work together and stop blaming each other for the shortcomings."

"The equipment would not fit through the door. We had to take out a section of the wall."

"Why we undertook this in the rainy season I will never know."

"At the last moment, neighbors complained that we did not have enough parking available. That delayed us a month."

"Our expensive experts messed up, then competed to blame each other, billing us all the while."

"The project manager got fed up and left in mid-project."

"The farther we got into the new system, the more our people resisted. My partner, I'm sorry to say, was one of the biggest resisters."

"After we had spent $50,000 and six months on the new software, the vendor went bankrupt. We had to junk the whole system and go back to our old way."

"Frankly, I ran out of money. Costs were much greater than expected. I should have secured the extra line of credit before I started the project."

"If we had checked, we would have found out that the city had already scheduled to dig up the street for a new storm sewer at just that time."

"Since it went way over schedule, we were still struggling with it during our busy holiday season."

Beyond such things, there is just pure bad luck. For example, in the midst of your transition, a completely different crisis strikes. You lose a key person, somebody gets sick, something else breaks down. You lose—or gain—a major customer. An event outside the business throws a monkey wrench into the process, or requires your urgent attention.

## HOW TO REDUCE THE HUMP

Since it is unrealistic to expect to level out the hump, our strategy is to minimize it and make it as painless as possible. Your goal is to find the "path of least resistance" from A to B. Here are some guidelines to do just that. Use these to brainstorm how you might ease your own company's transition:

1. Be realistic in your planning. Allow needed time and resources.

2. Decide the best time frame beforehand: a) Big Bang, just do it all at once, versus b) Spread it out over time. Each approach has its place. The risk is that Big Bang tends to get spread out over time.

3. Think through the entire process. Brainstorm all the things—including tangential activities—that will be affected.

4. Be pessimistic. Assume your Doctor Doom attitude.

5. Set priorities. See if you can identify particular processes that are the bottleneck, and especially processes that will result in being either a linchpin or catalyst.

6. If you spread it out over time, then make sure you produce good results on a manageable part of it. This validates and energizes further efforts. Achieve a small but significant result quickly to generate energy to continue.

7. Cut back on other activities. Defer some of your current tasks until afterwards. Free yourself up to focus more on the transition.

8. Budget for it with both money and time, but recognize that it will probably cost more of both than you expect.

9. Bring in an experienced advisor to help you avoid making some of the mistakes.

10. Get the help you need—from your staff people, outside professionals, and outside resources. Rather than relying on your already overworked staff members, it may be better to bring in a special transition team, e.g., outside temporary contract workers to deal with the transition.

11. Allow for the learning curve: installation, customization, debugging, training, overcoming resistance and inertia, refining, and upgrading.

## *Transition smoothers: money, time, skill, and luck*

To successfully navigate a transition hump requires a combination of money, time, and skill—and a dose of good luck helps as well. These three are somewhat interchangeable:

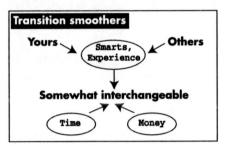

The smarts and experience can be yours (which requires your time) or someone else's (which requires your money).

If you spend more money you can get through the transition more rapidly. If you take your time, you can successfully get through the transition with less money. If you are skilled and experienced, so that you work smarter— say you have done it all before—you can traverse the transition with less time *and* less money. While none of this guarantees good luck, it's a good example of how you can create your own luck.

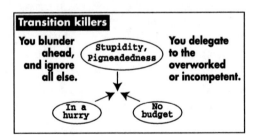

**The transition killer.** Unfortunately, all too often people approach these transitions with no money, in a big hurry, and display stupidity and pig-headedness. The stupidity can be yours (you blunder ahead, ignoring all else) or others' (you delegate to the overworked or incompetent). This assures bad luck.

An ironic rule of thumb is that any transition takes twice as long and costs four times as much as you expect. If anything, this is conservative. I have worked with people who estimated that installing a new inventory tracking system would take six months and cost $25,000. In actuality it took two years and well over $100,000. Your budget for your transition must include money, but also time and resources.

Here is the single biggest transition smoother:

**Get everyone involved in brainstorming** all the potential cost items. Think through all the steps, how long they will take, what must be done first, and where the bottlenecks are. Identify all the resources that will aid the process. Talk with your own key people, talk with vendors involved, and talk with others who have been through similar transitions. Ask them what they failed to take into account and for what they wished they had allocated more time or money.

Getting input from an experienced outsider is particularly valuable, for example:

- Suppose you are expanding into a neighboring town and making tenant improvements on a building you have leased. It may pay you to hire a general contractor who has worked with the local planning department and inspectors, who can make sure you don't skip small steps and can help you avoid costly mistakes.
- Suppose you are installing a large piece of equipment. You may hire someone in your industry who has previously used this machinery and has gone through the process of installing, troubleshooting and training the users. This may be safer than relying solely on the vendor's rep.

Obviously, you cannot anticipate every potential negative, but it helps a lot to brainstorm as much as possible. One of my clients has an employee who is called "Doctor Doom" because he is so good at thinking up all the worst case scenarios. While he can be very irritating, he has saved them a bundle because they have taken some of his gloomy warnings seriously. Ask yourself:

- How can you reduce or minimize the likelihood of any given negative occurrence?
- How can you reduce the impact if it does happen?

Asking these questions about a transition can lead to useful changes in your normal operation as well. For example:

What would happen if one of your key people left, got sick or incapacitated in the middle of the project? Asking this could lead you to cross-train key people involved so that the loss of any one person would be less devastating. This could be a valuable policy change even for the normal run of business.

What if it ends up costing a lot more than you anticipate? Asking this could lead you to secure an expanded line of credit from your bank long before you need it. (Even your banker will tell you that the best time to get money from the bank is when you do not need it. Do not wait until you must have it.)

One client asked, just before launching a major store redecoration, "What happens if the landlord does not renew our lease in three years?" This started them on a chain of thinking that led them to purchase their own building.

In each of these instances, a process that started as mitigating the hazards of a transition led to permanent beneficial changes in the way they did business.

From all this, develop your checklist showing activity, cost, time required, and resources needed. What are the critical periods and the bottlenecks? What activities have the greatest potential for going over budget and beyond schedule? The next couple of pages list many questions you can use for this purpose.

### Your role in the transition

What should you personally focus on during the transition? Presumably you are already working full time running your business. Are you going to take responsibility for guiding the transition on top of this? Unless you are Superman or Wonder Woman, that is a risky approach. Since you cannot do it all here are three options:

- You handle the transition and hand off some of your "regular" business activities to others.

- You run the business and delegate responsibility for managing the transition to someone else.

- A bridge position: you oversee both the regular business and the transition, but have strong people take over some of your major responsibilities in each area.

Another approach is to form a transition team that includes you and the key people involved, plus any outside experts. There are some real benefits to a team approach. You bring varied skills and contributions to the task. You share the burden. You brainstorm to work through the unfamiliar tasks. People can cross-train. The team continually debriefs and problem-solves.

*If you are already working full tilt, how can you also handle a major new project?*

Of course, there are dangers to a team approach. Lack of coordination, things falling through the cracks, disagreements and squabbles about who is responsible for what, or about who is running the store. But these are management issues that probably transcend your transition. A balanced team approach normally proves strongest.

The greatest benefit to the team approach is this: If you involve in its implementation all the people who will be affected by the new way of doing things, they get up to speed faster and have more ownership in the new way of doing things. On the contrary, if you present people with a *fait accompli* and tell them, "Starting Monday, you have to do it this way," you are likely to encounter resistance, subtle sabotage, and an incredibly long learning process.

### In-house or outsiders?

Can your regular people handle the transition? Should you hire a consultant? Or should you bring in a specialist to run the transition team? Often these options are complementary. Here are several typical options:

1. Your regular people handle the transition. They launch the new way, learn how to do it, and troubleshoot as they are doing their regular jobs.
2. A member of your existing team is reassigned to have sole responsibility for managing the transition.
3. You hire a consultant to advise you and help you plan and lay out the procedure. Then you and your regular people implement the new way.
4. You hire an experienced specialist who helps you and your people put together and launch the new way. The specialist takes charge of installation, customizing, training the users, and troubleshooting. His or her involvement is very hands-on in the beginning, but he or she leaves once the launch is complete.
5. You hire a specialist to get the new system up and running and who then stays to become the manager of the new function.

There are trade-offs with any of these:

- The outside consultant may have little commitment to seeing the project through to its completion, and will probably have conflicting obligations and be unavailable when needed most.
- The outside specialist may seem very expensive compared to one of your regular people.
- Your regular people may lack the needed skills, plus they already have a full-time regular job with you.

### Think through your transition beforehand

Use these questions to help you plan your transition to minimize the transition hump:

Describe the transition you intend to make.

Where are you beforehand at Point A? What is your current level of:

- performance and productivity?
- revenue and profitability?

- time use?

What difficulties impel you to make the change?
- Lost dollars, time or productivity. Customer dissatisfaction. Employee turnover.
- Lost opportunity. Inability to pursue opportunities.
- Being overworked and overburdened.
- Poor use of your time. A need to focus on different areas.

What is the desired end point? What is your target level of:
- Performance, productivity, and capacity?
- Expenditure, cost savings, margin, and reduced errors or waste?
- Better use of people's time, better teamwork, and better accountability?

What are your objectives regarding:
- Revenue and profit?
- Opportunities captured?
- Improved ease in your and your people's workstyle?

What sources of energy will sustain you through the tough transition?

Where can you get outside expertise to help you consider all relevant factors, plan realistically, and avoid costly errors?

List and describe all the steps. Get input from other people. Where are the critical steps and the bottlenecks?

Repeatedly ask, "To accomplish this, what else must be done first?" "What can go wrong?" "How can we ease this step?"

List all the cost items and amounts. If you don't know the amount, how will you get it? Is there a range of possibilities? How certain are you of each figure?

Estimate the time needed for each step: your time, your key people's time, and hired outsiders' time. Time needed for such things as hiring, negotiation, training, getting permits or approvals, and waiting for key resources to be available.

How will you mesh this transition with your ongoing operation to minimize disruption?

Who will take overall responsibility for shepherding the transition to completion? Define other key roles. Who will do what?

How will you free up the time needed—yours and your people's—to focus on this transition? What activities can you and your people defer or delegate?

What ongoing responsibilities must you continue throughout the transition period? What proportion of your and your people's time do these consume?

How will you finance the cost of the transition? How much cushion will you have available?

What outside events could affect the progress of your transition? Who should you check with; e.g., your landlord, neighbors, the city, local transportation department, utility companies, etc.?

What can hold back the process?

What do you fear might happen? What do your people fear might happen?

Where might breakdowns or confusion occur?

What obstacles might arise?

### Getting closure on the transition

This is a tough process you are going through. It is important to keep up the spirits of the troops. On the one hand, you need to debrief and review and problem-solve how to handle the glitches and make mid-course corrections. On the other hand, you need to acknowledge progress, success, and completion.

When you have indeed finished, declare completion, celebrate, acknowledge the contribution of the key people, and give suitable rewards. Then, debrief. What niggling details are left to be done? What trouble-shooting, what upgrades? And finally, now what? What is next for us? How will it be from now on?

### ASK YOURSELF . . .

1. What transitions are coming along in your business (or are already here)? How are you likely underrating the impact on your normal operation?

2. What are the biggest unknowns about this transition?

3. What should your role be during this transition?

4. Who should have what special roles during the transition?

5. What outside resources are available to ease your transition hump?

6. How can you minimize the impact and expense of this transition?

7. When you have successfully completed this transition, how will you celebrate?

## II. HOW TO GET THE BANDWAGON ROLLING

How can you introduce change so that those who are going to be affected by it will be enthusiastic, rather than resistant?

In your ideal business, once you decide upon a needed change, you would just announce it: "Starting next Monday, we will all..." and all your people would willingly accept that new way of doing things. Alas, it rarely works this way! Instead, you find yourself exhorting, cajoling and threatening—and sometimes backing off and giving up on the change.

> *You think you're asking, "Pretty please?" They hear you command, "You will do it!"*

Whenever a new way of doing things requires people to change their behavior, there will likely be resistance. This is true even when the people involved strongly back the change and will clearly benefit from it. The very process of changing things just raises resistance.

You can minimize this resistance and speed progress by the *way* you introduce the change. Here are some general guidelines on how to bring about successful changes of the type we have been discussing. But first, let's look at the worst ways.

### The 12 worst ways to introduce change

- Surprise your people by springing it on them.
- Issue a fiat: "Starting Monday, everyone must . . ."
- Introduce change on a whim: "Hey, I had a good idea; why don't we..."
- Assume you know best and ignore peoples' questions and concerns.
- Seek the input of your people and then ignore it.
- Say one thing, do another.
- Keep everyone guessing.
- Let negative rumors spread because you haven't said enough/anything.
- Play down the burdens and hassles involved.
- Start the project and then abandon it.
- Make the change seem like punishment or extra work.
- Wait until the change is forced upon you, then do it in crisis mode.

To discover the *best* ways to introduce change, look at the opposites of the worst ways.

## GUIDELINES FOR SUCCESSFUL CHANGE

The following guidelines are for changes that have a "political" element, that is, any change that will likely arouse strong opinions or resistance, and for which success depends on the support of the people involved. This includes a greater number and variety of changes than you might think. "All I wanted to do was change the type of fluorescent bulbs we use; I had no idea this would rouse such heated discussion!"

### 1. Treat the change as a shift in your business culture

Many of the changes we want to make seem, on the surface, to be just a new system, a new piece of equipment, and/or a new procedure. But they are really causing a complex change in the culture of your company, as we discussed in chapter 12, and need to be treated as such.

For example, you say to your people, "I want to replace our old way of relying on verbal instructions. We all see the flaws. Instructions are misunderstood. Steps get dropped out. Deadlines are missed. I want to replace it with this computer checklist system." It sounds straightforward to you, but people may think to themselves, "This is just the camel's nose under the edge of the tent. Before long everything will be systematized; we'll have to do everything by checklists. Our informal working atmosphere will be gone." Even if people don't verbalize this feeling, it can affect their morale and behavior. It's important for you to be attuned to these reactions and address them as I describe below.

### 2. Take leadership

Your business is not a democracy, nor is it a dictatorship. Your people want your leadership, and they want their voices heard. They want decisiveness, and they want decisions to make sense.

### 3. Do your homework; lay the groundwork

Thorough planning reduces the glitches that arouse resistance.
- Do a project plan, including budget, timeline, people assignments, and other resources. Assign project management. Delegate subprojects. Assign tasks, assemble the resources and set timelines and milestones.
- Include in your initial plan all the needed training, troubleshooting, follow up, and ongoing support.
- Brainstorm all needs and contingencies, including "worst case scenarios." Consider all the things around the change that will be affected.

- Select the best time to make the change. You might find a symbolic reason or starting point, e.g., New Year, a new employee coming in, or a new consultant or advisor is hired.
- Identify measurable milestones and results so that everyone can see the benefit of making these changes.

### 4. Involve all those affected by the changes

Often change in one area affects everyone; let them help create and plan for the transition. Address their concerns. "This new system will make us all more productive, but it will require some changes in the familiar methods, and it will take a little while to get accustomed to. I want you to help me figure out how to address these concerns."

### 5. Apply the Problem Solvent

What systems or procedures would help make this change?

What help or outside support would help make this change?

What skills or capabilities would help make this change?

What physical changes in the workplace or new equipment are needed?

How are your management style, practices, habits, attitudes, or beliefs a barrier to this change?

### 6. Build acceptance

Give people the big picture. Remind them of why it is important to make this change and how it will benefit them. Cast the desired change in ways that address their goals, aspirations, and motivations as well as their fears and reservations.

*There are early adopters, bandwagon jumpers, laggards, and change saboteurs.*

Start with your allies, then build outward. Who are your natural allies in this effort? Who will support your initial efforts and be enthusiastic? How can they help you build support?

Build a "bandwagon effect." When it comes to acceptance of new ideas or products, you often hear the terms "early adopters," "bandwagon jumpers," and "laggards." If you can, focus initially on the people who are comfortable with new things, who will adopt an idea and help you launch the new way. Others will climb aboard once they see results. Some laggards will hang back. They prefer the old way, yet many who initially resist will eventually come around.

A fourth group—those who will never get on the bandwagon—must ultimately be let go.

## 7. Address questions, concerns, and objections

Acknowledge that this is a significant shift from the old, familiar way. "It can be tough changing the way we're all used to doing things." Be frank about likely rough patches during the transition; don't try to be a Pollyanna and ignore them.

Listen for objections and watch for resistance. Sometimes you are the worst person to do this because you are so focused on the task. You may need someone else to watch the dynamics of the people in the situation.

Listen for the things that are not being said. What's the elephant in the room no one is mentioning? "We're afraid we'll have to work harder . . . there might be layoffs . . . schedules will change." If you spot those concerns—voiced or unvoiced—address them directly, "I recognize a lot of people are concerned about this. I take your concern seriously."

See if you can anticipate questions and concerns. Talk with the skeptics, the adversaries and the indifferent. Honor their points of view and listen for the validity of their concerns. Such employee concerns are like customer complaints. You can fear or resent them, or see them as an invaluable source of feedback.

How can you structure your plan of change to meet all legitimate concerns?

Deal with resistance and concerns by problem-solving face-to-face (whether in the group or one-on-one). Don't allow excuses or blaming. Come from the point of view that together you are going to make it work.

## 8. Tackle resistance

Resistance comes from supportive and well-meaning people—it isn't necessarily antagonistic. It can come from long-time employees, your partner, spouse, co-owner, or even from you. Yes, you! You, as owner, are an enthusiastic backer of the new system. You want the benefits, yet you resist the change and become part of the problem yourself. If your people sense this, then you give them tacit permission to vacillate and backslide.

Learn to recognize these common negative reactions to change. How will you address them?

- Inertia. Any change is resisted. Its value must be proved.
- Not invented here reaction. "If we didn't come up with the idea, it can't have much value."
- Busy-ness. "It sounds great, but we have way too much to do already."
- Bad timing. "We can't do this just now. We need to wait until after the summer season."

- "It's just another whim of the boss. If we drag our feet, she'll get tired and forget about it." This is an important comment on *your* management style.
- Fear. "I'm afraid I'll be held accountable for all of these tough things in the future."
- Resistance to your mandate. You think you are asking, "Will you do this, pretty please?" while others hear you demand, "You will do this!" Perception is reality!

How can you create allies from people who are initially indifferent or against you? By heeding their concerns, and producing positive results.

Some people will smile and say, "This is a great thing." But then they will pick it apart and criticize you behind your back. For example, a long-time loyal employee may subtly resist things you want her to do that push beyond her comfort level. These might include mastering a new technology, adopting new systems, logging time or activities, supervising others, or even participating in the coordination meetings for the big transition.

This puts you on the spot. You are loyal to her but you can't let her dictate the pace of change. She has done her job well up to now but now the job requirements are changing. Can she adapt? Is she willing to learn? How can you make it easier for her?

Her initial resistance may melt away once the change is made and positive results are apparent, but it may not. She may not be happy with the new responsibilities, and on top of that feel guilty for letting you down. She may well be happier elsewhere.

**The Foot Draggers' Club.** Some who resist turn out to be saboteurs. Unfortunately these might be long-time employees. They may pay lip service to the change yet drag their feet to the extent that the process is endangered. They may seek out others who don't want to change and reinforce each other in their resistance. Their hidden agenda may be to prove that the new process won't work so you will go back to the old way of doing things. It is dangerous and debilitating for you to allow this to spread. In most cases you will have no choice but to get rid of such people.

## 9. Watch for hidden barriers to change

Examine how the way your company does things hinders desired changes in behavior.

- Your company culture. Attitudes, beliefs and work styles of people within the organization, especially yourself, other owners, or your managers.
- Work rules, procedures, and performance standards. Look for conflicts and contradictions with what you want to implement.

- Company policies or incentive programs that reward performance that goes against what is required by the desired change. Even your mission statement may need to be re-examined in this light.
- How you and your managers monitor performance and give feedback.
- Standards of hiring, promoting, and letting people go. For example, if you want to increase commitment and productivity, there must be consequences for lack of commitment and low productivity.
- The workplace environment. How do the physical surroundings, individual work spaces and equipment limit desired changes in behavior?
- Attitudes or practices of those you work with, including customers or clients, competitors, suppliers, financiers, bankers, legal advisors, and other businesses in your community. For example, your customers always request to see you rather than working with one of your employees.

### 10. Stick to it

Once you get started, stick with it. Don't let people's resistance wear you down. Otherwise, people say, "Well, the boss had another crazy idea. But nothing's really going to change. If we just hold out for a few weeks, she will forget about this and it will go away." In the face of this, you get exasperated and think, "It's just not worth it. Maybe we shouldn't introduce the whole thing so fast. Instead, we'll phase it in over the next year." Then the resisters have won. They have stopped you from implementing the change you need. The next time you want to implement change, it will be even harder, because the number of those who say, "We can get the boss to give this up," will have grown. So it is very important for you to be steadfast.

- Make sure you use the data generated by the new system or procedure. Not doing so says, "This isn't really important."
- Cut people some slack, allow for the learning curve, but recognize that ultimately those who cannot get with the change must depart.
- You must set the example. Watch for backsliding on your own part, and if you do slip, handle it as the others must.
- Acknowledge people for their progress. You can do this one-on-one or in meetings. Learn to cheerlead.
- Handle backsliding only after you give people compliments for progress. Don't cast blame; instead problem-solve. "We did this part really well. On the second part, we slid back a little bit. Now, let's do

some problem solving and see how we can improve that over the next few weeks."

The process may get knocked off track. Interruptions and disruptions occur. How should you deal with the glitches that inevitably arise? Apply these guidelines iteratively, getting successively closer to success and completion. Ask the Problem Solvent questions above for whatever happens.

### 11. Know when to change course

Despite my talk of steadfastness, there will be times when the new way is not working and you need to change course. When you must do this, announce it. "We have been pursuing Plan A, but it is not working, so we are shifting direction, and now implementing Plan B."

Here's a story: A specialty manufacturer installed expensive new job costing and inventory tracking software. It was difficult to learn, but the president insisted that people stick with it. He refused to even look at reports prepared the old way. The new system was cumbersome but promised to provide all the reports they needed for their growing company.

Months passed with inadequate reports. He was angry when he saw his production people writing bits of data on scraps of paper. They responded, "Boss, we just can't get the spot product reports we need from the new system." His accountants agreed.

> *We've done it! Good job! Thanks for hanging in there!"*

He brought everyone together to compare notes. "We paid $50,000 for this system: are you saying you can't make it work?" His controller gave him a summary of the things it could and couldn't do. He made his decision: "We're dumping it. My mistake for not doing this months ago. Accounting recommends we go to this simpler system; it's more flexible, but takes more programming. Here's how I think we can make the transition. Give me your feedback."

If you have to change, change decisively. Debrief on the failed change only to avoid mistakes the next time. Do no blaming nor looking back. Move forward to the next thing.

### 12. Declare completion

When you are satisfied that the change is complete—or virtually complete—then announce completion. "We've done it! Good job! Thanks for hanging in there!" Have a celebration. Reward everyone.

## ASK YOURSELF . . .

These questions can help you think through any change situation before-hand:

- How is the change you desire to make in your company likely to engender resistance?

- How can you introduce the change so it is most likely to be viewed favorably?

- How can you make a small initial difference to show benefit right away?

- Who are your natural allies in this change? Who will support your initial efforts? What do you need from them?

- Who is likely to feel threatened by the desired change? How can you find out or anticipate their questions or concerns?

- How should you present your plan to them in a way that addresses their fears and reservations?

- How can you structure your plan to meet their legitimate concerns?

- How can you create allies from people who are initially indifferent or against you?

- How can you exert leadership in a way consistent with your goal?

- When should you review progress and make mid-course corrections? Who should be involved in these midcourse corrections?

## Chapter 15

# Calculate the Benefit and Cost

### *Is the benefit worth the cost?*

It can be very expensive to make the kinds of changes we have explored in this book. Are they worthwhile? Will they pay off for you? How can you figure this out? How can the benefits of making such changes be estimated? Here are some straightforward ways to look at both the likely benefits and the costs, and to compare them. Whether you scribble numbers on the back of an envelope, or use a sophisticated analytical program on the computer, these things are essential for you to know about the changes you want to make:

- Initial costs of the project
- Ongoing costs
- Revenue stream it will generate
- How soon this revenue will start
- The cost of capital

### *The cost of applying the Problem Solvent*

When you apply the Problem Solvent to boost your growth, profitability or ease, you must view it as an investment for which you put in time and money with the expectation that it will more than pay itself back. If it doesn't, then *economically* it is not a good investment, even if you choose to do it for other reasons.

### *The cost of changing your management style*

In chapter 5, The Inner Game of Growth, we discussed how you make changes in your management practices, habits, attitudes, and beliefs (M-PHABs). What is the cost? Part of this involves hiring and putting in new systems or equipment, thus should be evaluated by the tools in this chapter. The remaining "inner" part is largely a matter of your time.

But keep in mind that not all desired benefits are financial. For many of your desired changes—especially those related to increasing your ease of operation—making more money may not be your *primary* impetus, but it is important nevertheless.

| DESIRED CHANGE | | BENEFIT |
|---|---|---|
| Take more time off | *Leads to* | Better health, better relations with your family, time for other important activities |
| | *Also leads to* | A company that is organized in a more professional way so that its market value is increased |
| Reduce stress and improve my health | *Leads to* | More energy, renewed vigor and creativity, renewed sense of purpose |
| | *Also leads to* | Re-energized troops Improved competitive position |

What is the value of increased health, well being, happiness, satisfaction, and longevity? Priceless!

What is the value of a business that runs with greater efficiency, productivity, and profitability? This we can put a price on.

## HOW WILL THE CHANGE BENEFIT YOU?

Since many of the benefits you anticipate are tough to quantify, start out by answering some general questions like these:

1. What is the biggest desired change you want to make in your business?
2. If you accomplish this, your business would . . .
3. The benefit to you would be . . .

4. Estimate the monetary value of the change:
   The financial benefit could be as much as $ ____ But would surely be
   at least $ ____.
5. How else can the desired change help your operations, e.g.:
   Increase productivity
   Make better use of your labor, space, and expertise
   Allow you to react more quickly to opportunities or threats
6. If you accomplish these changes, how much would your business
   grow over the next few years: 10%, 50%, 100%, 10 times?
7. How much would your profitability improve? Put a number on the
   financial benefit to you personally.
8. Besides financial benefits, what are the most valuable effects the
   desired change could bring to your business? How long will it take to
   realize them? Can you put a monetary value on these non-financial
   benefits?
9. How would your ease of operation improve?
10. How would your personal satisfaction increase?
11. How would your lifestyle improve?
12. What is your *confidence level* that you will achieve the desired benefits?
    What is their likelihood?
13. What will it cost you if you do *not* make this change?
14. Given the benefits you identified, how much *should* you be willing to
    pay to make the change? Would you pay 10% of the increase in net
    profit for the first year? 50%? 100%?
15. Look at the desired change from the other side:
    The cost would be at least $ _____
    But could be as much as $ _____
16. If you make the changes, what are the largest costs you will incur in
    both money and time?

## THE COST OF *NOT* MAKING THE CHANGE

The cost of staying the same is an opportunity cost (i.e., the cost of an
opportunity not taken). Not making the change you know you need puts a
lid on your growth, requires you to keep working long hours, and prevents you from using your time for other things.

It's impossible to calculate money not made from a missed opportunity. After the fact, you see others passing you by. "How come her business
has made such great strides, and I'm still stuck here?" You have less capital to finance growth, less cushion for tough times, and less freedom to
pursue exciting new challenges than this other business that made needed
changes.

You can't stay the same. A business owner told me she was reluctant to put in the energy and money to upgrade her operation. "I don't want to put in the effort to grow, I just want to coast along as we are now." My response: "You can only coast if you are going downhill."

If the financial benefits are not substantially greater than the costs, you are not likely to undertake the effort, nor should you. But there are two problems with this:

- You may anticipate major non-financial benefits from the change, but even so you must pay for them in hard cash.
- You may see large potential financial benefits, but they are quite uncertain.

*You can only coast if you are going downhill.*

## HOW DO YOU JUSTIFY THE COST?

For many of the changes discussed in this book, the questions above are as far as you need to go to decide whether they are worthwhile. But if they require substantial investment of money and time, you'll want to make a more thorough analysis. To see if a change makes sense financially, start by comparing the cash you would spend with the new cash you would expect to bring in over time, using the Uses and Sources of Cash format that follows. This will help you answer either of these two commonly asked questions:

- When will it begin paying for itself?
- What is the payback period?

### Cash vs. profit

Should you estimate your increases in terms of profit or cash flow? In the long run they should even out, but in the short run they may diverge quite a bit. I recommend you focus first on cash. You can't use "paper profits" to cover your payroll or rent. You want to avoid this scenario: "The faster our sales increased, the tighter the cash squeeze we faced. Our P&L looked great, but all our so-called profit was in inventory and accounts receivable—not our bank account."

## USES AND SOURCES OF CASH

The Uses and Sources of Cash format (table 15-1) works for any change that costs money and takes time, from hiring a new person to building a factory. It is built from your answers to these questions:

- What are the up-front costs, including the cost of your time?
- What are the ongoing costs per month, including the cost of your time?

**TABLE 15-1**
**Uses and sources of cash format**

|  | 1. Start-up period of cash | 2. Pre-revenue period (no. of months) | 3. Revenue-earning period (for each month) | 4. Useful lifetime (in mos.) | 5. Total over lifetime |
|---|---|---|---|---|---|
| A. **Uses** of cash | Initial expenditures | Ongoing costs | Ongoing costs |  | Total lifetime costs, including cost of capital |
| B. **Sources** of cash | From cash on hand, current operations, or savings | Added working capital if needed | New revenue earned |  | Total revenue earned by the investment |
| C. Time as money | Money value of the time you and others put in | Your ongoing management time | Your ongoing time / Your time saved or leveraged |  | Net savings of your time; increased value of your leveraged effort |
| D. Uses minus Sources | Uses greater than Sources: Additional capital needed | Uses still greater than Sources: Working capital needed | Sources are greater than Uses: Generate funds to recover capital |  | Return on the investment |

- How much revenue (or savings) will this generate each month, including your time saved?
- How soon will the new revenue or savings commence? How long must you bear the cost before the revenue covers it?
- What is the cost of capital? What is the interest rate on money you borrow; or if you spend your own funds, what is the interest you forego?

I introduce the format here, and describe how you create your own tailored version later in the chapter.

## *Get all the costs*

If you start with the costs of the project—easier to quantify than the revenues—you can calculate a target revenue needed to make the project worthwhile. "Initial costs" are one-time costs near the beginning of the project, while "ongoing costs" are more regular periodic payments that may continue indefinitely. For example:

New employee **Initial costs.** Hiring costs, advertising, fee to employment agency. Training costs, salary paid until they are productive. Work station and equipment, phone, computer, software (installation and customization), supplies, tools, and equipment.

**Ongoing costs.** Salary plus payroll taxes, costs of benefits, health care, vacation, paid holidays. Ongoing training. Bonuses, incentives, raises.

New equipment **Initial costs.** Purchase price, shipping, installation, modifying the premises, electrical or data network connections. Related equipment, material and supplies. Changes to other equipment or workflow necessitated by the new piece. Work interruption. Debugging, customization, training the users, developing training and procedures materials, learning curve of the users.

**Ongoing costs.** Financing or leasing costs, salary of users, maintenance, materials consumed, spare parts and tools, electricity used, increased insurance, upgrades.

New software **Initial costs.** Cost of testing and selecting. Purchase price. Upgrading of computers to accommodate more powerful software. Installation, customization, debugging, training of users.

**Ongoing costs.** Upgrades. Troubleshooting. Ongoing training, especially for new users. Additional licenses.

| New or larger facility | **Initial costs.** Finding it. Negotiation and legal costs. Permits. Build-out. Fixtures, furniture, signage, equipment, landscaping. Contractors, designers. Phone, electrical, other utility connections. Deposits. Moving. Work disruption. Hiring new people and replacing people unwilling to make the move. New business cards, stationery, marketing materials. Disposing of old equipment and fixtures. Grand opening party. **Ongoing costs.** Increased rent, utilities, insurance, taxes. Equipment leases. |
|---|---|

## Time as money

In a traditional Sources and Uses of Cash statement, there is no provision for entering your time—except as you pay yourself a salary. However, for small businesses—especially sole proprietorships—the owner's time spent on a project is probably a major factor. Ignoring the value of your time (and the time of your other people involved in the project) distorts the true cost of an investment and makes it impossible to meaningfully compare two alternative investments.

*Your time is often the greatest cost of making the desired change.*

Assign a dollar value to your time (as we discussed in chapter 11), and compare time invested initially to either money earned or time saved later. You can do the same for any of your people. To do this, you must track how much of your time is used on the project. For example, in my case, I could compare the time it takes me to write this book to the increased revenue I can expect to earn later (except that it's too frightening to think about how much time it actually takes to write a book!). My expected returns come not just from selling books but from other opportunities the book opens for me. The return on your time invested take three forms:

- Net savings of your time. For example, you invest time developing a code book for standard design elements and teaching your drafters how to use them. Thereafter, you save ten to twelve hours a week on routine drafting design.
- Increased return on your leveraged effort. For example, you train three of your technicians to handle inspections only you could do before. You now have three more people conducting the inspections, thus tripling your capacity while freeing you to focus on the toughest (most lucrative) jobs.
- Increased return on your creative effort. For example, you laboriously create a job-tracking system tailored to your type of business. By

advertising this system through your industry association, you end up licensing it to other companies all over the country.

## WILL IT PAY FOR ITSELF?

Here are two simple "back of the envelope" approaches to check the financial worth of a potential investment.

You are more likely to ask, "Will it pay for itself?" when the initial investment is relatively small compared to the stream of revenue (or savings) it generates, e.g., hiring a sales rep, renting space, leasing equipment, or launching a marketing campaign.

If you add something that costs a regular amount per month, how much must your revenue increase to at least break even, i.e., make you as well off as you were beforehand?

A key point: you must recover this cost not by increased revenue, but by increased gross profit, i.e., what is left from sales revenue after covering direct costs, such as cost of goods sold.

For example, suppose you hire a new person at $3000 a month, including benefits, payroll taxes, etc. Suppose your cost of goods sold (CGS) on sales is 60%, i.e., from $1000, your direct costs are $600, leaving $400 gross profit. Thus your gross margin (gross profit divided by gross revenue) is 40%. Using these figures, you can calculate how much your sales must increase to cover the cost of this new employee:

| Required increase = in revenue | Increased cost: $3000 per month | ÷ Gross margin: 40% or .4 | = $7500 per month |
|---|---|---|---|

Turn this around. If your sales increase by $7500 per month, the cost of those sales is 60%, or $4500, leaving you $3000 per month, enough to cover the pay of the new person. You would break even.

Here's the *wrong* way to look at this: "I hired Joe at $3000. He brought in $4000 more in revenue, so I am better off." Not so. You are actually losing $1400 per month compared to before, if your cost of goods sold is 60%.

Now of course you don't want to hire a new person and go to all the trouble of training and managing them if you are only going to break even. You want a new hire to bring in much more profit than they cost. But now you know the break-even floor: any revenue lower than $7500 per month means you are worse off financially than before.

This $7500 per month might be produced directly by the person you hire—e.g., sales they make that wouldn't be made otherwise—or by making the crew they join $7500 more productive. Perhaps the new hire allows you (or other key people) to be more productive, as in this example:

"If I hire a second project manager, it will free me up to bring in more business. If I'm not managing projects myself, I gain ten to fifteen hours per week that I can devote to selling. I should be able to bring in two or three more projects per week; say, ten more per month. With a new project manager, we'll be able to handle that added work."

"Our jobs average $5000 with a gross margin of 30%. Ten more jobs per month means 10 x $5000 x .3 = $15,000 per month increased gross profit. The new project manager will cost about $4000 per month. Net profit increases $11,000 per month, or $130,000 per year. I'd be crazy *not* to hire a project manager."

## The learning curve

If a new person takes awhile to get up to speed, then the amount you pay during the learning period must be recovered by later productivity. This amount goes into column 2, "ongoing costs of pre-revenue period" in the Uses and Sources of Cash format above.

## WHAT IS THE PAYBACK PERIOD?

Ask this when the initial investment is large and the payback takes quite awhile, e.g., when moving into a larger facility or building a factory. This is an inexact tool, but gives an easy-to-calculate first approximation of whether a potential investment makes sense.

Once you have your best estimate of the initial and ongoing costs, you can calculate how long it will take for the increased profit to repay the investment.

A) Initial and ongoing investment        $_____

B) Months/years until the new person or thing begins generating profit _____.

C) Estimated monthly/annual profit due to this investment thereafter $_____.

D) Payback period = B + (A ÷ C)

For example: "Our new inventory tracking software cost us $50,000 by the time it was fully operational and all our people had been trained to use it—which took about five months. By using our materials and components better, we cut our cost of goods sold by ten percent. That added four percent to our bottom line. Since our monthly sales are $100,000, we recovered the cost of this system in only thirteen months after it became operational." (4% x $100,000 = $4,000 = monthly increase in profit. $50,000 cost ÷ $4,000 = 12 to 13 months. Add the 5 pre-operational months; thus the payback period is 18 months after it was purchased.)

Remember to use increase in profit, not just increase in revenue.

This approach ignores the cost of capital, which can be a drawback. But for many projects, the uncertainty in your initial cost estimates, added revenue, or savings is much greater than the cost of capital.

It can be difficult to put meaningful numbers on the financial benefits generated over time. But give it a try. If you can't justify these changes financially, why are you making them?

## Useful lifetime

**Staff**. It may seem callous to talk about the useful lifetime of a new employee, but look at it in terms of turnover rate. How long will a new employee likely stay with you? For high-turnover positions you cannot justify very high hiring and training costs. Conversely, if extensive training is essential, you'd better make sure you have a workplace that will keep people satisfied and productive.

**High tech**. When making such a capital investment, ask how long this item will be a useful asset. Make sure the payback period is much less than the useful lifetime. For example, a print shop installed a sophisticated $50,000 electronic device, figuring it would boost their sales and keep them competitive. It did boost their profit—by about $1000 per month. However, because the technology was changing so rapidly, the competitive lifetime of the equipment was only about three years. By the time it was obsolete (albeit still fully functional) they had recovered only about three-quarters of its cost.

**Equipment**. Unlike high tech, the useful lifetime of a quality piece of equipment that doesn't become technologically obsolete may be greater than your lifetime. The owner of a custom frame shop showed off a strange contraption: "It's a mat cutter that cuts ovals. The technology hasn't changed much in a century."

**Real estate**. If you lease a facility, link calculations of useful lifetime that depend on that location to your remaining lease period. If you have three years left on your lease, don't make expensive office upgrades that will take six years to pay for themselves unless you have locked up your option to renew.

If you purchase commercial real estate—especially in my part of the country—its value will probably increase. This can put an upper limit on the useful lifetime of continuing your business at that location. Rents may increase faster than you can raise prices of your products to compensate. Your business rents from you, but you may not charge yourself the market rate. One man shut down his business and became a commercial landlord when he discovered he could make more money renting out his building

than using it for his own business. Another company I work with antici-
pates making this transition in about five years. Thus the useful lifetime
for any new project they undertake now would be five years at the most.

You may not know the useful lifetime of an asset or project. It may be
adequate to ask if it is long enough to assure a substantial payback. How
long must it be useful in order to pay for itself? Does this seem likely with
a substantial margin for error?

### How to nail down the benefit

These calculations ask you to estimate the revenue stream from the investment you're going to make. But how can you really know how much your
cash flow will increase by hiring a new person, upgrading a system, or
installing a piece of equipment? There's a lot of intuition and guesswork
involved.

> *The most important benefits may be intan-gible—and very hard to put a number on.*

When you ask whether the benefit is worth
the cost, you may have to compare cash costs
with non-monetary benefits. You must compare apples with oranges. For example, is the
benefit of expanding your operation throughout the five-county area worth the cost in
increased effort and stress on your part? Many
people answer this question with a resound-
ing "No!" That's why growth is not the only thing we discuss.

Large companies do sophisticated analyses of net present value and
internal rate of return to compare alternative investments. They state their
conclusions with high precision. However, this doesn't mean they turn out
to be right any more often than you do with your educated guess. The
accuracy of a conclusion is only as good as the data on which it is based.
You've heard the maxim, "Garbage in, garbage out." But when numbers
are run through a computer and printed out to two decimal points, the
danger is that you might believe them—"garbage in, gospel out." If you
are unsure whether your project will cost $50,000 or $100,000, or whether it
will take six months or a year, calculating the return to the nearest percent
is a waste of time.

So turn it around and ask these two questions instead:
1. What does the return need to be for you to be as well off as you are
   now?
2. How likely is it that you can make *at least* that much? Hopefully,
   you'll make many times more, but this establishes a floor.

For example: "The new point-of-sale software will cost $20,000, includ-
ing customization and training. It would pay for itself if it saves us just

$20,000. However, it *should* save us $100,000 in the first year—in reduced need for cashiers, reduced losses from incorrect ring-ups, etc. And its lifetime should be at least five years. So there's a high likelihood that it will pay for itself many times over."

In this example if it were to cost you twice as much and save you only half as much, it would take two years to pay for itself and therefore still be worthwhile. So you have a substantial margin of error in which to work.

However, if all the stars have to line up just right in order for your desired project to pay for itself, it probably won't because there's always some part of it that will cost more and pay back less than you optimistically estimate.

## HOW TO CREATE YOUR OWN *USES AND SOURCES* STATEMENT

If the "pay for itself" and "payback period" approaches don't allow you to account for all the detail in your project, you should create a Uses and Sources of Cash statement (table 15-1). Typically you would lay out this format on a spreadsheet, with a column for each period (say, each month). The top row would be labeled "Cash Balance Carried Forward" from the preceding month.

 In the "Uses" section, create rows for everything you use cash for: initial and ongoing expenditures, payments on accounts payable, loan or interest payments, tax payments, owner's draw, deposits made. In the "Sources" section create rows for revenue from sales, payments received on accounts receivable, loan or investment proceeds, refunds or deposits received. Working capital, once deposited into your bank account, is a source of cash. List also ways this project will save you money by reducing other costs. Since you are tracking cash, it doesn't matter whether the entries are from your Profit and Loss Statement or your Balance Sheet.

"Uses minus Sources" represents the balance at the end of the month. If Uses are greater than Sources, then unless you deposit additional funds, your checks will bounce. If this number is negative, it indicates the needed working capital infusion that month. If it is positive, it shows the amount available to pay down your line of credit or for other uses.

You can integrate the project spreadsheet into the Uses and Sources statement for your entire business. Initially, the uses of cash predominate; you must spend and spend to launch it. But not all at the same time: expenditures are spread over several months. Assuming you are currently profitable and generating positive cash flow, this will show how much additional working capital you will need until it begins paying for itself.

You can build in leads and lags. Suppose, for example, that for a sale made in May you must purchase materials in March. In April you pay for the materials and the production labor. You don't get paid till June or July. Then in May you pay for sales you expect to make in June and get paid for in July, and so on. Build formulas for these leads and lags into your spreadsheet and let it calculate how much capital you need to finance increased sales. You quickly discover why growing companies are strapped for cash.

After you enter into the appropriate months all the anticipated costs and new revenue (and build in the needed formulas), your spreadsheet will calculate everything in a flash and tell you when it will all pay off (assuming all your numbers turn out to be right). Here's what you might observe:

"Not until Month 6 does this investment begin generating any return and not until Month 14 is the return greater than the outlay. Finally, in Month 26, the cumulative return exceeds the total outlay. At this point, the investment will have paid for itself, and thereafter should be an increasing source of profitability throughout its expected seven-year lifetime."

In doing this, you may discover that it will never pay for itself, or that the margin of error that you can allow yourself is too narrow. The beauty of the computer spreadsheet is that you can change assumptions, enter new numbers, and instantly see the impact. "What if we lease instead of buy? Find a lower-rent facility a bit farther away? Spread the cost out over a year? Contract the work out rather than doing it in-house? Redefine the jobs so that we need two fewer people? Wait for six months to get started?"

In its simplest form, the Uses and Sources spreadsheet ignores the cost of capital. But you can factor it into the spreadsheet by having it calculate a percentage of the cumulative deficit each month. If, for example, you can borrow money at 12% per annum, then your spreadsheet can calculate 1% of the total amount you owe each month and add that in as a use of cash.

Use this spreadsheet to answer these questions:

- How soon does this investment begin to pay for itself?
- How can you spread out the cost?
- Can you take small initial steps to generate some cash flow that will help pay for more costly steps later?
- How much of the cost can you pay out of ongoing cash flow without borrowing money?
- What can you do to begin making it pay for itself more rapidly? For example, aggressive marketing, better systems and procedures, etc.

You can also use the above approaches to compare alternatives, such as these decisions made by business owners:

- Hired two assistant managers rather than one top-level manager
- Hired an entry-level staff person at the bottom of the hierarchy, rather than another skilled technician at the top
- Put in high-speed phone/data lines connecting the facilities at $2000 per month, thus freeing up time of the accountant and production manager worth much more than $2000 per month.

## WHERE WILL THE MONEY COME FROM?

It's a common mistake to secure insufficient working capital to cover the initial investment plus the ongoing shortfall until the project starts generating a surplus. How will you pay for the desired change? Here are four approaches:

- Earn it before you spend it. Calculate what level of business you need to attain before you take on the increased cost. "Before we lease a larger office and hire more staff, I must be convinced that our monthly revenue will stay consistently above $200,000."
- Phase in the changes over time so that you can afford to pay for them out of ongoing cash flow, without taking on more debt.
- Borrow the money, by expanding your line of credit or taking out a working capital loan.
- Get an outside investor to put in money, or invest your own money.

Each of these has pluses and minuses. The downside of the first two is that you may miss a lucrative opportunity by not being able to pursue it in time. The risk of the last two is that your investment will not generate enough return to repay these obligations. If you borrow more money, remember these guidelines from chapter 13:

- Spend no overhead before its time.
- Don't use short-term capital to pay for a long-term obligation.
- Secure needed financing up front. It's usually easier and cheaper to get financing when you are not desperate for it.

*The cost of capital will be much lower if you lay proper groundwork.*

- Lease rather than buy. As leasing becomes flexible you may be able to lease a package of related items—especially if they are acquired through one vendor.

By not laying the proper groundwork, business owners often pay much more for capital than they need to. Table 15-2 ranks types of capital available to small business owners, with the most expensive at the top. The better you prepare, the farther down this list you can go to get the capital you need, and the lower your cost of capital will be.

## TABLE 15-2

### Costs of capital compared

Types of business working capital ranked from most to least expensive:
- No capital; thus missing out on a lucrative opportunity
- Taking on a partner who makes a "sweat equity" investment
- Taking on a partner who makes a financial investment
- Venture capital
- Private placement capital, i.e., from family member, business associate, or customer
- Additional investment from an existing partner or stockholders
- Factoring accounts receivable
- Late payment interest and penalties, especially from paying taxes late
- Run up credit card balance; use cash advances
- Failure to take trade discounts
- Unsecured loan
- Personal savings (Your effective cost depends on the lost return on alternative investment.)
- Secured loan, second mortgage, or co-signed loan
- Renegotiate existing loan for lower rate; larger balance
- Stretch out payables as long as possible without incurring interest or penalties
- Aggressively collect overdue receivables
- Invoice in timely fashion
- Finance from cash flow; make expenditures that are tax deductible

## ASK YOURSELF . . .

1. What change to your business would have the greatest financial benefit?
2. What change to your business would have the greatest non-financial benefit?
3. In order to compare the costs and benefits, what cost figures will you have to collect? How will you obtain this data?
4. What revenue streams must you estimate? What is your level of confidence in your estimate?
5. What could you do to increase your level of confidence in the financial benefit of your desired change?

## Chapter 16

# Setting a Plan of Action

*Some businesses act like they are at the mercy of unpredictable, uncontrollable forces.*

*Other businesses act to predict, plan for, and influence outside forces.*

*The latter prevail.*

### Why bother planning?

When I ask an audience of business owners how many of them have a business plan, it's amazing how few raise their hands. When I ask why they don't bother planning, I hear things like, "My business is at the mercy of unpredictable forces. I never know when projects will come through. If I do set a plan, I can guarantee that what I plan for won't happen." I have gathered all these excuses together on Table 16-1, "Planning Zappers for Small Business Owners." Do any of these resonate with you?

Small businesses that take the time to plan do better, and are more likely to prevail. No one can deny that small businesses are buffeted by the winds of business fate. So to create a plan that is a useful guide to action, follow two principles:

1. Plan for what you can.

2. Then plan on how you will deal with the things you can't plan for.

## Three types of plans

There are three kinds of business plans:

1. The Prospectus is a slick, flashy plan that you put together to impress someone, such as a financier, of your long-term potential, rather than to accurately estimate short-term details. Such a plan may be necessary for your business, but it is a poor management tool for you. So you put it on a shelf where it gathers dust and seldom look at it again. This is what most people have in mind when they say they want a business plan.

2. The Action Plan is dog-eared and smudged, covered with hand-written edits and coffee cup stains, because you continually refer back to it and agonize over it. This is the kind of plan I am interested in.

   You do your best to estimate revenue and expenses, specify marketing strategies and activities, and describe operational requirements. You use the plan to help guide your actions and inspire you to achieve your targets. But you also review your actions to make sure your goals and target are realistic. If not, you revise them. This is a working plan.

3. The Project Plan helps you organize a major, dominating activity, such as a move into a new facility, a marketing campaign a new region, or the introduction of a new product. It has a beginning, middle, and end. You should create a project plan to implement the changes we have discussed in this book.

   *I've got my plan in my head," you say. That way, you never have to be held accountable.*

   A Project Plan must be incorporated into your Action Plan, since no matter how large the project, you have to run your regular business at the same time. If you fail to take this into account, then both your project and your regular business will suffer.

## The annual plan

Every December and January, we hold day-long planning workshops during which business owners set a plan of action for the coming year. You start with your life goals and long-term business objectives. But the Action Plan format itself (shown on table 16-3) is just one page. In my experience, if you cannot write your action plan on a page or two, you can't get it done in a year anyway.

   This action plan is more than a to-do list for the coming year. It's carefully thought through to move you toward your long-term objectives. If you adapt this plan format for yourself, you can of course change any of the categories to fit your needs, but the ones shown are things every business needs to think about.

Your action plan must not just project your numbers but spell out everything that must be done for these numbers to be accomplished, starting with the details of marketing and operations. We spend a quarter of the planning day focusing on dilemmas or choice points you face: questions, uncertainty, and confusion, the impact of uncontrollable outside influences, and the deficiencies in the way you do things.

Too often, business plans fail to address these questions and negatives—especially plans written to impress others. But I cannot emphasize this enough: any business plan that fails to address the dilemmas, uncertainties, and negatives is bound to go awry.

## A DOZEN STEPS TO A PRACTICAL PLAN OF ACTION

1. Start with the big picture: your long-term objectives.
2. Plan for the short term: about a year.
3. Keep it short and simple.
4. Base your plan on recent performance as well as long-term aspirations.
5. Build your plan around what is most important for you.
6. Cover all the bases: not just the numbers, but all aspects of your operation.
7. Tie short-term goals to the big picture.
8. Tie your goals and targets to specific strategies and actions.
9. Plan how you will deal with dilemmas, uncertainties, and choice points.
10. Balance business with the rest of your life.
11. Focus on your critical challenges.
12. Build in review and accountability.

## TABLE 16-1

# Planning zappers for small business owners
*Do any of these apply to you?*

- **Nose to the grindstone.** You're so busy on day-to-day stuff, you can't take the time to think through a realistic plan, much less stay on it.

- **Lost in the woods.** You don't know where you want your business to take you, or what you ultimately want from it; you just go along year after year.

- **Can't connect the dots I.** Your short-term goals and activities are not connected with your long-term desires and objectives.

- **Can't connect the dots II.** Your strategies and activities are not linked to your financial goals. (Should be, e.g., "If I intend to increase sales by 25%, then I must make 10 additional sales calls each week." "If our sales increase 25%, we'll need three new staff people.")

- **Dreamer.** Being unrealistic; not grounding your goals in what you can actually do. ("I want to double my sales." However, "My health and energy just aren't what they used to be.")

- **Bead of mercury.** Unwilling to be pinned down to concrete goals; being fuzzy; not having any real idea of what can be accomplished. "My plan is in my head."

- **Leaf in storm.** "Why plan? I'm at the mercy of the winds of business fate anyway!"

- **List maker.** You produce a laundry list of activities rather than a strategic plan. ("My marketing goals are: get new business cards, install a marketing database.")

- **Whoops!** You leave out key aspects of the business, especially how to deal with problems, dilemmas, and challenges; thus they are bound to sneak up and surprise you.

- **Lost in the trees I.** You fail to think through the "what-ifs" and set contingencies for things that may not be likely to happen, but will have a huge impact if they do. ("What if I lose my lease? . . . lose a key employee? . . . get a bigger project than we've ever had?")

- **Lost in the trees II.** You don't anticipate and think through the impact of outside events, e.g., what your competition may do, changes in your customer base, in the technology, the economy, or in laws and regulations. ("What if my major competitor gets much more aggressive?" "What about this e-commerce stuff, anyway?" "What if the city prohibits parking on my street?")

- **Artiste.** Beautiful plan, admired from time to time, but gathering dust.

## 1. Start with the big picture: your long-term objectives

(Section 1 of table 16-3)

Ask and re-ask the basic questions: Why are you in business? What do you want from your business? How does your business support your life goals? What is your vision of success? What is your exit strategy? Refer back to chapter 3, where we covered these questions.

*Your business plan flows from your life goals and core values.*

A plan that does not address these questions cannot be practical for a small business owner. The plan of a large corporation can ignore the personal dreams and aspirations of the people running it, but you cannot.

If your business plan flows from your life goals and desires and core values, if it moves you toward an inspiring yet reachable vision, then you have a plan that harnesses your commitment and energy.

Your long-term objectives might include:

- Wealth build-up; increase in shareholder value
- Market share; growth target
- Personal accomplishment or contribution
- Exit strategy

## 2. Plan for the short term: about a year

Should your plan of action always be for a year? There is nothing magical about a year—especially a calendar year. Perhaps March through February is better for you, or this January through next June. An action plan needs to cover a limited period of time for which you can foresee events, lay out activities, and predict results with some confidence. A five-year action plan is way too long because, for a small business, things change much too quickly.

You should have a five-year—or even longer—strategic planning horizon. Within this, each year, develop a plan of action. Your short-term goals may include:

- Revenue/Earnings/Profit
- New customers
- Develop new products/services
- Lay groundwork
- Get needed investment capital

If may be difficult to assign a particular time for some major event to happen. For example, suppose your plan states that by October you will move into larger quarters, but then October comes and you aren't ready to move. You get discouraged because you can't stick to your plan. Instead, set a contingent goal: "When A happens, then we will do B." For example:

- "When sales reach $2 million, we will open our second location."
- "When our new cost-tracking and project-scheduling system is up and debugged, we will launch our profit sharing plan."
- "After we close the Alpha and Beta contracts, we will bring in Phase 2 financing."

Of course you should include target dates for these events, so that you can organize activities to accomplish them, but these are not carved in stone, because there are too many elements you cannot control.

### 3. Keep it short and simple

On our annual action plan format, goals are boiled down to fit just one or two pages. Newcomers to the process complain, "There just isn't room in this tiny space for me to write all the marketing activities I must do." My advice to them: "You'd better prioritize, and put some of them off till the following year." Another rookie mistake: everything has to get done first! It's all crammed into the first quarter, with nothing left for the rest of the year. You know that's not realistic.

### 4. Base your plan on recent performance as well as long-term aspirations (Table 16-2)

Review your past performance; there should be continuity in many of your goals. At the same time, some goals will be brand new; your business may go in a new direction.

Evaluate your past year's performance using a three-column format as in Table 16-2. Recap your goals in Column A, and your results in Column B. How did you do—right on target, better, or worse? Use Column C to explain the difference between goal and actual result.

If you did not set goals last year, or if you have a new business since then, fill in column B so that you will have a baseline for the coming year's goals.

**Practice makes perfect.** You learn to plan more accurately by reviewing how your past plans fared. Once you have done annual plans for a few years, comparing performance with goals you set a year earlier, you begin to plan more effectively. You notice where you were overly ambitious, where you failed to anticipate key events, and when you shifted goals in the middle of the year. These things help you develop a more realistic plan for the coming year.

If you did not achieve a goal last year, why not? What can you learn from this that will affect your goal setting?

What missed goals, unsolved problems, unanswered questions, strategic issues, etc., need to be incorporated into your planning process for the upcoming year?

**Look for past trends.** To establish your baseline for the coming year's plan, you might review your performance over the past several years. Overlay your month-by-month performance for the last several years on one bar graph. Do patterns emerge? Is February always slow and June always booming? Or do your February figures jump all over the graph? If there is a useful pattern—e.g., on average, June sales are always double February—you can use this pattern to project your monthly or quarterly revenues for the coming year.

**Cope with variability.** On the other hand, if your revenue figures jump all over the graph with no pattern, incorporate this lack of predictability in your plan using strategies like these:

- Keep overhead low so that you can weather the troughs.
- Build up a larger cushion during the peaks to carry you through the troughs.
- Secure a line of credit. Borrow against it during troughs and pay it back without fail during the next peak.

| **Table 16-2** <br> **Review last year's performance** | | |
|---|---|---|
| A. Last year's goals | B. Your result | C. What accounts for the difference? |
| Financial | | |
| Marketing goals | | |
| Operational goals | | |
| Strategic goals (taking advantage of opportunities) | | |
| Balance between business & rest of life | | |
| Key challenges | | |

### 5. Build your plan around what is most important for you

The head of an engineering firm said to me, "I'm not sure why I should take the time to plan. Our revenue is steady. We've got more work than we can handle and I've got good, committed people. It's hard for me to project revenue because I never know precisely when jobs will come in, how big they will be or how long they will last. So how can I make a plan?"

"Does that mean you have no problems?" I asked him.

"Not exactly. My problem is that I work way too many hours and I do things that should be handled by the others working for me."

"Then build your plan around changing the way you run your company so that you can focus on desired responsibilities and work the desired number of hours. Plan how you will reorganize management responsibilities, provide training for your managers, refine systems and procedures, and make this transition stick."

Emphasizing what was important and difficult to accomplish shifted his attitude from "Planning is a humdrum, marginally useful activity," to "I've got to have a plan to make these crucial changes in our operation!"

He did indeed need a plan. If he could have made these organizational changes easily, he would have done so years ago. But he'd been grappling with the issues for several years. It involved not just him but all his managers and other staff people. He saw that the situation was unlikely to change without thinking it through, putting it into a plan, having an ongoing process for making desired organizational changes, and having outside review to keep him on track.

> *A useful plan is dogeared, smudged, covered with hand-written edits.*

In this context, he also needed to look at how they select clients (and who they refused), how to price and invoice, and how to best use their computerized systems.

Your plan for tackling your key challenge should be at the center of your plan; then see how this one issue impinges upon all other aspects of your business.

If a key to your success—and one of the toughest challenges you face—is making a shift in the way you manage your business, then the concrete activities for making that change must be included in your plan or it will turn out to be useless.

### 6. Cover all the bases: all aspects of your operation

For some people, planning involves projecting revenue, spending, marketing performance, and raising capital. While essential, the numbers are only one aspect of a useful plan. Make sure your plan covers all the parts of your business, plus intangible factors such as dilemmas, choice points, and questions to be answered.

Goal statements can take several forms besides financial and numerical targets:

- Specific action items with a target completion date. "Finish the web upgrade by June 30."
- Ongoing activities. "Make twenty marketing contacts each month."
- Guiding principles. "Give top priority to our most profitable clients."
- Unresolved strategic questions. "How should we decide whether to lease, buy, or build a larger facility?" "Should I groom my kids to take over or figure on selling my firm to a larger company?"
- Goals for future years. "Defer south-county expansion effort till middle of next year."

In these last two, your plan should specify action items for this year that will help you resolve the questions or lay groundwork for an action to be completed in a future year.

### 7. Tie short-term goals to the big picture

Your goals and targets should move you toward your long-term vision and objectives. Start your plan by recapping your objectives in concrete, quantifiable terms. All your subsequent goals should be selected to further these objectives. Ask yourself what part of your long-term objectives can be accomplished in the coming year.

### Balance vision and aspirations with business realities and needs

How can you balance your vision and aspirations, your personal needs, and your business reality? Write a brief description of these for your business.

**1. Making steady progress toward your dreams and aspirations.**
What level of performance is needed in the coming year to move your business along toward your vision and long-term goals?

**2. Providing for your personal needs.**
What revenue is needed to cover your needs, pay down obligations, and pay yourself well—both now and in the future? How much of this must come from your business?

**3. Staying in line with your recent business performance.**

What has happened so far? What track has your business been on? What are the demands on you? What opportunities have opened for you? What barriers or limitations have you encountered?

Set your goals based on each of these. Ideally, they are in alignment. If the three diverge widely, then your plan should focus on how to get them into alignment.

### *Financial goals* (Section 2)

**Financial targets** must be adequate to support you and your business, and must contribute to your long-term objectives.

### *How to set revenue goals:*

You can use several different approaches to set revenue goals:

- **Percentage of last year:**

  "We think sales in our service department should increase 25%."

  "I expect Direct Labor to decrease from 22% to 20% due to our new scheduling system."

  "Prices will go up 8% across the board."

- **Sum of the parts.** Look at how you expect to do in the different parts of your business and add up the figures.

  "I told our division managers that revenue should increase 20%, but I don't want to plug that into the plan unless they can convince me that their divisions can produce that growth."

- **Other criteria:**

  – How much you need to take out of your business (pay yourself). How much must your business bring in to make this possible?

  – How much you need to generate from operations to lay groundwork for longer-term objectives, create a fund for incentives, pay down debt, pay dividends, etc.

- **Best guesstimate.** For new sources of revenue, for which you have no historical numbers, it's best to make a conservative estimate. You may even assume *no* sales from them, so that your business does not rely on something so unpredictable for its health over the next year. You might calculate the level of sales needed for that line to break even or to recover your investment in it, and then ask yourself how likely it seems that you can sell at least that amount.

- **Project revenue several years out.** If your goal is to reach a particular revenue, profit, or net worth within, say, five years; show a progres-

**TABLE 16-3**

| **Format for one-year action plan** |
| --- |
| *Keep it short and simple* |

### 1. LONG-TERM OBJECTIVES (from chapter 3)

| 2. NUMERICAL TARGETS | Baseline (last year) | Q1 | Q2 | Q3 | Q4 | Total (coming year) |
| --- | --- | --- | --- | --- | --- | --- |
| $ Revenue | | | | | | |
| $ Your pay | | | | | | |
| % Profit | | | | | | |
| $ Cost reduction, capital raised, debt paydown, etc. | | | | | | |
| # Customers, contracts, new products/services | | | | | | |

### 3. MARKETING GOALS/STRATEGIES

| Goals/targets | Action items/ milestones | Q1 | Q2 | Q3 | Q4 |
| --- | --- | --- | --- | --- | --- |
| | | | | | |

### 4. OPERATIONAL GOALS

| Goals | Action items/ milestones | Q1 | Q2 | Q3 | Q4 |
| --- | --- | --- | --- | --- | --- |
| | | | | | |

### 5. STRATEGIC GOALS – take advantage of opportunities, deal with threats & dilemmas, lay groundwork

| Goals | Action items/ milestones | Q1 | Q2 | Q3 | Q4 |
| --- | --- | --- | --- | --- | --- |
| | | | | | |

### 6. BALANCE – business & the rest of your life

| Goals | Action items/ milestones | Q1 | Q2 | Q3 | Q4 |
| --- | --- | --- | --- | --- | --- |
| | | | | | |

### 7. KEY CHALLENGES – toughest challenges to accomplish your goals

| Challenge/ desired change | Action items/ milestones/ accountability | Q1 | Q2 | Q3 | Q4 |
| --- | --- | --- | --- | --- | --- |
| | | | | | |

sion of annual revenues that will reach your target. Will your plan for the coming year produce the amount needed to keep you on this trend? If not, perhaps you are being overly-optimistic in your five-year goal.

Whatever approach you use, write the assumption on which the goal is based. Having this in writing will help you a year hence when you are scratching your head trying to figure out where these numbers came from.

If it makes sense for your business, set quarterly, seasonal, or monthly revenue targets for the whole and the parts of your business.

**Billings vs. collections.** Unless your business is run on a cash basis, when you project your revenue, you must choose whether to focus on billings or receipts. For example, the billings for Jane's rapidly growing consultancy had been increasing twenty- to thirty-percent per year. However, her major customers are public agencies that are notoriously slow payers. Jane exceeded her annual sales targets, but was always scrambling for cash because of the sixty- to ninety-day day lag in receivables. She had to pay her employees and subcontractors—and herself—long before she was paid by her customers. She had to learn to build this lag into her plan. She did separate projections for sales and cash receipts.

BASELINE FOR THE YEAR. For each financial goal, enter figures for the end of the last year, for comparison purposes.

**Set other financial goals besides revenue:**

- Your paycheck. How much do you intend to pay yourself from the business? On what schedule? For a one-person business, you may set your desired paycheck first, then calculate how much revenue your business must bring in to pay you that amount.

- Plans for changes in major outlays. These might include:

    – **Overhead**: changes in labor, rent, marketing

    – **Direct costs:** changes in direct labor, components or raw materials, vendors or subcontractors

    – **Balance sheet items:** changes in inventory, facilities, equipment

- Funds needed for capital expenditures. What are the costs of expansion or upgrade needed to achieve major marketing or operational goals and by when? What is the source?

- Bringing excessive or unpredictable expenditures under control, based on your budget. For example: "Last year our overhead got out of control." "Warranty work ate up our profit."

- Clearing a profit from operations adequate to cover the needs of your thriving business, e.g.:

- Fund for bonuses, financial incentives
- Retirement program for you and your employees
- Fund for expansion or upgrades
- Calculating how profitable your business should be, *beyond what you pay yourself*. Estimate either the dollar amount or percent of revenue for the items below:
  - Working capital for growth or acquisition
  - Debt repayment
  - Taxes
  - Dividends, return on investment

Calculating a target profit rate helps you set prices, submit estimates or proposals for profitable jobs, evaluate and compare profitability of different parts of your business, etc. Most importantly, it helps shift your perspective toward *maximizing profitability* and away from merely *maximizing gross revenue*.

## 8. Tie your goals and targets to specific strategies and actions

When members present their annual plan to their business owners' group, here are some common responses they hear: "You say you will increase revenue by a third, but I don't see how your marketing will get you a third more business." "You're already complaining of capacity constraints. Where will that added work get done?" "You'd better factor in the cost of hiring more people—and providing them all with tools." You must convince your advisors—and yourself—that your marketing and operational activities will produce your projected revenue.

Sections 3 through 7 of the Action Plan include columns for Goals/ Targets, Action Items/Milestones, and for a quarterly breakdown of the Action Items. For each goal in the left column, write the action items beside it in the next column. Where appropriate, you can further break down the action items for each quarter. For example, see the Action Plan on the next page.

**The difference between a goal and an action item.** When filling out your Action Plan, your initial goal statements may resemble a laundry list of things to do over the coming year, for example:

- Rearrange the office furniture and equipment
- Hire someone to do mailings and make follow-up calls
- Design and produce a new marketing package

To me, these look like action items. If your goals look like these, ask yourself two questions for each one:

| ACTION PLAN | | | | | |
|---|---|---|---|---|---|
| GOAL | ACTION ITEM / MILESTONE | QTR 1 | QTR 2 | QTR 3 | QTR 4 |
| **Marketing goals** 20 new projects | 10 marketing calls/week; 1 project per 20 calls | 4 projects | 6 projects | 6 projects | 4 projects |
| Make website the primary conduit of info for prospects & customers | Rebuild website by June 30 | | Web graphics & pro-graming | Review results | Refine site |
| **Operations goal** Bring office pro-cedures into compliance with regulations | Rewrite employee and procedures manuals | Complete employee manual | | Complete procedures manual | |
| **Balance goal** Have more time for family | Schedule 5 weeks of vacation | | May-Mexico 1 week | Sept.-Italy 3 weeks | Christmas Hawaii 1 week |

1. "Why am I doing this? What business goal does this serve?"

2. "How does this goal advance my long-term objectives and my financial targets for the year?"

Your responses are likely to sound more like goals:

- To be able to take on the larger, more lucrative projects I want, I will create a more productive and flexible work space.

- To free me up to focus on getting the number of projects I want, I will hand off routine tasks and responsibilities to others.

- I will create marketing materials and presentations adequate to attract the larger clients I seek.

By restating these specifics in a more general form that is directly tied to your core objectives, you tie the plan together in your mind and in the minds of those working with you.

Furthermore, it may expand your thinking. If you state your goal as, "Have the workspace I need," and not just, "Rearrange the furniture," it may open you to the possibility of moving to a workspace that is larger or has a better layout. If you adopt the more general goal, "Improve my market presentation," this may lead you to question the relative merit of printed brochures vs. an upgraded web site. If your goal is, "Get the help you need," rather than, "Hire someone," it opens you to look at contracting with an outside service or bringing someone in on an as-needed basis.

### *Marketing Strategies, Targets, and Activities* (Section 3)

Marketing goals complete this sentence: "In order for the business to achieve the revenue and profit goals stated above, I/we must . . ."

**Marketing strategies.** Here is a set of condensed topics you should address in your marketing plan, taken from my book *The Magic Chain of Marketing*.

Description of your company, its products and services. Your place in the industry. How you stack up against your competition; why people buy from you.

Your market. Your target customers for each segment of your business, now and in the near future.

Your mission statement. Your core competencies or technologies. What you do and don't do.

Your long-term objectives and strategy, including growth goals.

Marketing goals, numerical and financial.

Marketing outreach or penetration strategy for each part of your business. Your message, marketing channels, materials, presentation, location, selling processes, etc. The actions you will take to achieve your goals.

Pricing strategy and policy.

Marketing budget; tie expenditures to intended results.

Tracking. How you keep on top of your effort.

Market intelligence. How you keep on top of market conditions.

Which of these do you need to emphasize in your Action Plan? Set numerical targets and milestones needed to achieve your marketing strategy and attain your financial goals. Below are some examples. You should focus on just a few.

### Marketing or selling targets

number of sales or projects or jobs
types of sales or projects or jobs
sales in each part of your business
division of sales by region or salesperson
number of prospects or proposals
number of customers per day or month
size of average transaction or sale
mix of different size projects
number of new customers
number of repeat customers, retention rate

## Marketing milestones

opening, remodel, refurbish
completion (e.g., website)
expansion (e.g., showroom)
design or redesign (e.g., brochures, portfolio)
simplification, reduction (e.g., product line)

How much marketing and selling must you do to produce your target revenue? Here are some simple formats to help you figure this out.

## How many customers do you need?

Do this calculation for each profit center or product category of your business.

A. Target revenue for the coming year

B. Average purchase, job size, or customer expenditure per year

C. Your new price as a ratio of the old price.
  (E.g., if you make a 10% price increase, then new price is 110%, or a ratio of 1.1. If no price change, then ignore C.)

D. Number of customers needed this year = $A \div B \div C$
  (You divide by C because if you raise prices, you need fewer customers to achieve your revenue goal, assuming that raising prices won't drive any customers away.)

If you do this exercise for several parts of your business, then you must figure out the desired proportion of each part to attain your target revenue.

## How much selling must you do to produce target sales?

Do this for each type of business you have.

E. Number of customers needed for the coming year (from D above)

F. Number of prospects to get one customer  (Your close rate)

G. Prospects needed per year  (E x F)

For example, suppose you need 100 clients to reach your annual goals (E). You know from experience that your must talk with three good prospects to complete one sale (F). Thus your marketing effort must produce 300 qualified prospects a year (G).

However, if you have 80 *continuing* customers, then you need only 20 new ones, or just 60 good prospects. So be good to your customers!

How does your needed marketing compare with last year?

H. Number of customers you had last year

J. Needed percentage growth in your marketing effort    $100 \times [(E \div H) - 1]$

This looks more complicated than it is. Suppose you had 75 customers last year (H) and you need 100 this year (E). 100 divided by 75 equals 1.33.

Subtracting 1 leaves .33. Multiplying by 100 gives 33%, which means you must increase your marketing by a third.

This assumes your size of sale or job remains about the same and your marketing continues to work as well as it did last year.

## What kind of customers do you want more of? Fewer of?

One of the best ways to develop these profiles is to think of particular customers you love or hate, and list their qualities. You can add to my list:

|                      | Preferred customer | Marginal Customer | Customer from hell |
|----------------------|--------------------|-------------------|--------------------|
| Who they are         |                    |                   |                    |
| What they buy        |                    |                   |                    |
| Size of purchase     | Just right =?      |                   | Too small = ?  Too big = ? |
| Profit from purchase |                    |                   |                    |

How can you make a *marginal* customer into a *preferred* one?

### *Operational Goals and Targets* (Section 4)

What changes in your operation do you need in order to support your marketing goals and achieve your financial targets? This includes the way your work is performed or production is done, how your sales are made, hiring, training, upgrading skills, making changes to your office or plant, or upgrading systems. It includes shifts in your organizational structure and how you run the business.

Again, I have listed examples of some categories. You should focus on just a few.

## Operational goals & milestones

> your facilities, shop, factory, office
> remodel, refurbish, reorganize
> hire, train
> publish, design, create
> purchase or upgrade equipment
> work organization, work space
> simplify, redesign, create
> upgrade or expand an operation
> acquire or sell off assets

## Administrative goals & milestones

> your office, other facilities

software, hardware, equipment

systems, procedures

contracts, agreements

financial policy, procedures

work organization

policy, manuals, checklists

hire, outsource, bring in-house

train, retrain, cross-train

re-organize, create, upgrade

track, evaluate, analyze

**Management.** Goals and action items to work on your own management style or practices (from chapters 5 and 8).

## *Strategic Goals* (Section 5)

A strategic opportunity opens a new door to achieving your long-term objectives. It could be a new way of conducting your business, a new market niche, or a new way of selling what you already have. It has the potential of making a far-reaching improvement in your business. Examples of some types of strategic goals:

a new niche, location, region, etc.

strategic alliance with other companies or organizations

a larger company is interested in acquiring yours

expand by acquiring another company

take advantage of weakness of competitors

exploit a special strength or advantage

a window of opportunity if you move on something right away

A strategic challenge, on the other hand, can seriously affect the operation of your business. If you ignore these (or even fail to see them coming) they can be very damaging. These might include:

a shift in the business climate or economy

technological change

demographic shifts in your customer base

the competitive climate in your industry

laws and regulations that can have an impact on you (especially tax law changes)

the plans of your city

It's apparent that the same event can be both an opportunity and a challenge, depending on how you respond to it.

What strategic *opportunities* do you already have, or want to create for yourself? To do so, what must you include in your current action plan?

What strategic *challenges* do you face or see coming? To address them effectively, what must you include in your current action plan?

### 9. Plan how you will deal with dilemmas and uncertainties

We spend a quarter of our all-day planning workshop on the inevitable dilemmas, choice points, uncertainties, and sticking points that business owners face. People ignore these questions in their business plan, then wonder why their plans go awry.

- Dilemmas you face; tough choices you must make, for example:
  Balancing two lines of business
  Doing paid work *and* developing new work
  Sustaining the old while allowing the new to emerge
  Caught between what you love to do and what you feel you have to do
  Retaining your personal touch while improving efficiency and productivity

- Unanswered questions, uncertainties, or fears, for example:
  You know where you want to go but don't know how to get there.
  You want to grow, but don't have the resources, ideas, or knowledge needed.
  You want to grow your business, but are afraid of the consequences of growth.

- Your own limitations; personal and family realities
  You want to push for expansion, but don't have the energy you used to have.
  Despite years of grooming, your son just doesn't have what it takes to step into your shoes.

Any issues like these must be addressed with specific goals and action items in your plan. You can add a column to your Action Plan headed "Questions and choice-points." Beneath that, for each aspect of your plan, note the questions you must address and the choices you must make. Under Action Items, state how you will answer the question and make the choice. In our workshops, we have business owners work one-on-one to help each other brainstorm the best course of action for these.

## 10. Balance business with the rest of your life

What are your goals regarding the desired balance between business and the rest of your life?

As a small business owner, your plan must be built around your life.
I have urged you to make sure your business fits into your life, and not try to force your life to fit around your business. You must include concrete measures for doing so in

*Build your business plan around your life, not vice versa.*

your business plan. These are very individual goals, but here are some of the most common areas:

- Number of hours you work, days off and vacations.

  If your goal is to reduce your workweek from 60 to 45 hours, what specific actions must you take during the year to accomplish this, so that you can work less without cutting your profitability?

  What days off will you take? How many hours per week will you work?

  What is your schedule of vacations?

- Taking care of yourself

  What regular recreation or rejuvenation will you schedule? What health care or fitness activities? What will you do to recharge your batteries?

- Family time

  How will you mesh family activities with your work schedule?

- Avocation, volunteer activities, pro bono work
- Community involvement
- Spiritual concerns

The final two requirements are the topic of chapter 17.

## 11. Focus on your key challenges (Section 7 and chapter 17)

A key challenge is not the same as a goal. Rather, it is the toughest thing you must grapple with in order to accomplish a goal. Your plan should describe the biggest challenge you face in the coming year, what you will do about it, and how you will measure progress.

## 12. Build in review and accountability (Chapter 17)

After you complete your plan, you must set up a procedure to keep on track throughout the year.

## RESOURCES FOR PLANNING

*Success in 20*— (a planning workbook published by The Business Group, and updated each year).

*Pay Yourself First,* by Mike Van Horn (a workbook and template that helps you calculate how much you need to pay yourself from your business, and how large the business must be to pay you this amount).

*One Page Business Plan,* by Jim Horan

Computer templates

- Action Plan

- Accountability trackers: Project Tracker, Key Challenge Tracker, Work On Yourself Tracker

Complete information on these publications is in the Book and Resource List at the end of this book.

## Chapter 17

# How to Stay on Track With Your Toughest Challenges

### Accountability templates

*Anybody can write a plan; it's sticking to it that keeps you up at night.*

It's tough enough to accomplish the regular goals of your business plan—revenue targets, marketing activities, production quotas, etc. In addition, throughout this book we've been talking about changes you can make to boost your growth and profitability and work with greater ease. This effort can make it all the more difficult to get everything done—on schedule and within budget—without driving yourself nuts. It's like having two full-time jobs.

For most business owners—including me—this seems like the normal state of affairs. There are always special projects we must undertake in addition to running our business. As we finish one, another comes along. That's if we're lucky. Oftentimes they pile one on top of another. Sure, it's easy for me to say "Prioritize. Do just one at a time." Sometimes a bunch of things get thrown at you and you just have to dig in and do them.

I'm a perfect example. This past year—in addition to running my company and leading several of our groups—I decided to write this book. At the same time, we were making a major upgrade in our web site. On top of this, I had to update several workshops during the year. Through all of this I tried to lead a normal life. So believe me, I'm writing from first-hand experience.

You need a way to keep yourself on track, and to get back on track when you slip. In this chapter, I will describe two essential tools: tracking systems and an "accountability team." You should track two kinds of things:

**1. Key Performance Indicators** (KPIs) track your regular, ongoing business goals and targets—as you set in chapter 16. You should select numerical Key Performance Indicators based on your past performance.

**2. Key Challenge Trackers (KCTs)** follow the progress of your toughest challenges—such as the kinds of changes you want to make after reading this book. It may be harder to attach numbers or definite completion times, yet each needs to be broken down into discrete events and a schedule, using the Key Challenge Progress Tracker (Table 17-3).

These two are complementary and they overlap somewhat. Whether you emphasize one or the other depends on whether staying on top of either regular performance or special challenges presents more difficulty.

## 1. KEY PERFORMANCE INDICATORS (KPIs)

You might tell me that your toughest challenge is just keeping your business on an even keel day in and day out. When you also have special projects or major challenges, you must be all the more vigilant to keep on top of your regular business.

What are the best indicators of your business performance? You already watch (or should be watching) the standard measures, e.g. your profit and loss statement, bank balance, balance sheet, inventory levels, labor costs, accounts receivable aging, and so on. Do these give you all the data you need? Let's ask this question in a different way. What numbers would allow you to:

- get an "early warning" of future performance—especially potential problems
- make the best day-to-day management decisions
- track progress toward your annual goals and targets

In chapter 13 I suggested you ask yourself, "What do I need to know to make the best management decisions?" rather than, "How can I use the data my accountant gives me?" Your wish list of desired indicators may not appear on any standard financial statement. You must select—or create—the indicators and reports that are most useful to you. Here are some business owners' answers to this question:

- The weekly cost percentages of food, labor, and beverages (for a restaurant whose goal is to increase profit margin by decreasing cost of goods sold).
- The number of overtime hours paid (for a maintenance firm whose night crews spend too much time on jobs).
- The proportion of patients that requests one of the associates rather than the owner (for a physical therapist who can grow her practice only if patients are willing to see her associates).
- Requests for bids compared to signed contracts (a general contractor who thinks he spends too much time going after jobs he won't likely get)
- The rate of on-time order completion (for a print shop for whom late delivery hurts customer satisfaction).
- The number of customers that come from various types of advertising (for a retail store that spends too much on unproductive ads).

These KPIs were created to answer the question, "What data would help me make the best decisions?" In the first bullet above, the restaurant's weekly cost percentages could in principle be read directly from the financial statements, but the owner created a table that included *only* these figures, and a graph that showed the trend week-to-week. He—and his managers—could grasp the significant data at a glance.

> *What data will help you make the best decisions? How should it be displayed? When do you need it?*

Simple, easily-grasped measures work best. A contractor I work with creates a bar graph for each job after it's done: estimated labor, materials, and sub-contractors vs. actual. If the actual costs exceed the estimate, the graph displays this in red; if the job is within budget, it shows green. These are shared with the foremen at the regular safety and training meetings, where they hash out the causes of exceeding budget and figure out how to do it better next time. These shared graphs are potent motivators for the foremen to stay within budget, and for the estimators to get the bid right.

This illustrates several rules for creating the most useful KPIs:

- Select just a handful of indicators. A dozen is way too many for one person to pay attention to; however, you may have different indica-

tors aimed at different people in your organization.
- Tie KPIs to the goals on your annual Action Plan (from chapter 16). Ask yourself which goals— financial, marketing, operational—you need to track with a key performance indicator. Not every goal requires one. Then ask how you will measure progress toward the goal, what data you must collect, and how you will display it.
- As you can see, much of the data in these KPIs never appears on your financial statements, and even if it does ultimately, your financials may not be timely enough to help you make forward-looking decisions. So you must set up different data tracking systems.
- Select KPIs that point to progress or danger in your business. Use them to watch for significant trends and shifts.

Tracking a KPI brings into consciousness something you tend to neglect or lose sight of, especially something important but distasteful or intimidating, such as making marketing calls. For example, if you graph the number of marketing calls you make per week, and one week the number declines, your graph will dip. This shows graphically that you need to take corrective action.

Here are a couple of useful variations to Key Performance Indicators.

## *Leading indicators*

What measure of current activity gives you a leading indicator of the future performance of your business—and in time for you to respond appropriately? For example, keeping track of the number of sales calls you make each week may be a very good indicator of the amount of work you have three months later.

*What measure can tell you where your business will be in six months?*

What data could you track now that would give you an advance indication of how your business will be doing in a few months?

Number of marketing contacts made, especially *qualified* prospects

Proposals submitted

Backlog of projects, or size of projects in your backlog

Proportion of your work done for your three largest clients. (For example, you might decide that if these three account for more than 20% of your work, you are getting too dependent on them, and should put in more effort to diversify.)

Conversion rate, i.e., number of contacts you make per sale closed. (For example, if you have been closing one out of three, then it slips to one out of four, this is a danger signal: new competition is moving in,

---

**TABLE 17-1**

**Examples of key performance indicators**

- Revenue, billings, collections
- Your paycheck
- Your hours worked, weekends off, and promises to yourself kept
- Sales compared to target
- Sales compared to break-even point
- Cash position compared to target
- Gross margin for the period, for each product line, or for each job
- Accounts receivable aging
- Actual expenditures compared to budget for key items
- Ratio of billable hours to work hours
- Schedules met, on-time delivery rate
- Non-billed consultations that should have been billed
- Requests for bids or estimates compared to signed contracts
- Marketing contacts made
- New prospects or customers by source
- Inventory turnover
- Average job or transaction size per month

---

you're trying to sell to unqualified prospects, there's a shift in what your customers want, etc.)

### *Personal performance indicators*

Since you are the most important asset of your business, indicators relating to your performance are crucial, both for current performance, and for the future growth of your business. Here's an example:

Suppose you are a professional who lives by the number of hours you sell. The more hours you sell the better, right? Not necessarily. When will you develop new business? You must allocate a certain proportion of your time for marketing and selling, and then track your time use to see whether you stick with it.

Suppose you decide that for the long term health of your business, you need to spend an hour in marketing and business development for every two paid hours. Your ratio of Paid Hours to Marketing Hours is 2 to 1. (And of course you spend time on other things as well: administration, planning and monitoring, driving to and from jobs, etc.)

$$\frac{\text{Paid Hours}}{\text{Marketing Hours}} = \frac{2}{1}$$

Deviation in either direction is a danger signal. Suppose you track your time use for  several months and discover that this ratio has changed to 1 to 1—that is, you are spending as much time marketing as doing billable work. This is a clear danger signal: you are not closing sales, you are trying to sell to the wrong people, or your business is drying up.

On the other hand, suppose the ratio changes to 4 to 1—four billable hours for each hour of marketing. This is also a danger signal: you are spending so much time working that you aren't lining up customers for the time when your current projects finish. Eventually you'll head from boom to bust.

"But I know whether I'm putting in enough marketing effort without the bother of tracking my hours," you say. Many people fool themselves into thinking this—especially workaholics who would really prefer not having to market. It's easy to ignore the reality that there is often a long lag time involved. Marketing you do now may translate into sales six months or a year hence; so if you cut back now on marketing you may not notice any decrease in work for many months.

If you don't rigorously track your current marketing and selling efforts, you may fool yourself into thinking all is well when in fact you are about to fall off the cliff. By the time your cash flow is hurting, it will take you more months to build your business back up. This is the source of the notorious "boom or bust" cycle bemoaned by consultants and other professionals.

The discipline of tracking this ratio alerts you to potential problems on the horizon long before you would otherwise feel discomfort from them.

The biggest objection to this is the requirement to track time use. But no professional objects to tracking *billable* time; you just need to extend the system a bit. On your schedule, treat your marketing and selling effort as a client. You don't need to track marketing time to the nearest five minutes; just close enough to calculate an approximate ratio. "Today I went to the chamber breakfast, then spent half an hour doing follow-up calls, then maybe forty-five minutes reviewing the new ad copy." You will surprise yourself how much time you spend on these things.

## Criteria for key indicators

To sum up, you should select measures that are:

- important and related to the goals that are crucial for you to keep an eagle eye on
- few in number: three, four, six; but not a dozen
- quantifiable so you can attach a meaningful number
- easy to track: derived from your current record-keeping systems, or from new records you will keep
- easy to compare from one period to another
- timely: they come out often enough and quickly enough so that you can take timely action
- easy to interpret: you can tell at a glance what you need to know, and effective remedial action is suggested.

## Tracking your key performance indicators

KPIs do you no good unless you monitor progress and take appropriate corrective action. Follow these steps:

1. **Selects indicators** and **set reasonable monthly targets** that will reach your goal. Your target may be the same each month ("Ten marketing calls per week") or may progress ("1st quarter sales $225,000; 2nd quarter $275,000 . . .)
2. **Set up a tracking system** if you don't already collect the data, and a **procedure** for collecting it. This must be something that is minimally burdensome, otherwise it won't be done.
3. Create an easy-to-grasp **report** or **display** format. Is there an alarm to warn you of slippage?
4. Decide how you will respond to slippage or divergence from targets.
5. Create a regular **review procedure**, and put review dates on your calendar. Review progress toward your goals and problem-solve the causes of slippage. Also review whether the above steps are working well. Have you selected the right indicators? Are you keeping track? Are you using the data?
6. **Report to someone** besides yourself. This last step is vitally important. The review procedure—conducted by a consultant or a support group—will help keep you on track, especially when you are falling behind your target, and might neglect to look at it.

It may take you several tries to come up with a set of key indicators and a display format that is meaningful for you. Your key indicators evolve over time. You may find that you need to track other data, or refine them so they give you better early warning

## 2. Key Challenge Trackers (KCTs)

A key challenge is different from a goal. It's the hardest part of achieving your most important goal. It's something that is very important for you to do yet it is difficult to complete. It may have been bugging you for a long time. Maybe it keeps you up at night. It may be the bottleneck to your getting what you want in your business.

> *What is toughest for you to do? Most critical? That's your key challenge.*

A key challenge might be attached to a particular goal, or related to the entire operation of your business. For example, suppose your key challenge is to cut back the number of hours you work without hurting the profitability of your business. You wouldn't say that your business goal is "Work fewer hours." Yet you know that working fewer hours is central to your energy, enjoyment from the business, and ultimately for its success.

After you have set your business goals, ask yourself "What will be the toughest aspect of attaining this goal? What will give me the biggest headaches?" That is your key challenge. For example:

| GOAL | KEY CHALLENGE |
|---|---|
| Move your business into a larger facility | Do everything needed for the move and run your business day-to-day without driving yourself crazy |
| Increase your ease of operation by cutting back to four days a week at the office | Train your people to handle things in your absence, and resist the pull from employees and customers—and yourself—to be there five days. |

As you can see, very often your toughest key challenge involves making a change in your own management style or work habit.

To help you identify your key challenges in accomplishing your goals, ask yourself: To accomplish your goals:

- What will be the hardest part for you to get done?
- What are you most likely to let slip?
- Where do you feel the least certainty? The most discomfort?
- Where are you likely to get overwhelmed?
- What has given you the most trouble in the past?

These are your key challenges.

## Five varieties of key challenge

I've listened to hundreds of business owners describe their key challenges. I notice that they fall into at least five categories:

1. A big project, such as moving to a new facility or installing a complex new system. The challenge is handling the complexity of an unfamiliar task, focusing on the project at the same time you are running the business, and integrating the new thing into your operation.
2. Handling a temporary load that you know is too ambitious. The challenge is balancing the demands that pull you in different directions.
3. Making a big shift in your management style or habitual way of doing things. Working on yourself is always a challenge.
4. Clarifying a choice point or resolving a dilemma; redefining or re-energizing your business; sustaining the old while allowing the new to emerge. The challenge is having to operate on two levels at once—running the business and changing it at the same time.
5. Responding to an unpredictable, uncontrollable circumstance, such as economic downturn, a huge opportunity, changes in your industry, or personal health problems. The challenge is finding a way to get a handle on this and adjusting your operations and the way you do things.

## How many challenges can you juggle?

How many key challenges can you effectively deal with in a year? Probably just one or two. If you have more than that, you may need to put some off till next year. So prioritize. Choose just one to focus on initially. If it comes to completion, then replace it with another.

## HOW TO TACKLE YOUR KEY CHALLENGES

Think of a your plan to tackle a key challenge as a project, and develop a project plan. Define the project, state your goal, and lay out your approach or strategy. Ask the Problem Solvent questions. Then ask the questions on table 17-2, Key Challenges Worksheet.

You can track progress in a variety of ways:

**1. Set a numerical measure or target.** These examples also specify what you will track and report, including the question you must address if you miss the target.

| KEY CHALLENGE WITH MEASURABLE TARGET | REVIEW/REPORT |
|---|---|
| "Pay myself $5000 per month." | Actual paycheck. If you are not able to pay yourself this amount, why not? |

## Table 17-2
## Key Challenges Worksheet

Answer these questions for the #1 key challenge you identified:

1. Regarding your goal or goals of _____, what is your key challenge?
2. What is the desired outcome? How do you want it to be?
3. To address this key challenge, what is your strategy or approach?
4. To tackle this key challenge, can you apply the Problem Solvent? For example, by:
   - making changes in your management style or habitual way of doing things
   - getting needed help; e.g., delegating
   - changing the way you do things: i.e., upgrading your systems and procedures
   - training; i.e., upgrading your skills or those of your people
   - making changes in your workplace or equipment
5. How much will it cost? How much of your time will it take? (Create budgets for both time and money.)
6. How will you track progress on this key challenge?
7. Where will you need help/accountability from others?
8. How will you review progress and make mid-course corrections if necessary?
9. What is success? How will you know when this challenge has been overcome?

KEY CHALLENGE WITH
MEASURABLE TARGET

REVIEW/REPORT

"Reduce my work week from 55 to 45 hours."

The number of hours you worked. If you worked more than 45, what happened?

"Hold staff meetings twice monthly."

Number of staff meetings and their results. If you didn't hold the meeting, what happened?

"Make 10 marketing calls per week."

Number of calls actually made. Results. If you didn't make the calls, why not?

"Review my financials each month with my CFO."

Was the meeting held? What did you learn? If you didn't hold the meeting, why not?

## 2. Lay out a timeline with concrete milestones and dates.

| Goal | March | April | May | June | July | August |
|------|-------|-------|-----|------|------|--------|
| Move into larger space | Begin looking | Select location, complete lease | Get permits, begin improvements | Move in (old lease expires) | Complete improvements | Grand opening party |

| Goal | March | April | May | June | July | August |
|---|---|---|---|---|---|---|
| **Get the book completed** | Chaps. 1-4 Cover design, testimonials | Chaps. 5-9 ISBN #, page design | Chaps. 10-12 Production bids | Complete copy editing, galleys | Complete layout | Review copies printed |
| Goal | March | April | May | June | July | August |
| **Take a month-long vacation** | Brainstorm with my managers what they must master. | List all the invoicing codes only I know. Train managers. | Take 4-day weekend as "trial run" | Adjust schedules to cover for me | Go to Italy | Debrief upon my return; avoid backsliding |

**3. Have an indicator of an intangible state,** for example, a "Happy Meter." "How will I know I'm making progress? By the smile on my face. I'll put a happy face sticker on my calendar for each week I'm satisfied with the results." Then track and report your level of satisfaction.

Remember, your key challenge may relate to several goals. For example: "Regarding my goals of increasing revenue 20% and opening our third store, my challenge will be staying on top of both activities without going nuts."

Some key challenges are large, formless beasts. If they are too unwieldy, they may need to be broken down into something smaller. But don't be too reductionist: one of the most common challenges is having to grapple with a large, disparate set of goals.

Keep separating challenges from goals by asking yourself, "What is the toughest part of this goal for me? What am I likely to let slip?" As you list actions and milestones to tackle the challenge, other roadblocks will come to mind. How will you attack that new barrier? This is an iterative process. You progressively clarify the core problem in this way.

This is a great exercise for a group, since you can often see others' key challenges—and how to tackle them—better than your own, and you learn from each other.

Once you have answered the questions on the worksheet and described the milestones, summarize them on the Key Challenge Progress Tracker (table 17-3). The top row recaps the worksheet. Then fill in column A with the period you choose (week, month, half-month) or with dates for particular activities or milestones you enter in column B. Enter these for as many periods as you can. Then at the end of each period, review progress. Enter the actual result or the actual date completed in column C.

You may not be able to fill out all the rows. You may be able to see ahead only one or two months at a time. That's fine: make sure that each review period you add in what you need to do for the next period.

There is nothing magic about six periods. If the challenge is resolved in less than six months, that's great! If it takes longer, add rows to your Tracker. One woman figured it would take about six months to retrain and reschedule her office staff so that she could take Fridays off. But a month later, she said, "It's done! I told them to come up with a plan for how they would cover for me on Fridays, and they did. It's working just fine. No more Fridays for me!"

### When you get off track

The schedules you set will slip if your key challenge plan has a couple of things in common with a personal goal, such as losing weight or stopping smoking: you are likely to get off-track, and when you do, you just need to get back on track.

*Try it. See how it works. Refine it. Try it again.*

**Rule #1. No blaming.** I like to sail on San Francisco Bay. If we set course for the Golden Gate Bridge, we're bound to get blown off course. The winds shift and the currents change. Does it help to say, "Oh, drat, we're off course! Why can't this boat stay on course? What a lousy sailor I am!" No. I just trim the sails and get back on course, time after time, until we reach the goal. I have sailed—and worked—with people who yell and fuss, and blame others or themselves, when things don't go according to plan. It doesn't help. It takes all the ease and satisfaction out of your work.

Every time you get off course, ask yourself:
- What happened to get you off track?
- How can you get back on track?
- How could you do it differently next time? Apply the Problem Solvent to this situation.
- Are your goals and timelines realistic?

Make refinements based on your answers, then move forward again.

## USE AN ACCOUNTABILITY TEAM

To whom will you be accountable? To yourself or to someone else? Business owners who come out of the corporate world comment that one of the things they miss most is having others to report to. In your business, you are on your own. It's all too easy to get in the habit of relying on fuzzy goals and timelines. You may be way too easy (or too tough!) on yourself. You may be your own worst critic; you make over-ambitious goals, don't accomplish them completely, and come down hard on yourself.

A corporation has a board of directors, but even so the CEO may have more power than the board members, and pay them little heed. This is all the more likely if your privately-held corporation has a rubber-stamp board that meets no more than mandated by law. In a partnership, the partners can be accountable to each other, but many have developed ingenious ways to avoid holding each other accountable: "If you don't remind me of my commitments, I won't remind you of yours either."

This is why there will always be work for coaches and consultants.

I'm a strong advocate of getting outside help to stay accountable to your plan. I recommend you form an "accountability team"—independent peers to whom you present your plans, make commitments, and report progress. You can develop your own brain trust—or use a coach or consultant for this purpose. The next chapter tells you how.

Here's how we do it: If you were in one of our business owners groups, each year you would go to our planning workshop and create an action plan for the coming year. Then, at the next meeting of your group, you would stand up at the flip chart with a pointer and present your plan to your peers. Making this presentation forces you to think it through, state your plan concisely and realistically and lay out the timeline, deadlines, and milestones:

"Here's my plan; these are my commitments for the year. This is my long term objective and right here is the part of it I can accomplish this year. Here are my revenue and profit goals and how much I will pay myself. Here's how I will accomplish these: my marketing strategies and activities, and my operational targets. Here are my goals regarding balance between business and the other parts of my life. And right here I described my toughest challenge. Your job is to help me stay on track all year."

Thereafter, the group helps you stay accountable to your plan throughout the year. The requirement of making regular progress reports keeps you mindful, and makes it harder for you to let your commitments slide when the going gets tough. When you get stuck, they problem-solve with you; when you complete a goal or reach a target they celebrate with you.

This support is doubly important for your key challenges, which are by definition the most critical parts of your plan and the parts that you are most likely to let slide.

If you slip from your goals during the year, they don't let you beat yourself up. Instead they help you figure out how you can get back on track, or else urge you to change your targets to reflect more realistic assumptions.

In this way, your plan becomes an effective management tool throughout the year. You will know you are using it well by the number of scratch-outs and coffee cup stains.

## TABLE 17-3
## Key challenge progress tracker

Your name _____ Date _____

| Regarding your goal of | Your key challenge is | Your desired outcome is |
|---|---|---|
| | | |

| A. Time period or projected date | B. Desired milestone or accomplishment. Concrete measure or "Happy Graph" | C. Actual result |
|---|---|---|
| 1 | | |
| 2 | | |
| 3 | | |
| 4 | | |
| 5 | | |
| 6 | | |

*Success!* declared on _____. Your reward: _____

## ASK YOURSELF . . .

1. When you consider your goals for the year, what will be the toughest aspects to accomplish?

2. If you had to pick just three or four numbers to watch, which ones would give you the most useful information about the performance of your operation?

3. Where could you most use some help to tackle your toughest business challenges?

4. If you don't already have an "accountability team," list the names of the people you'd most like to have on it.

## Chapter 18

# The Power of the Group

### *How to join a business owners' group*

*"I have no one to talk with about my business challenges. I can't talk with my employees or my spouse. I feel isolated in my decision-making."*

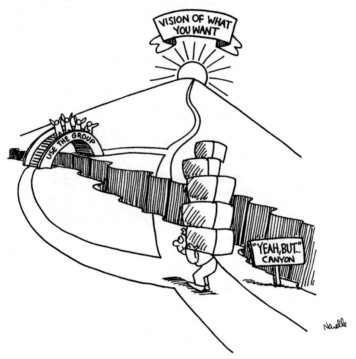

I f you feel this way, you are not alone.

Overcoming the barriers and challenges we discuss in this book is no easy task. I know first hand: I have grappled with these same barriers in my own businesses. If these things were easy, you would have resolved them years ago.

It is a lot easier if you have some help. The best help comes from your peers—other business owners. Find a few other business owners who feel the same way and form a problem-solving group.

I admit I am biased: we're in the business of putting together and leading such groups. There is great power in a peer group of CEOs. Tackling the barriers to growth and working on your personal management styles are difficult to do on your own. Working with a group of other successful business owners helps tremendously to stay on target and to problem-solve.

A larger corporation has a board of outside directors. Most small companies lack this valuable resource. You can however, create this resource for yourself. Here are some criteria for a good group:

- **Ongoing groups.** Hold regular meetings; have a stable membership. Work only with people who will get to know and understand you and be there for you. On the other hand, some turnover is fine: as some members leave and others join the group; the new energy and ideas are valuable.

  Our groups meet once a month for four hours and have a maximum of ten members. The group is small enough that your voice gets heard, yet large enough to provide lots of energy and varied ideas.

- **Be there.** Emphasize the importance of attending almost every meeting, getting there on time and staying till the end. One of my groups instituted a late fee of $1 a minute! Make sure all cell phones and pagers are turned off at the door.

- **Peers.** Bring in people you can respect, from whom you can learn, and to whom you can contribute as well. You often learn best by teaching others.

- **Variety.** Don't get a bunch of people from the same industry who will just talk shop. There should be no competitors; no-one with an ax to grind. Our groups tend to divide along number of employees. Bigger companies want to discuss employee problems; one-person companies say, "Thank goodness I don't have those problems."

  We keep our groups as diverse as possible. We deal with the challenges of growth that cut across all kinds of businesses. You never know where your next $10,000 idea will come from.

  All our members are business owners, but there is no reason similar groups couldn't be built around top managers or people who run non-profits. We have found it difficult to mix these types in one group.

- **Stick to business.** Grapple with real, eye-level problems, rather than "interesting" topics. You want hard-headed, practical feedback that you can apply tomorrow. This is much more valuable than the latest management buzzwords or theories. We sometimes bring in outside speakers to a meeting, but only if the topic is applicable to most of the group members.

- **Accountability.** Help each other hold to the goals you set. Our members attend an all-day planning session each year, then present their "action plan" to their group, followed by a mid-year review of progress. If you don't have a concrete plan with numbers and time-lines, then it is hard for others to be effective advisors for you.

- **Confidentiality.** Make sure the meeting is in a place where you feel safe to reveal any business issue. Our members sign a confidentiality agreement.
- **Be wary of doing business with each other.** You don't want customers present when you are digging into your toughest problem.
- **Have a leader,** someone to keep things on track, even if members take turns leading. But you can't be both leader and participant at the same time. Having a paid leader who is a good facilitator and who takes responsibility for scheduling and logistics helps extend group longevity.

You can form your own group, join an existing group, or work with an organization that puts on such groups. You can also get involved with a group under our auspices. (Check our website for details on this.)

**Want to get trained** to lead one of our groups in your area? Call me. This could be a valuable supplement for a coach, consultant, or CPA with a client base of small-business owners. Any business owner can become a leader. The leaders of our existing groups own businesses ranging from print shop to self-storage business to financial advisor to marketing consultant. We have a leader training program, with a Leaders Manual. Our workbooks and leader's guides are available to our trained leaders.

# Conclusion

The rule for authors and public speakers is "Tell 'em what you're going to tell 'em, then tell 'em, then tell 'em what you told 'em."

With that bit of wisdom in mind, here's what I have told you in this book:

**1. Learn to apply the Problem Solvent**—the set of five questions—to any business problem you encounter. Ask yourself, to tackle this problem, how can you:

- get needed help and outside support?
- improve the way you do things by upgrading your systems and procedures and getting "secret knowledge" out of your head?
- improve your own skills or expand the capabilities within your company?
- make changes in your workplace, your equipment or your materials?
- work on your own management practices, habits, attitudes, and beliefs—or those of your people?

**2. "Work on yourself"** is the most important element of the Problem Solvent. Your habitual ways of doing things are almost always part of the problem.

- What can you change that will help you solve the problem?
- How can you go about making this change in your management style?

**3. It helps to get help.** Don't be a lone ranger. Find others from whom you can learn and whom you can also help. This might be a consultant, a coach, or an informal advisor. Or form a community of peers and work together. Get help clarifying the issue, problem-solving, setting goals, getting feedback, staying on track, getting encouragement when the going is tough, and celebrating your successes. This makes your problems seem smaller and getting to the solution much more enjoyable.

**4. Insist that your business be profitable** and that you get paid very well. Profit is a signal of how well you are doing. If you are not profitable, then you are not doing something right. Look to see how you can change things to become profitable.

**5. You are in business to get what you want.** To do this, you must *know* what you want—not just revenue and wealth, but also doing what you want to do, working the way and with whom you want to work.

**6. Keep the desired balance** between business and the rest of your life. Make sure that your business supports your life.

**7. Trust yourself.** You already know most of what you need. Getting help applying what you know will usually pay bigger dividends than applying the latest management theories and buzzwords. Take your own counsel. Pay attention to your own inner wisdom. Sleep on new ideas; see how they sound in the morning.

**8. Don't be too hard on yourself.** Lighten up. You are not your business. Business is something you do; it is not who you are. Retain your sense of perspective.

**9. Be patient.** Take a step at a time. Tackle problems in bite-sized pieces. Don't beat yourself up for a seeming lack of progress, because changes don't happen instantaneously.

**10. Keep your sense of humor.** Keep a lightness about you as you operate your business. Laugh about your problems. Your problems are not unique; many people have survived much tougher problems than you have. A lot of those people aren't nearly as smart or determined as you are. If they can do it, you can surely do it.

*   *   *

I learned everything in this book from the business owners I have worked with over the years. To all of them I say "Thank you!"

But the process is never complete! I am still learning. I always love to hear your words of wisdom. Please write or email to add your voice to what I have said here.

Let's finish with a toast:

> *May your business bring you prosperity, satisfaction, and a sense of community.*
>
> *May you always do what you love and what you do best.*
>
> *May your work be a real service to your customers and a contribution to your community.*
>
> *When you are finally ready to turn out the lights, lock the door behind you, and go on to the next thing, may you do so with a sense of completion.*
>
> *Most of all, may your business grow without driving you crazy!*

*"Grow Your Business Without Driving Yourself Crazy" series*

# More Books and Workbooks for Small Business Owners

by Mike Van Horn

*Get the workbooks you need to take this farther. Give extra copies to your favorite entrepreneurs. Get on our mail list for new titles and templates.*

## ___Success Tips From Small Business Owners

A pocket-sized book with common sense tips and questions taken from the *Grow Your Business* book. Guaranteed to stimulate your thinking! Some samples:

- How do *you* balance "Spend no overhead before its time" and "You have to spend money to make money"?
- What is *your* "sweet spot of business success"—where these three circles overlap?

  What you love to do

  What you do very well

  What people will pay for
- A Zen master says, "Every day I meditate an hour, no matter how busy I am. Except on those days when the crush of work is overwhelming. Then I meditate for two hours."

48 pages, ©2001, ISBN 0-9714114-1-7, 4.25 x 5.5. $5.95

Some of these workbooks are companions to chapters of this book, which are indicated. Workbooks are $8\frac{1}{2}$ x 11, and range from 48 to 96 pages. $14.95 each.

## ___Grow Your Business Without Driving Yourself Crazy
(Chapters 1 – 10)

Tackle the barriers to growth, profitability, and ease.

## ___Success in 2003 Plan Workshop. (Chapters 16 and 17)

Goals, strategies, and activities for the coming year. From "Why are you in business?" to a plan to tackle your toughest challenge. Create a brief Action Plan for the year. *This workbook is updated each year.*

## ___ *Magic Chain of Marketing*
Your marketing is only as strong as its weakest link. How to take advantage of your strengths; and redress your weaknesses.

## ___ *Promote Yourself to CEO* (Chapters 8 and 12)
How to build the executive skills, management style, and team needed to run a growing company. How to groom your key people to take on more challenge.

## ___ *Recapture Your Time* (Chapter 11)
Don't save time; invest it! Forget time management; use time strategically. Use "time triage" to ease the busiest schedule. Maximize your "ROT" (return on time) and "ROC" (return on creativity).

## ___ *The Sweet Spot of Business Success* (Chapter 3)
Do what you love, what you're best at, and what people will pay for. Find where these three circles intersect for you.

## ___ *Pay Yourself First*
Link your marketing, finances, and paycheck. How much do you need and want? How large must your business be to pay you that much?

## ___ *Increase Your Cash Flow*
Find the cash hidden in your business. A dozen often-overlooked sources. *With David Levinson, CPA*

## ___ *Boost Your Profitability* (Chapters 13 and 15)
A dozen steps to establish a "business culture of profitability." The basics for those who are *not* financial whizzes.

## ___ *How to Get a Bank Loan*
For small business owners. How to make your company "bankable"—now or as soon as possible. *With David Levinson, CPA*

## ___ *Finding & Keeping Good Employees, part I* (Chapter 6)
Hire smart so you don't have to manage tough. Guidelines for job descriptions, interviewing, selecting, getting new hires started off right.
*With B.J. Van Horn, Senior Professional in Human Resources*

## ___ *Finding & Keeping Good Employees, part II* (Chapter 6)
Create a work environment that is firm, fair, and consistent. Retaining good people is cheaper than replacing them. Training, grooming, reviewing performance, handling problems. Employment practices, compliance questions.
*With B.J. Van Horn, Senior Professional in Human Resources*

## ___ *Hiring Your First Employee*
A step-by-step guide for first-time employers, with instructions and forms, to minimize the hassle. *With B.J. Van Horn, Senior Professional in Human Resources*

## ___ *Employer Assertiveness Training*
Change your management style for a more productive workplace.
*With B.J. Van Horn, Senior Professional in Human Resources*

Tables of contents will be emailed to you upon request.

Ask about volume discounts for bookstores, consultants, coaches, and business support organizations: 1-800-367-9848 or books@businessgroup.biz. For the latest titles, check our website: **www.businessgroup.biz**

--------------------------------------------------------------------------------

# Order Form

|  | No. | Price each (US$) | Total |
|---|---|---|---|
| **Books** |  |  |  |
| How to Grow Your Business Without Driving Yourself Crazy |  | 19.95 |  |
| Success Tips from Small Business Owners |  | 5.95 |  |
| **Workbooks**. Enter your desired titles and the number you want |  |  |  |
|  |  | 14.95 |  |
|  |  | 14.95 |  |
|  |  | 14.95 |  |
|  |  | 14.95 |  |
| Subtotal |  |  |  |
| Sales tax – California purchases   7% of above total |  |  |  |
| Shipping –  $4 per US address  (any number of copies) |  |  | $4.00 |
| **Please Pay This Amount** |  |  | $ |

❑ **Credit card.** Include card number, name on card, expiration date

Card #                                                              Exp. Date

Name on Card

❑ **Check**. *Payable to* **The Business Group**. Mail to 135 Paul Drive, Suite 300, San Rafael, CA, 94903
**Shipping address.** Books will be shipped via US Postal Service

Name

Company

Address

City, State, Zip

Tel:                                              Email

**1-800-367-9848      fax 415-491-1855        www.businessgroup.biz**